刘是
LIU SHI

无名画集 卷三
WUMING (NO NAME) PAINTING CATALOGUE Vol.3

王爱和 主编
Edited by WANG AIHE

香港大學出版社
HONG KONG UNIVERSITY PRESS

香港大学出版社
香港田湾海旁道七号
兴伟中心十四楼

Hong Kong University Press
14/F Hing Wai centre
7 Tin Wan Praya Road
Aberdeen
Hong Kong

ISBN 978-988-8028-23-8

中国北京 北京彩之林图文设计有限公司承印
Printed by Beijing Caizhilin Picture and Text Design Co., Ltd., Beijing, China

主编：王爱和
英文编辑：陶格

Editor: Wang Aihe
English Editor: Greg M. Thomas

本画集出版获得如下各方资助：
香港研究资助局角逐拨款资助研究项目
香港大学徐朗星基金会
香港大学查良镛基金会
雷耐包赛先生、徐芝韵女士
广东省佛山市顺德工业设计园艾万学研中心

Financial support has been provided by the following:
The Hong Kong Research Grants Council: Competitive Earmarked Research Grant
The University of Hong Kong: Louis Cha Fund
The University of Hong Kong: Hsu Long-sing Research Fund
Mr. René Balcer and Mrs. Carolyn Hsu-Balcer
Guangdong Foshan Shunde Industrial Design, A-One Research Centre

目录
TABLE OF CONTENTS

艺术家小传
ARTIST BIOGRAPHY

刘是，男，1955年8月8日出生在北京。1968年至1971年北京65中学。1972年至1981年被分配在北京市东城区服务公司任厨师、服务员、看砖工人、看煤气工人。1972年学习绘画，结识马可鲁、邵小刚，后结识赵文量等无名画会众人。1979年、1981年参加无名画会画展。1982年离职。1982年至1984年深圳都乐书屋画廊，北京科技导报，北京创造者俱乐部，北京妇女杂志社工作。1985年至1991年流浪北京，结识冯国东、孙大力等画家。1986年至1991年在黄建中工作室任电影美术师。1989年举办个人画展。1992年进入广告界。2005年至今从事纪录片拍摄、编剧、制片人、导演。

Liu Shi, male, was born in Beijing on August 8, 1955. From 1968 to 1971, he studied at the Beijing No. 65 Secondary School. From 1972 to 1981, he was assigned to the Service Company of Beijing Eastern District as a cook, a waiter, and a guard for a brick warehouse. He started to learn painting in 1972 and met Ma Kelu and Shao Xiaogang, as well as Zhao Wenliang, who were all from the *Wuming* Painting Group. He then participated in the *Wuming* Painting Group art exhibitions in 1979 and 1981. In 1982, he resigned from his job. From 1982 to 1984, he went through a number of different jobs at the Dule Gallery, the *Beijing Technology Daily*, the Beijing Creator Club, and the Beijing Women's Magazine Press. He lived a vagabond life in Beijing from 1985 to 1991 and met painters like Feng Guodong and Sun Dali. From 1986 to 1991, he worked as an art director in the Huang Jianzhong studio. He held his own art exhibition in 1989. In 1992, he entered the advertising profession. From 2005 to the present, he has been working on filming, screenwriting, producing, and directing for documentary films.

无名：特殊历史条件下的艺术和团体

王爱和

1979年7月7日，无名画会在北京北海公园首次公开展览。数月前，“新春画展”和“四月影展”在北京开幕，上海办了“十二人画展”。数月后，星星画会在美术馆外举行露天展览，更多的展览在其他城市举办。这些非官方艺术展览，如雨后春笋破土而出，宣告艺术已突破政治的长期奴役。从宏观历史角度来看，1979年值“民主墙”被禁，公众的表达由政治转向文化领域。这些展览是80年代“文化热”的前奏，[1] 标志一个泛政治时代的终结和社会文化生活的苏醒。

无名画集十三卷讲述着一个故事，即独立艺术如何在草根下生成，涓滴凝聚，涌而成溪，溪川成势，最终改变了历史的地貌。这不是一个完整的故事，不过是冰山的一角，但可由此窥见莫测的海下那庞大的文化现象。这个故事讲的是艺术，也讲产生艺术的那个团体——其凝聚力、其生存条件和共同努力。本文不评价无名的艺术成就，而是为它产生的历史条件、过程和方式提供一些线索。

“无名”和“四月”、“星星”一样，都是为办展览而现起的名字。但名字本身也是故事的一部分。“无名”不标志一个团体在筹展时诞生，如“新春”或“四月”；也不宣告燃起“今天”之“星星”以志明日之燎原。“无名”是一个回顾性的描述，描述一条漫长曲折之路。在严禁结社的年代，这个团体只可能是无名、无形、自发、自然，没有章程、没有会员制度，没有统一的艺术理念及绘画风格。所有的只是年复一年的集体艺术实践；实践将我们系为一体，成为每个人每一天存在的中心。因此，在1979年，我们发现没有名字可以描述这个无形而多层面的集体。简言之，“无名”不是东方哲学的抽象，不是前卫艺术的宣言，而是对一些平凡生命具体存在的描述。

我们从哪里来？我们来自两代人、不同的社会背景、各种工作职业、和几个朋友圈子。年长的一代有许多共同之处：他们都生于1949年以前；家庭出身都不好；都报考美术院校落榜、其后自学绘画。赵文量（1937年生）、张达安（1941年生）、杨雨澍（1944年生）和石振宇（1946年生）四人先后入私立熙化美术补习学校并在此相遇，1962年后常在一起画画。赵文量曾在苏联油画展上临摹原作，他创作的《同学肖像》入选北京市画展。但政治压力开始加码。1960年，杨雨澍因出身问题被迫去白虎涧采石场准劳改两年。1964年，社教运动深入，闲散“社会青年”必须安排工作。石振宇入工厂学徒，张达安去永乐店农场务农，赵文量、杨雨澍去黑龙江农场不成后被分配到工厂做工。接着，“文化大革命”的风暴席卷了全国。[2] 1966年，杨和石的家被抄，杨全家遣返农村，赵的父母回东北老家。经过45天在红色恐怖中的隔离，赵、杨、石三人再次相聚，互相支持，坚持绘画。他们将画箱改小，藏在书包内，在休息日去远郊写生。在当时的条件下，他们的题材由室内的静物、人像改为户外风景为主，画幅变小。艺术成了他们生命的支柱，大自然成了他们的画室，在社会底层他们创造着独立的艺术。

风暴中，一代年轻人长起来了。1966年我们在学校目睹打老师、砸教室，在家看抄家烧照片书画。1968年，上山下乡运动开始，无论是被红卫兵打死祖母的张伟，还是革命干部的女儿杜霞，一律下乡插队。次年，郑子钢去黑龙江农场，1970年马可鲁平谷插队。1972年田淑英赶上插队末班车。[3] 高中废除，大学关闭。父母下放，郑子燕、刘是、王爱和各守空巢。[4] 成长为人所必须的社会纽带全部破裂，知识的源泉干涸，学校、家庭、社区支离破碎，暴力横行，宣传充耳，没有图书、电影、音乐，也没有榜样。在这样的环境下，人何以超脱“动物凶猛”成长为人？[5] 在史无前例的教育废墟和文化荒野中流浪五年，我们到了十六、七岁，被分配作工人、农民、厨师、幼儿园阿姨……成为群众社会的沙砾，混入水泥，去浇铸共产主义的大厦。[6] 此时，我们有幸抓到一支画笔，绘画成为我们创造自我的主要行动。没有院校画展，我们的艺术启蒙来自巨大的宣传机器。政治宣传发动了无数工农兵写作组、宣传队、创作组，生产了铺天盖地的批判稿、样板戏、主席像、宣传画。[7] 据马可鲁回忆，他第一次感到油画的震撼，正是看韦海在学校操场整面墙上画巨大的宣传画。

权力总是在自身机体内产生反叛权力的抗体。年长的三位在工厂画主席像，因而获得颜料和画布，得以在下班后实践自己的艺术。年轻的也在学校、工厂搞宣传，由此产生的反叛令他们转而探求独立的艺术。画画，画出一个与四周宣传不同的世界，用以突破宣传的包围，用以建树独立自觉的人格；这不完全是有意识的反抗，而更多的是一种本能。要超越群众社会的沙砾，我们先要改变如何看世界。

我们如何相遇？同一历史条件不仅使艺术成为我们生命之必需，也使团体的出现成为必然。艺术是社会行为，没有艺术可以在孤立隔绝中产生。当正常的公共空间不存在时，我们更需要小团体内部的亚公共空间。而当时的历史条件——下乡下放、抄书禁书、宣传、分配——提供了我们聚合的资源、地点、和向心力。文化部宿舍大院里，有八间库房锁着抄禁的图书。史习习和郑子钢多次夜盗，盗出数麻袋的书籍画册。这些书开始流传，吸引了众多饥渴的心灵。这个叫203大院的宿舍，住着许多像习习这样父母下放的青少年，因而相对自由。1972年习习遇马可鲁，马带来老同学韦海、新朋友张伟，张伟带来李珊。1973年，郑子燕在文化宫画游园彩车，遇到在那里上工人业余美术班的王爱和。刘是、邵小刚、马可鲁在脱产搞宣传时相遇。1973年秋，习习带赵文量、杨雨澍、石振宇到203大院，两代人、几个朋友圈子合而为一。

1973年秋，时值林彪事件后的短暂解冻再遇严冬，怀疑“文革”的种种读书会、地下沙龙在萌芽中惨遭霜冻。[8] 自上而下的政治运动：批右倾回潮、批林批孔，掀起了“二次革命”。新工人民兵诞生以加强无产阶级专政。[9] 这样的环境使团体牢牢凝聚。它提供了我们仅有的社会空间，在这里我们可以自由交换思想、传阅禁书画册，共同实验现代艺术。在“批判无标题音乐”运动中，我们围在老唱机旁，偷听贝多芬。我们去看黑画展，企图发现我们的联盟。[10] 团体凝聚的最重要标志是1974-1975年冬的地下画展。[11] 地点选在张伟家，因为那幢苏俄式大楼，漆黑的走廊较容易躲过街道委员会的监视，更因为张伟的母亲勇敢地接纳了我们。我们先把画藏在大衣里分批运到摆好。那天两间屋挤满了十几人。至今没有人清楚记得参展都有哪些画，但人人都忘不了当时的激动和振奋。许多人把这次展览看作是加入地下团体的洗礼。

我们如何作画？我们每月工资在十六至四十几元之间，没有画室也没钱买颜料画布。我们绝大部分的油画是画在纸上，从二毛五分钱一开的素描纸到七毛五分的水彩纸，上面涂上骨胶或立德粉。大家常合伙刷出一批纸，分而画之。有时谁找到一批废弃的包装盒，如获至宝，也拿来分享。石振宇最有本事，能把画主席像的颜料画布顺出来，让三位老将画一些大幅布上油画。但我们早期的绝大部分作品是A4 纸大小的纸上油画。

画幅小是无名的一个特点，但却非我们的美学追求。它不但受制于物质条件，更取决于我们生存的社会环境和时空结构。我们每周六天劳作，每天八小时工作加两小时政治学习，能作画的时间只有每周一天休息日和每天下班的几小时。多数人都上倒班，为节能所设的轮休制令我们不能在同一天休息。定时的聚会和长期作画都成为不可能。自然而然我们学会知道何时何地可以找到大家，上班把画箱藏在包里，下班就奔那个地方去。有时去某某家，画人像静物，临摹画册，从伦勃朗到梵高、塞尚、毕加索、表现主义、野兽派一概不拒。我们也看中国画，黄公望的雪景、倪瓒的山林，金农的梅花、八大的枯荷；文人画的美学意境滋养着我们去创新。

但我们大多数人没有自己的居室，街道委员会看得又紧。所以一般我们在户外作画并相聚。最常去的是玉渊潭：一条河，两岸伸着白桦林和荒草地，三面环着农田。那里荒野无人，最接近我们想象中的“自然”。在这里我们画不尽落日、河流、农舍、山林。此外，我们追着春天到植物园画丁香，到后山画桃花；夏天画紫竹院的柳岸荷塘。郊外的香山、八大处、颐和园、十三陵，市内的故宫、天坛、文化宫、北海，都是我们作画的场所。上班的六天，我们在下班路上画街道、胡同，天黑了就画夜景。在被革命现代化遗弃的古迹上，我们与文化传统相连；在工业化都市的夹缝和周边，我们寻找大自然。

寻找大自然，我们集体远游，最重要的一次是十三人去北戴河画海。1975年十一国庆，我们得公假三天外加个周末。有人伪造了一张介绍信，以此我们通过了工人民兵的盘查住进招待所。有人拿不出二十几元买火车票，习习替杨雨澍付票钱；张伟、李珊则晚走一天，等我们把用过的票寄来，改改再用。招待所床位九毛钱一晚，馒头二毛五一斤，大家凑钱买馒头，分享杨雨澍带来的一大罐咸菜，开始了四天的乌托邦公社。张伟、李珊第二天到达，当晚即遭工人民兵盘问并责令次日离开。次日天不亮，大队人马去鸽子窝画日出，小队人马等食堂开门为大家买馒头。两路人马走差了道，大队人马饿了一天。最后一天我们直画到天擦黑。习习吟诵普希金《致大海》，含泪挥别“自由的元素”，我们跑向车站。等火车时，刘是因“形迹可疑”被抓，石振宇使出浑身解术将他赎出。

我们画什么？我们的画大多为风景：山水、落日、月光、树木。为什么画月光、树木？在那个时代，社会主义现实主义已成为严格的形式教条，统治着一切文化领域。绘画题材必须是人物画，主题必须是革命，形象必须是“高、大、全”的工农兵典型，形式必须是“红、光、亮”。红色象征革命，黑色则暴露画家的反革命意识。[12]风景只能作革命形象的背景，作人定胜天的战场。1974年“黑画展”大肆批判那些用黑色画风景动物，因而违背了这些形式教条的画家们，引发了“反文艺黑线回潮”运动。[13]戏剧界，历史剧《三上桃峰》遭到批判。[14]同年，文化部长带头批判无标题音乐，指其为“为资产阶级夺权掌权制造舆论的工具”；而那些以“月光”、“泉水”、“松树”为题的音乐则同样是掩盖资产阶级荒淫腐朽的生活和病态情感的面具。[15]正如布莱克特(Brecht)所描述，在这样的时代，“言树木几乎是犯罪”。[16]在这样的时代，我们画树。

树木、风景不仅提供了正统之外的艺术题材，而且帮助艺术家塑造体制之外的自觉主体。我们在风景中找到自由空间，想尽办法从体制的齿缝中挤出时间，在风景中投射我们的理想、创造不同于现状的新的现实，并同时创造自己。画，记录了这种过程，数百张画，把日复一日零碎的经验连成一个延续的整体，这种延续形成“存在的力量”。[17]这是一个想象和创造的过程，而非反映或描绘现实。在一个视自然为斗争对象的时代，我们在自然中找到自己，也重新确定了人对自然崇敬的关系。

我们也画人物、静物。在人像中我们挖掘人性的相通和人的尊严，尽管每人画人像多少不等，形式各异。这些人物静物虽然数量不多，却是无名的珍品。它们见证我们不懈的人文关怀、对社会的参与而非漠视或逃避。这些人物画的反叛力量在1979年公开展览时可见一斑。当时正是人物画引起最大争议，有几张被美协要求撤除，多亏美协副主席刘迅先生的坚决抵制，才得以公开面世。

反思无名。与插队学生的读书会、诗会不同，无名的组织构成特别多样，这种多样正是团体生命力所在。除家庭、职业和性别之差，两代人的组合尤为重要。1973年，无名的长者年龄在二十七至三十六岁之间。无名的青年晚生十五至二十年(1951－1957)，年龄在十六至二十二岁之间。今天，有批评家提出有两位长者是无名的导师和灵魂人物，引起激烈争议。成员们公认最年长的赵文量最具影响力，他主动帮助别人克服绘画上的困难，他对艺术的执著感染了每个人。但多数人强烈感到，如果把无名定义成一群学生跟一两位老师学画则完全曲解了无名的真实性质。赵文量对大家的最大感召，是他坚信画不可能由他人教会（学他），而只能从心中发现自己（自学）。青年人敬重他，最根本是把他看作是反对一切权威的独立艺术家的榜样。正是为了共同的反叛、追求独立的自我，我们走到一起。

集体不是个人的总和或延伸，如生物体，它靠各部分相互依赖形成生命。每个人都以独特的方式为团体的存在作出不可或缺的贡献。年长者领队，传授宝贵的经验。年少者激励长者，令团体充满青春活力。老练机智者应付警察和街道，确保集体的安全。童稚者的纯真令人耳目一新。女画家以独特清新的感觉丰富了无名的艺术。勤学者带来《印象派画史》、《罗丹谈艺录》。雄辩者争论理念和政治。嗜文者传阅雨果、托尔斯泰和普希金。好音者分享贝多芬和德彪西。思辩者讨论尼采、萨特。善社交者将无名与外界联络，扩展了它的资源和机会。至关重要，是每一个人对集体的忠诚和友谊，创造了这个自由空间。在一起我们敢说犯忌的话，敢想叛逆的思想，实验离经叛道的艺术。在一起我们走过个人不可能单独逾越的距离。归根到底，把我们凝聚在一起的，是不自由时代的自由，是文化饥荒中的食粮，是无情社会中的友情。无名是我们追求真理、发展真我的空间，是我们最重要的身份。在一个扼杀精神生活的世界，无名是我们创造的精神家园。

今天，我们清楚地知道，历史产生无名，也决定了它的局限。在一个封闭的社会，它遗传了封闭。缺乏信息令我们难以系统学习而依赖自发本能。没有公共空间令我们自省内心感觉多于关怀公众。反对外面的个人崇拜，我们崇拜自己的英雄。一旦意识到这些局限，每人都努力突破之。我们拒绝任何统一艺术理念；“为艺术而艺术”是争论的热点但不是信条。我们反对任何形式标准；一旦创造了共同的题材和画风，就开始创新个人风格。1977年“文革”结束后，集体整体活动渐由个人或三两个人的独立活动取代。1979年展览同时体现了集体的认同和个人风格的多样。1981年春为准备二展，几位成员成立了一个常务委员会领导班子并拟定了“无名画会会员章程”和“会员名单”，这一重整组织的努力恰恰反映了团体的分裂。七月无名画会二展如期举行，其后自然解体。无名的存在目的在于追求真理和自由，它完成了这一历史使命。

画集。画集共十三卷，十三位艺术家人各一卷，以姓氏拼音排序。每卷以无名时期作品为中心，展现个人艺术发展的全程。画家本人为画集选画、排序，并提供目录信息。每卷在本文之后刊登艺术家的自述文章，讲述个人和艺术创作的经历。无名的作品绝大多数未记时间未署名，目录中的作品年代多靠各人记忆而定。因而这些年代只应作某画家作品相对年代的参考，不可作横向比较的绝对年代。每位艺术家的成就有画为证，恕不赘言。画集未能收录所有的参与无名活动的画家。1979年有二十二位画家参展，包括成员们的同事和朋友。史习习，无名的沙龙主人和重要成员，于2005年英年早逝。习习一生不满自己的作品，使之遗失几尽。出版之际，“遍插茱萸少一人”，令人伤怀，唯有在画集中珍藏对他的怀念。

无名有幸获众多朋友和支持者。艰难岁月，父母亲人分担我们的窘困，勇敢地打开家门接纳这个集体。很多朋友提供了珍贵的书籍画册。1979年，北京美协副主席刘迅先生刚出监狱，就担着风险全力支持无名画展，与极左势力做了艰苦斗争。刘海粟大师为展览书写“无名画会”匾额并在著作中评论无名作品。批评家高尔泰、栗宪庭，艺术家马建、朱金石等撰文介绍无名画会。美术史家高名潞策划“无名回顾展”并著专著研究无名。[18]美术史家孙志新为画册的出版给予宝贵建议。画册的出版获得多方资助，鸣谢另见画册版权页。这个名单不可能全，对所有朋友和支持者，我们在此深表谢意。为他们的期待，为纪念无名画会走出地下三十周年，我们谨献给公众这套画集。

2008年8月于香港

Wuming: Art and Solidarity in a Peculiar Historical Context

Wang Aihe

On July 7, 1979, the first public exhibition of the *Wuming* painting group opened in Beijing's Beihai Park. A few months earlier, the "New Spring" Painting Group and "April" Photographers Group had staged exhibitions in Zhongshan Park and the "Twelve Persons" Painting Exhibition was held in Shanghai. Months later the "Stars" would hold an open-air exhibition outside Beijing's China Art Gallery. More exhibitions were opening in other cities. These unofficial art exhibitions, sprouting suddenly, announced that art had broken the tight grip of ideology and political enslavement. 1979 was also the year when the Democracy Wall of Beijing was banned and public expression was forced to seek a new outlet—in the cultural domain. These exhibitions, therefore, presaged the decade of "cultural fads" in the 1980s.[1] From a macro-historical perspective, they marked the end of an era of total politicizing of society, during which all domains of human experience had been reduced to crude political struggle, and the revival of social and cultural life.

Paintings collected in this thirteen-volume catalogue tell a story of how independent art came into being at the grass roots level, accumulating through years of clandestine practice, like drops of water silently merging into a stream, and streams into a river, finally changing the cultural landscape of history. It is not a complete story, but a chip of a hidden cultural phenomenon in a murky era of an immense country, where a complete story has been impossible to obtain. It is a story about art, and about the group that produced it—the group's solidarity and shared practices against shared conditions. This essay does not survey or evaluate *Wuming* art, but situates it in its historical context, providing some clues to the processes and means of its production.

Like "April" and "Stars," "*Wuming*" (meaning No Name or Nameless) was a name invented for an exhibition. The name itself, however, is part of the story. "*Wuming*" did not signal the time of a group's birth, as did "New Spring" and "April." Nor did it declare avant-garde futurism, as did "Today" and "Stars," which could become tomorrow's prairie blaze. Instead, it was a retrospective description of a winding path stretching back into the nights of the Cultural Revolution. In an era when free association was a crime, the group had to be nameless, shapeless, and spontaneous. There were no regulations, no membership, no unified artistic principles or style. All we had was years of collective artistic practice that bound us together, molding the center of everyday life for each person. That was why, in 1979, we felt that no name could describe such a formless, fluid, and multifaceted collectivity. "*Wuming*" was not an Oriental philosophical abstraction or an avant-garde manifesto, but a description of the tangible existence of ordinary lives.

Where Did We Come From? We came from two generations, diverse class backgrounds, various working positions, and some pre-existing circles of close friends. Figures of the older generation have much in common: all were born before the establishment of the PRC; all came from families defined as "class enemies" by 1950; all took entrance examinations and were rejected by art schools or academies; and all learned art largely by themselves. Between 1957 and 1962, Zhao Wenliang (b. 1937), Zhang Daan (b. 1941), Yang Yushu (b. 1944), and Shi Zhenyu (b. 1946) began attending the private "Xihua" Art Preparatory School, established by an artist who had studied in Japan. Zhao Wenliang copied paintings in public art exhibitions, and his portrait entitled "Classmate" entered a municipal exhibition in 1959. After 1962, the four often painted together. But political pressure was increasing. In 1960, Yang Yushu was sent for two years to Baihujian Quarry, a semi-labor camp, simply because of his problematic family background. By 1964, the Socialist Education Movement started to clean up free-floating elements of society—the unemployed, descendants of dispossessed families, school dropouts, and failed university candidates—all of whom had to be institutionalized and put to work. Under pressure, Shi Zhenyu took a factory job in 1964, while Zhang Daan volunteered to work on the Yongle Dian Farm in 1965, the same year Zhao Wenliang and Yang Yushu tried unsuccessfully to join Heilongjiang Farm. They were soon assigned to different factories. As soon as these art students turned into workers and farmers, the Great Proletarian Cultural Revolution stormed the country beginning in 1966.

During the storm, Zhao, Yang, and Shi bonded tightly. In 1966, the homes of Yang and Shi were raided, Yang's family was deported to the countryside, and Zhao's parents left Beijing for their hometown. Meanwhile, mob violence was unleashed, the state was paralyzed in anarchism, and long-suppressed social divisions erupted into mass factionalism that ravished schools, universities, factories, government agencies, and villages.[2] After forty-five days of separation in the Red Terror, the three reunited to help one another continue painting. They made small painting boxes that could be hidden in normal shoulder bags, met at bus stops, and went to sites far outside the city. Painting under this historical condition resulted in smaller sized works and a shift in motifs from predominantly figures and still life to landscape. The difficulties of the Cultural Revolution led them to anchor their life to art, establish their belief in art and its independence, and develop their artistic styles outdoors, in nature.

In the midst of the same storm, a new generation came of age. In elementary school, we witnessed beatings of teachers and the trashing of classrooms, at home we saw the raiding of houses and burning of family collections of art and photographs. None of us was old or red enough to be perpetrators of the revolution, but none was too young to escape its effects. By 1968, the carnival was over and the bill came. Zhang Wei, whose grandmother had been beaten to death and whose house had been raided six times by the Red Guards, was now sent down to the countryside as all middle school graduates were wantonly punished for the Red Guards' deeds. Also sent down was Du Xia, daughter of two upright revolutionary cadres. The following year, Zheng Zigang went to Heilongjiang farm, where he spent the next ten years. In 1970, Ma Kelu went to a village near Beijing and in 1972, Tian Shuying caught the last sent-down bus.[3] High schools were abolished and universities closed. Parents who were cadres or intellectuals were sent down to the provinces.[4] Those sent down from both generations left most urban families fragmented, and Zheng Ziyan, Wang Aihe, and Liu Shi lived in empty homes.

Throughout our teenage years, all the social fabrics needed for forming personhood were torn apart, and all sources of knowledge vanished. How could one transcend the state of being a "vicious beast" to become human, a person, while living through formative years in broken homes, ravaged schools, and crumbling communities, with violence and frenzied propaganda shoved down your throat and no libraries, no books, no cinema, no music, no museums, and no role models?[5] After five years of unprecedented cultural famine and educational ruin, we reached our late teens and were assigned social identities—factory workers, kindergarten teacher, cooks, truck loader, construction worker, and peasants. We thus entered adulthood as indistinguishable grains of sand, tossed into the cement mixture of the masses to build the communist grand fortress.[6]

While tossed, however, we had the good fortune to find a brush. As with the older generation, these specific historical conditions made painting the center of our lives, our primary self-inventing action. But where they had been initiated into art at a relatively normal time—seeing western art, attending art classes, and visiting exhibitions—initiation for the younger generation came in the middle of the Cultural Revolution, when elaborate propaganda and political ritual mobilized a vast grass roots population. Numerous workers' writing groups, propaganda teams, performing troops, and art workshops became producers of texts, performances, and images to popularize the models of correct conduct.[7] Most of us gained access to the brush and the right to make images when our talent was put to use for such mass production. Ma Kelu recalls his first experience of the power of oil painting, in 1968, when watching his schoolmate Wei Hai paint a giant propaganda poster covering an entire wall of the school's sports field.

Power never fails to produce its own antibody and its own rebels from within. The older generation of *Wuming* artists painted Mao portraits in their factories yet turned this into a source of precious oil paints and linen canvas, with which they experimented after work. Most of the younger artists painted propaganda posters in their schools, villages, and work units, which spurred them to rebel by seeking their own art, also after work. It was during that one day off each week, and a few moments each day after work, that we could paint, paint something completely different from the all-enveloping red propaganda, something to break through it, something to enable one to be a real person, an authentic, self-determining human being. This was not so much a conscious act of subversion as an instinctual drive to transcend being a grain of sand, by changing one's way of seeing the world.

How Did We Meet? The same historical conditions that made art the center of our lives also made the group's formation inevitable. All arts are social actions, and no art can come into being in total isolation. When the normal sense of public space disappeared, we needed that semi-public space created by clandestine groups. Such groups came into being also from within the very system of political control that provided our resources and meeting points. In a dormitory yard of the Ministry of Culture, truckloads of books were locked in storehouses, waiting to be recycled. Shi Xixi and Zheng Zigang broke into these houses at night, filling cargo bags full of books and art catalogues, which soon started to circulate, attracting young minds starved for intellectual nourishment. The yard, called 203 yard, provided a relatively free space, camouflaged by teenagers like Xixi living alone, unsupervised. In 1972, Xixi met Ma Kelu, who soon introduced him to old schoolmate Wei Hai and new friend Zhang Wei, who then introduced Li Shan. In 1973, Zheng Ziyan was assigned to decorate parade trucks in the People's Cultural Palace Park, where she met Wang Aihe and Ma Kelu, who were attending a "Worker's Art Class." Liu Shi, Shao Xiaogang, and Ma Kelu also met when painting propaganda posters. By the fall of 1973, the preexisting circles of older and younger generations met at 203 and merged into a complex group.

The birth of this group at this particular moment was directly related to historical circumstances. After the Lin Biao incident shocked the nation in 1971, people began questioning the Cultural Revolution, and various underground reading groups, art and literature salons, and dissident writings began sprouting. This temporary thaw, however, met with a deep freeze.[8] Dissidents were jailed and executed, and a series of nationwide political campaigns initiated the so-called "Second Cultural Revolution." If the first can be characterized by romantic revolutionary illusion, fervent faith in a great leader, and bottom-up mass turmoil, its second coming was marked by widespread disenchantment, cold-blooded dictatorship, and top-down suppression by force.[9] This Second Cultural Revolution bound the group in unwavering solidarity. Under increased ideological control and social surveillance, the group provided a shared space where we could exchange our unorthodox ideas, circulate smuggled books and catalogues, paint together, and comment on one another's work. During the 1974 campaign against "music without titles," we gathered at a friend's home around an old record player to listen to Beethoven. In February that year, we all went to the "Black Painting Exhibition," not to join the public criticism but to look for potential allies.[10] The more pressure the large society exerted, the more freedom our small society offered.

Group solidarity manifested itself in an underground exhibition held at Zhang Wei's home in the winter of 1974–1975.[11] We chose his apartment because it was in a Soviet-style building with pitch dark hallways and isolated staircases, making it easier to evade the neighborhood committee's surveillance. Zhang's mother bravely opened her home for such a risky event. We delivered our paintings furtively, with some even planning a coded knock. Inside, about fifteen people gathered. No one can remember for certain which paintings were displayed or when the exhibition began, but no one can forget the zeal and exhilaration of that day and evening. For many, this was the rite of passage into true art and a clandestine art society.

How Did We Paint? As laborers, most of us made salaries between sixteen and forty-some *yuan* per month. We had no studios and little money for paint and canvas. Where did we get the material, space, and time to paint all these paintings? Human beings have always made art with whatever material is available. We usually used paper, from ordinary drawing paper costing twenty-five cents per sheet to thicker watercolor paper costing seventy-five, and we brushed boiled bone glue or gesso paste on it to prepare the surface. Often several friends did this together, preparing a bunch to share. At times someone would pick up a pile of packaging cardboard, then for weeks everyone would be painting on cardboard, sharing its deep brownish grey background. Shi Zhenyu was the most capable at smuggling real canvas and paint from painting Mao portraits, and he supplied Zhao and Yang, enabling the three to paint some larger works on canvas. But most of our paintings from that time are small, about the size of A4 paper.

This small size was not a conscious aesthetic pursuit; it had to do not only with our material life but also with our social conditions and the space-time structure of our everyday existence. We labored six days a week, eight hours plus two hours of political study per day. The only time we could paint was in the few hours after work and on our one day off. Most of us rotated between day- and night-shifts, and workers had different days off due to electricity shortages, so a regular schedule of gathering was impossible. Spontaneously we developed an instinct for finding one another at the right time and place. We concealed our small self-made painting boxes in shoulder bags when going to work, and after work we went by bicycle or bus to sites where everyone knew to go. We also gathered at one another's homes to paint still lifes or portraits and to circulate books and art catalogues. These enabled us to study and copy reproductions, from Michelangelo and Rembrandt to Corot, Monet, Van Gogh, Cézanne, Picasso, Expressionism, and Fauvism. We also studied and discussed Chinese literati paintings such as Huang Gongwang's snowy mountains, Ni Zan's wintry trees, Jin Nong's blossoms, and Ba Da's withering lotus. Literati motifs and aesthetics nurtured us in creating collective motifs and styles.

Meeting at home, however, was not easy. Few of us had the luxury of a private bedroom, and neighborhood committees would monitor who came and went. So we met most often outdoors at painting sites, the most important of which was Yuyuantan. This park had been built in the 1950s in the style of a Russian landscape—a curving river flanked by white birch trees, tall grass, and a hill of aspens. It lay at the west end of the city, deserted and unmanaged, bordered by villages and fields. We found it a communal space of freedom, almost exclusively our own. On a typical evening, a few painters dotted the riverbank, with some arriving after work as others left for the nightshift. Whoever remained lingered on to catch the sunset, and then a night scene on the way home. Before finally parting, we would check with one another about where and when to meet the next time.

Over the years, we accumulated a repertoire of sites, where we developed a shared body of motifs. Yuyuantan was the landscape we understood as nature—deserted and unmanaged, surrounded by fields and woods, with little trace of artificiality. Here we painted the sunset, woods, river, farmhouses, and fields. In spring, we went to imperial gardens and the Botanical Garden for peach blossoms and lilacs. We painted the willows and lotus pond at Zizhuyuan and the lake at the Summer Palace. Within the city, we painted the ancient pines and imperial palaces of the Forbidden City and Temple of Heaven, as well as allies and streets around our homes and factories. On days off and public holidays, we would venture far outside the city to the Fragrant Hills and Ming Tombs, which lay at the limit of our monthly bus pass. When daylight waned, we painted sunsets and night scenes, then painted by memory as well. In 1976, Zhao Wenliang opened his home to the group. He lived at Shishahai, and this neighborhood of small alleys and traditional courtyards surrounded by three lakes became another communal painting site. At all these sites, we connected to the past through cultural relics standing neglected by revolutionary modernity and carved out 'nature' from the outskirts and cracks of the industrialized city.

In search of nature, the group made several trips by train. The most important was made by the group of thirteen to the sea in 1975. For National Day (October 1), we all had three public holidays plus a Sunday. Someone forged a "letter of introduction," with which we passed the local militia and public security and checked into a "Reception Inn" at Beidaihe, a beach town deserted in autumn and winter. Some could not afford the train fare of twenty-some *yuan*, so Xixi paid for Yang Yushu, and Zhang Wei and Li Shan waited for a day to reuse tickets that we mailed to them the minute we arrived. The rooms cost ninety cents per person per night, steamed buns were five for twenty cents, and Yang Yushu brought a large jar of salty vegetables to go with the buns. We pooled our money to cover the costs and started a four-day utopian commune. Zhang Wei and Li Shan arrived the second afternoon, but that evening they were questioned by security officers and ordered to leave by the next day's train. The next morning, a group of early birds went to Pigeon Nest rock, while the late birds, responsible for buying the buns, took a different route. The early birds starved. On the last day, we painted until evening. Xixi recited in tears Pushkin's *To the Sea*, waving farewell to the "element of freedom" before we ran to the train station. While waiting, Liu Shi got caught while wandering around, just for looking "fishy", and Shi Zhenyu used all his wit and wile to get him released.

What Did We Paint? A large proportion of our paintings are landscapes, made in and out of Beijing, depicting mountains and water, flowers and trees, sunshine and moonlight. Why trees, why landscapes, and not some real resistance, loud as a marching band? In our time, "Socialist Realism" became a dogma of crude stylistic dictates dominating all cultural domains. In painting, the genre had to be figure painting; the subject was revolutionary splendor symbolized by the ageless models of workers, peasants, and soldiers; images had to be "tall, grand, and complete (*gao da quan*);" and the style had to be "red, bright, and shining (*hong guang liang*)." Red symbolized the revolution, while the use of black indicated an artist's counterrevolutionary intentions.[12] Landscape served only as a background for these beaming figures, showing the abundant productivity brought by the red sun (Mao) or the victory of people conquering the earth under it. Art that did not strictly follow such stylistic dictates subjected an artist to incrimination. The "Black Paintings Exhibition" (1974) displayed just such stylistic disobedience—the color black, with motifs of landscapes and animals—to persecute artists and the "figure behind them" (Zhou Enlai), and to denounce the restoration of the "black line of literature and art."[13] In theater, the Shanxi opera *Going Up to Peach Peak Three Times* (*san shang tao feng*) triggered a criticism campaign.[14] In music, the Minister of Culture wrote a series of articles in early 1974 denouncing European classical music as "weapons to shape opinions to serve the bourgeoisie for seizing and consolidating political power." While untitled music is "merely a means by which bourgeois composers conceal the class content of their works," the titled music, taking inspiration from such things as pines, fountains, and moonlight, masks the "decadent, chaotic life and depraved sentiments of the bourgeoisie the weird cacophony represents."[15] This was literally a time when, as Brecht depicted, "to speak of trees is almost a crime."[16] In such a time, we painted trees.

Trees and landscape not only offered an alternative, non-dogmatic motif, they also helped fashion an alternative subjectivity for the artist, outside the processes of institutional subject formation. At a time when most people were preoccupied with the revolution, we found in landscape a space of freedom, and we squeezed hours and days from the claws of our work units to live there. In such space-time we studied nature, projecting onto it our dreams for a different existence, an alternative future. While experiencing nature, we were simultaneously inventing ourselves. Painting recorded that process, and hundreds of paintings by each person connected fragmented experiences into a coherent continuity, "forces of being."[17] This was a process of imagining and inventing rather than "reflecting" reality or "depicting" sites. In a culture that treated nature as the object of struggle and conquest, we redefined people's relationship to nature, as its worshipers rather than destroyers.

We also painted human figures and still lifes. Again, we were not reflecting the people or material surroundings, but exploring humanity in these figures and objects. In images of friends, neighbors, and strangers, we searched for compassion, empathy, and dignity. Some painted more figures than others, and each artist's style was distinct, but all our figures opposed the revolutionary stereotypes. What we tried to discover in these figures was subjectivity breaking institutional molds. These figures and still lifes, though not numerous, are gems of *Wuming*. They evidence our persistent humanistic concerns and our engagement with our own time. The subversive power of these figure paintings was evident even at our 1979 public exhibition, when they caused the biggest controversy. Members of the Beijing Artists Association, which sponsored the exhibition, called for removing some of these figure paintings, but Mr. Liu Xun, fresh from jail and newly appointed Vice-President of the Association, successfully fought to keep them in. "While they were painting, what did you people do during the Cultural Revolution?" Liu challenged, silencing his opponents.

The Group in Retrospect. Unlike reading groups or poetry societies formed by sent-down students, the *Wuming* group was exceptionally diverse, and this diversity fuelled its vitality. The combination of the two generations was an important structural feature. By 1973, the older painters were between twenty-seven and thirty-six years old, while the younger ones were sixteen to twenty-two. Today, some critics say two of the elders—Zhao Wenliang and Yang Yushu—were the "teachers and spiritual fathers" of *Wuming*; this statement triggered fiery controversy. Few in the group deny that Zhao, the eldest, was the most influential; he regularly helped other members overcome technical difficulties, providing commentary and encouragement. But most feel that to define *Wuming* as a group of students learning from one or two teachers is to fundamentally misunderstand the group's true nature. Zhao Wenliang's greatest appeal to the rest of us was his affirmation that art cannot be taught by academies or teachers, but must be discovered within oneself. The young generation respected him above all as a model of the self-determined artist defying all authority. Pursuing such individual self-discovery was the true common pursuit that bound all the diverse members of the group together.

The collective, therefore, was not an extension of any one person. Nor was it merely a collection of individuals. It was an organism, in which parts existed in mutual interdependence, with each person contributing in unique ways, each vital to the group. The elders naturally took more of the lead, more responsibility, and shared their experience. The young reciprocated by affirming the elders' causes, rejuvenating their art, and giving *Wuming* vibrant energy. The experienced and tactful protected the group from trouble with the police and neighborhood committees. The innocent refreshed our eyes with their child-like visions. The women contributed to the diversity and richness of *Wuming* art with views and experiences that were distinct from the men's. The studious brought in *History of Impressionism* and *Rodin on Art*. The eloquent debated theory and politics. The literary circulated Hugo, Tolstoy, and Pushkin. The philosophical discussed Nietzsche and Sartre. The musical shared Beethoven and Debussy. And the sociable connected the group with other groups and friends to provide further resources and opportunities. Most importantly, the loyalty and friendship each person dedicated to the group ensured our common safety and freedom. Within this community, we dared say the taboo words, think the dangerous thoughts, experiment with the forbidden art, read the banned books. Together we ventured to distances nobody could reach alone. Above all, the magnet binding us was the space of freedom in a time not free, cultural nourishment during cultural famine, and a solidarity sustaining us in an age of unprecedented alienation. *Wuming* was where we pursued truth and lived out our true selves without having to pretend as in all other social circumstances. It gave us our most important identity. In a world where spiritual life was smothered, *Wuming* was the spiritual home we created.

We fully realize today that the history that produced the group also dictated its limitations. At a time when the country was completely closed up, we inherited that closeness. The lack of information hindered systematic study of multiple traditions and promoted reliance on instinct and the subconscious. Absence of public space limited our vision, forcing us to introspect personal sensations rather than reach out to the public. Opposing the worship of Mao, we worshiped our radical heroes instead. Once these limitations became evident, each person tried to overcome them. As a result, we rejected any orthodox artistic theory for *Wuming*. "Art for art," "pure art"—these were topics of debate but never a common doctrine. We also rejected any collective stylistic standards; as soon as we created a repertoire of shared motifs and styles, everyone began breaking through them, resulting in a diversity of personal styles and motifs. From 1977, with the end of the Cultural Revolution, group activities diminished and individuals or groups of two or three friends painted more independently. The 1979 exhibition therefore revealed both our well-established collective identity and our assertion of personal styles. Early in 1981, in preparation for the second public exhibition, several members created a standing committee of leadership and established honorary chairs for eminent masters, a *Wuming* membership list, and a set of member regulations. This attempt at formal organization revealed further rifts within the group, and after the July show, the group ceased its existence. *Wuming*'s raison d'être was pursuing truth and spiritual freedom, and that historical mission had been fulfilled.

The Catalogue includes thirteen volumes, each about a single artist. The sequence of the volumes is alphabetical according to the artists' last names. Paintings within each volume are centered on the *Wuming* period while stretching throughout the artist's career, thereby allowing study of both group and individual development. Following the present essay, each volume includes an artist's essay about personal experience and the social conditions for creating his or her art. Each artist has selected his or her paintings and provided the catalogue information. Since most *Wuming* paintings were not dated at the time of completion, most dates in this catalogue are based on memory. Therefore, they should only be seen as a relative chronology within the artist's own body of work and should not be used as absolute proof of who did what first. Each artist's artistic achievement and personal style are apparent in the catalogue and will not be discussed here. Unfortunately, the catalogue could not include all the artists related to the *Wuming* group. Twenty-two painters participated in the 1979 exhibition, including friends and co-workers of some members. Shi Xixi, a key member of *Wuming*, passed away in 2005. He was our salon host, poet, generous friend, and a perfectionist who abandoned most of his works; missing him from this catalogue is our greatest regret, yet each volume preserves a memory of him.

Wuming has been fortunate to have many supporters and friends. In the most difficult years, parents and families shared our hardships and opened homes to host us. Many friends helped provide access to books and art catalogues. In 1979, recently released from prison, Liu Xun shouldered all the risk and fought hard to open the first public *Wuming* exhibition, with the determination that this "would cause nothing more than being in jail again." Master Liu Haisu came to our opening in heavy rain, wrote the calligraphy "Wuming Huahui" for the show, and commented on our art in his books. Critics Gao Ertai and Li Xianting, artists Ma Jian and Zhu Jinshi, and others have written essays on *Wuming*. Art historian Gao Minglu curated the *"No Name" Group Retrospective Exhibition* and published the first monograph on the group.[18] Curator Sun Zhixin has also provided valuable advice. This list can only be incomplete. For all friends and supporters, we express our deepest gratitude. To fulfill their expectation, and to commemorate the thirtieth anniversary of the 1979 *Wuming* exhibition, we offer to the public this catalogue.

1 甘阳，《八十年代文化意识》，上海：世纪集团、上海人民出版社，2006；查建英，《八十年代访谈录》，牛津大学出版社，2006。

2 Roderick MacFarquhar and Michael Schoenhals, *Mao's Last Revolution* (Cambridge and London: The Belknap Press of Harvard University Press, 2006), pp. 102–31.

3 Between 1967 and 1979, the number of rusticated "educated youth" totaled 16,470,000, over ten percent of the urban population. MacFarquhar and Schoenhals, *Mao's Last Revolution*, pp. 251–52; and Thomas P. Bernstein, *Up to the Mountains and Down to the Villages: The Transfer of Youth from Urban to Rural China* (New Haven: Yale University Press, 1977).

4 Beginning in 1968, between 70 and 90 percent of the original employees in most ministries were sent down to "May Seventh Schools" in remote provinces to be "reeducated". MacFarquhar and Schoenhals, *Mao's Last Revolution*, p. 160; Yue Daiyun and Carolyn Wakeman, *To the Storm: The Odyssey of a Revolutionary Chinese Woman* (Berkeley: University of California Press, 1985); Yang Jiang, *Six Chapters from My Life "Downunder"*, trans. Howard Goldblatt (Seattle: University of Washington Press, 1984); etc.

5 *Vicious Beast* (动物凶猛) is the title of a novel by Wang Shuo (王朔), portraying the generation growing up during the Cultural Revolution under the same situation described here.

6 Hannah Arendt, *The Origins of Totalitarianism* (San Diego et al.: Harcourt Inc., 1968), pp. 305–26.

7 Stefan R. Landsberger, "The Deification of Mao: Religious Imagery and Practices during the Cultural Revolution and Beyond," in *China's Great Proletarian Cultural Revolution: Master Narratives and Post-Mao Counternarratives*, ed. Woei Lien Chong (Lanham, Maryland: Rowman and Littlefield, 2002), pp. 139–84; 147.

8 Song Yongyi, "A Glance at the Underground Reading Movement during the Cultural Revolution," *Journal of Contemporary China* 16, no. 51 (May, 2007), pp. 325–33; MacFarquhar and Schoenhals, *Mao's Last Revolution*, pp. 352–54.

9 Frederick C. Teiwes and Warren Sun, *The End of the Maoist Era: Chinese Politics During the Twilight of the Cultural Revolution, 1972–1976* (Armonk and London: M.E. Sharpe, 2007), pp. 110–85. For contrast with the first Cultural Revolution, see Carma Hinton, Geremie Barmé, and Richard Gordon, *The Morning Sun: A Documentary Film*, 2003; and Jonathan Unger, "The Cultural Revolution at the Grass Roots," *The China Journal* 57 (January 2007), pp. 109–37.

10 Ellen Johnston Laing, *The Winking Owl: Art in the People's Republic of China* (Berkeley: University of California Press, 1988).

11 The exact date of the exhibition is uncertain. It was most likely during a public holiday of the New Year. According to all my interviews, there are at least three possible dates: January 1, 1974; December 31, 1974; and January 1, 1975.

12 Landsberger, "The Deification of Mao;" and Julia F. Andrews, *Painters and Politics in the People's Republic of China, 1949–1979* (Berkeley: University of California Press, 1994), p. 360.

13 Teiwes and Sun, *End of the Maoist Era*, p. 160; and Laing, *Winking Owl*.

14 Richard Kraus, "Arts Policies of the Cultural Revolution: The Rise and Fall of Culture Minister Yu Huiyong," in *New Perspectives on the Cultural Revolution*, eds. William A. Joseph, Christine P.W. Wong, and David Zweig (Cambridge, Mass.: Council on East Asian Studies, Harvard University, 1991), pp. 219–42; 229.

15 Quoted in Kraus, "Arts Policies," pp. 230–31.

16 Cited from Nadine Gordimer: *Living in Hope and History: Notes from Our Century* (New York: Farrar, Straus and Giroux, 1999), p. 203.

17 Gordimer, *Living in Hope*, p. 198.

18 朱金石，〈优美的旋〉，《读书》，（2007）7，33–38页；刘迅，〈因势利导，繁荣群众美术活动〉，《美术》，（1979）9，8–9页；马建，〈现代派艺术的开拓者——无名画会〉，《人生伴侣》，香港：新世纪出版社，1996，24–32页；高名潞，《"无名"：一个悲剧前卫的历史》（*The No Name: A History of a Self-Exiled Avant-Garde*），广西师范大学出版社，2006；高尔泰，〈"无名画展"印象记〉，《论美》，兰州：甘肃人民出版社，1982年，104–107页；刘海粟，《齐鲁谈艺论》，济南：山东美术出版社，1985；栗宪庭：〈再访赵文量和杨雨澍〉，《新潮》（2001）8，73–78页.

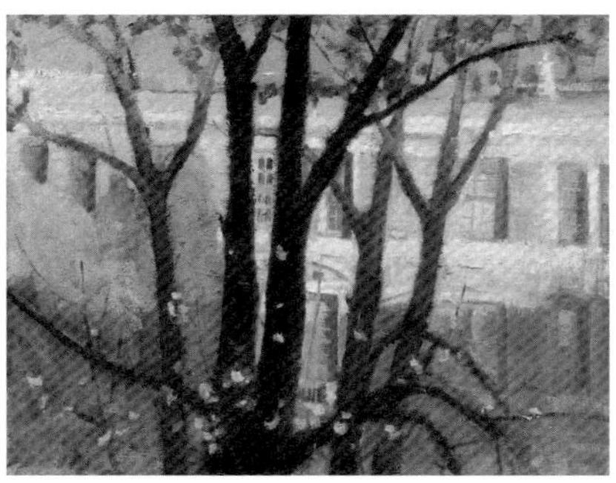

1

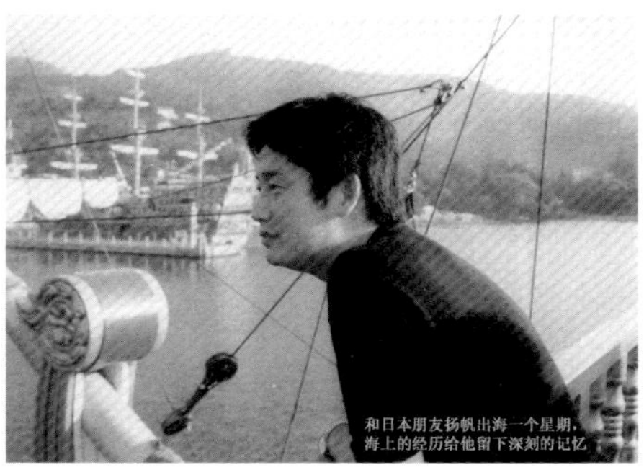

2

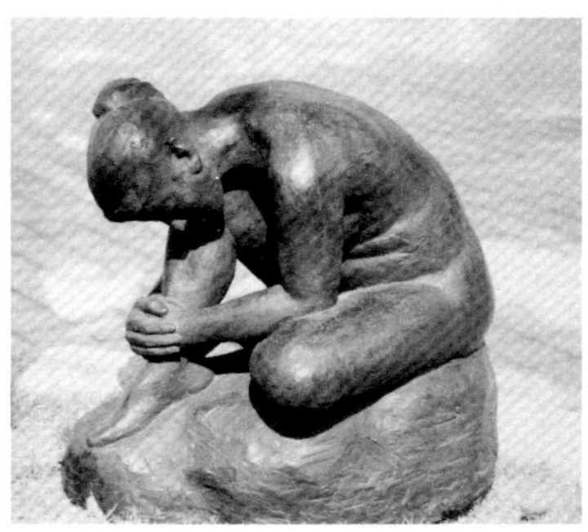

3

1 史习习：203大院东楼
1974, 40cm × 53cm
Shi Xixi, **The Eastern Hall of 203 Yard**

2 史习习在日本出海一星期，1990年
Shi Xixi sailing in Japan for a week, 1990

3 史习习：北方的夜
1992, 70cm × 50cm × 55cm
Shi Xixi, **Night of the North**

酿花时节
——记“无名画会”的那些年

刘是

“禔柳辰光参冷暖，酿花天气半晴阴。”这是我父亲在1978年写的律诗中的一句。

今天坐下来写起我自己的成人之初，就像果实回忆自己的酿花时节。

过去的事像遥远的恋爱，似止似行。

我是个很晚熟的人，那个时代的人都比现在的人晚熟。我更特殊一些，可能是各种营养都不良，又没有现在这么多激素。1971年底，朦朦胧胧中毕业于65中初中。初中学习，是三年的农村、工厂、军营的劳动；还有拆老城墙、烧砖坯、挖防空洞的快乐时光。我不记得当时学到了什么文化知识，只记得出了不少期的黑板报，画了不少个毛主席像。这就是我绘画的开始。

我那时所谓画毛主席像就是临摹画他的画像。当时市面上有很多不同版本画毛主席的画像，我一般是临摹木刻画。临摹在黑板上、墙上、大字报上、十字绣上。临摹得很像时，就很有成就感。在我们排（班）里，有能力临摹的人好像只有徐海林和我，他比我画得好。每一、两周出一期的黑板报上，一定要有毛主席像。我们每次都是等着女同学把文字内容写完，在她们留空白的地方画上毛主席画像。那种感觉很“腕儿”，很“大爷”的。

最让我迷恋的是放学后，在父亲所在的政府机关的大院里玩耍。那里原本是乾隆女儿的公主府，“五四”运动时期是北京大学的理学院。院子里前部分是办公楼区，后边、西边是家属区，巨大的迷宫一样的府院。父母下乡了，姐姐哥哥也陆续下乡了。他们去了哪儿我当时不知道，只知道他们去的是干校。家里没人了，外婆来跟我同住，看家看我。院里的大人们都像我的父母一样去了乡下，剩下一群看家看孩子的老太太和一群孩子。

一大群我们这样大的孩子主宰了大院。我们很少走出院子的高墙，住着上百户人家的院子好像一天都跑不完。院里是我们的世界，院外是大人们的争斗。要知道，在小学那六年，我是住在外婆家狭小的四合院里的，而且从不允许走出院门。我的天空只有几十平方米，上面是一棵老枣树的枝杈。

大院儿里一派欢乐景象，社会的波澜丝毫影响不到我们。每一家都在养动物，鸡鸭鹅兔鱼猫不算，蚕蛇老鼠乌鸦燕子刺猬无奇不养，奇怪的是没有狗。每家都种地，门前屋后，有的地块只有枕头大小。有一家人是用带把儿的尿盆种“死不了”，摆在门前一溜儿。我们无花不种无菜不栽。当时种了很多现在已经见不到的菜，紫红色的华丽的扁豆，一米长巨大的蛇豆，跟军用手雷一模一样的苦瓜。我们还用自己拉的屎尿做粪肥。

我们什么都敢吃，蜜蜂肚子里的蜜囊，护城河里的小虾，老槐树下的“狗尿苔”。气得院里的老太太们大呼小叫。十几米高的大殿房顶，满是尘土的老洋楼密室，深邃黑暗的防空洞，都是我们的游戏场。最让我惊奇的是大门站岗的士兵，有枪没有子弹，子弹袋里竟然是棉花！这段时光基本上是我上中学这三年。随着我毕业、工作，大人们陆续回来了，他们把社会上那股沉闷的气息也带回来了。我们的天堂结束了。

16岁的我，在朦胧中被政府分配到了一家小饭馆工作。1972年初，寒冬，一个大脸盘大屁股的男人，骑着三轮车来到我报到的东城区饮食公司，接走了我。我和另外两个新来的学生坐在他油腻腻的车上，慢慢地在胡同里走着，没有人说话。深深的蓝天下，满街空荡荡白花花的阳光。骑车的人就是我们的党支部副书记，他以前是个著名的烤鸭师傅。

我就这样只身走进了社会，像一个梦游的人。跟今天的我相比，当时的我就像没睡醒一样。发生了什么也不明白，也不知道自己想干什么，在干什么。有人说我们71届的毕业生很幸运，不用去插队，我完全没有这个感觉。那些跟我毫无关系的工作无聊而沉闷，让我不明白缘由的无尽无休的各种革命讨论，使我感到倍受煎熬。我就像在一个锅盖下活着一样，闷死了。

由于中学时画过毛主席像，就成了单位里有美术专长的人。每逢佳节，就由区公司组织到公园参加布置十一、五一的庆典。在一些大牌子上涂些巨大的黄色白色的标语，涂上鲜红的底色，画上一些梵高画的那种葵花，它在当时的政治含义是忠诚。有的牌子上要画上满面红光笑嘻嘻的工农兵，笑的原因是正值佳节。要是在某个政治运动的宣传画里，工农兵的表情就变得凶狠而愤怒难耐了。愤怒的表情就是把眉毛画成像耐克的LOGO，眼角向上嘴角向下，脸色还是红扑扑的，因为红色是好人的颜色。

我们还要做一些零碎的工作，用彩色皱纹纸条，向一个方向拧很多圈，轻轻拉直，成了旋转的花带。把它挂在公园的树杈之间，就有了佳节氛围。05年去朝鲜看到他们准备国庆庆典，很感熟悉。

好像在1973、74年的布置庆典时，结识了同样参加布置工作的邵小刚、马可鲁。马可鲁当时能在大板子上画工农兵像令我佩服。开始一段时间，他带着我和邵小刚到东、西交民巷去过几次，画那些清末民初时期的使馆洋房，练习写生。当时我们的写生风格与主流学院派的苏联风格差不多。

1973-74年，我父亲已经可以经常回到北京了。他看我总是在画画，就介绍我去找他的同学一个中央美院画家，让我跟他学画。你能想象他的画室里也都是那些虚假沉闷的革命主题的绘画，我肯定受不了。没有半年，我离开了。

似乎是在1974年前后，一个下午，马可鲁带着我和邵小刚去到玉渊潭公园。那时的公园里是没有什么人的。我们走进公园的深处，寂静的湖，泥土的岸。萧疏的树林里散落着几个人，他们离得很远。他们像当时所有的人一样，穿着蓝色的、灰色的毛制服，普通人的发型。每个人面对自己选择的风景，画着，没有人说话。天快黑了，他们竟然变得快乐起来，大声地说，唱，旁若无人，引来一些怀疑的目光。快要走到街上时，他们的声音压低了，谨慎了。我开始进到了这个圈子里，和他们一起画画。

他们就是后来“无名画会”的画友们。那时不叫无名画会，没有组织。当时我们就是一圈在一起画画交往的朋友，但是来往很密切。比天天在一起上班的同事要密切得多，差不多所有的业余时间我们都聚在一起。我的家人叫不出我当年同事的名字，可是他们至今还记得我的画友的名字。在1970年代这个朋友圈几乎是我们唯一的社交圈子。

1972年，有一个本来跟中国毫无关系的意大利人，导演米开朗基罗—安东尼奥尼Michelangelo Antonioni。据说是毛夫人江青请他来拍中国的纪录片。他不懂中国的规矩，客观地拍了他看到的。用他那善良的眼睛深切地关注着最普通的中国人。江青在电影里没看到她习惯的粉饰现实，对时代的歌颂。她怒了，她竟然让全中国的人批判安东尼奥尼。要知道当时我们没有一个人知道安东尼奥尼是谁，更没看过这部叫《中国CHUNG KUO》的电影。开批判会的时候大家就胡说八道，什么难听骂安东尼奥尼什么，什么好听说毛主席什么。还有那做作的人，声泪俱下。安东尼奥尼是怎么回事不重要，保护自己是第一的。这就是中国人讲的：顺我者昌！逆我者亡！这样的革命讨论在每一天下班后都要举行两个小时，只是那些莫名其妙的题目不断变换。《中国CHUNG

KUO》就记录了这样的情景。

七十年代，红卫兵不再喧闹了，家也没人抄了，不再见到跪在街头被批斗的可怜的老人了。被点燃的人性的恶也渐渐歇息下来。毛主席也不再每隔几夜就讲句莫名其妙的话，让我们连夜上街呼喊。似乎全中国都失去了方向，人民是倦怠的状态。激情被耗尽，沉闷就随之而来。但是社会依然是高压的社会，社会只有一个声音，任何不同的思想都是异己。对异己的制裁依旧是很严厉的，轻则批判重则关押乃至处决。在当时的报纸、广播、所有你能触及的媒体，在每一个人的嘴里，日夜不停地，无休止地叨唠着、拷问着：你对毛主席忠诚吗？你对他的主义、他的事业、他的国家忠诚吗？只要是有人的地方，只有这一个话题。

记得有一次我跟这群画友们去北戴河画海，我发着烧，躺在沙滩上还画。我不是用毅力在坚持、在克服痛苦；其实我是在享受自由、风、阳光。做自己想做的事情，在那时是何等的惬意。尽管那时我正为着被这群朋友里的个别人排挤而痛苦，那又算得了什么。我无法离开这个小集体。在这个团体里，我的反叛，躁动，求知，追求艺术的欲望，都是不受禁锢的。它与大的时代背景相比就是自由天地。

在那个年代，无名画会是一群很特别的人，他们脸上有着当时人们脸上很少见到的性格、自信、热情。他们唱着在外面的世界从没听到过的西方歌曲，谈论那些普通人从没看到过的谜一样的外国电影，讨论那些我根本不知道的印象派、野兽主义、立体派的外国现代派画家，画那些风格在官方媒体或中央美院里从没看到过的画，……。

我甚至结识我的女朋友，第一件事就是带她进入我画画的小圈子，带她看画，画画；她后来成了“无名画会”的画家。她是一个极其少见的人，她画中的世界永远都是那么无邪而又那么沧桑。在单位我有个极好的朋友，孟庆国，他有苦难的家事。我们成为好朋友时，我兴致勃勃地带他来到我画画的朋友圈，他也画得很好。直到后来，殷小林、徐海林、赵峰、冯健、小鞠，我很多好友都被我带进这个朋友圈。

七十年代地下状态中，艺术氛围还是很活跃的。不只是有我们这一圈画画的人，还有不少画画的小圈子活跃在社会上。估计当时北京至少有十几圈人这样画画。大家相互都认识。文学的，摄影的，也都有这样的圈子。那时很少有一个人画画的，因为资讯贫乏，更因为大环境那么高压，一个人画画在精神上你就很难撑得住。几个人十几个人，一圈朋友来往画画，相互产生的作用力确实有一种精神支撑。就像原始人赤身裸体地面对大自然，必然形成一个个部落，才能生存下去。

那时画画是半公开的。没有人禁止你，因为没有明文规定不允许画画，没有人可以证明画画是不热爱毛主席的活动。可是一小群人的活动是很扎眼的，在一双双质疑警觉的眼睛下，你必须小心谨慎，最重要的是不能让人们感觉到这群人有反现政权的倾向。万一被革命群众抓住你一句半句的反革命言论，打你一个“现行反革命”是很容易的事情。一旦到了这个地步，你就会知道什么叫“无产阶级专政”的威力。不仅你的个人命运会很惨，还会连累到这群人。这里没有玩笑的成分。

热爱艺术的青年们自发地聚集在一起。年长的对付社会，经验丰富、老到，自然成为中心人物。有不少小圈子里都有一两个年龄稍长的人物。年长的人，经常不断地告诫着不知深浅的青年。无名画会成员平安地渡过那个高压年代，跟我们那些年长的成员的经验和警惕有很大关系。像荒原上的一群野生动物，老的总是在队伍的外围，警惕地观察着四周，把那些离队的、要惹事的赶回到队伍里。

冯国东很早就跟我说：艺术不是职业，艺术是一种瘾。他真实地反映了那个时候画画青年的心态。我那时不管不顾地要画画，真是心里像有条虫样的无法控制。不是为了娱乐自己，不是为了改变自己的处境。好像只有画画才活得像个人，我心目中的“人”是那些能留作品于世的艺术家。

为了有时间画画，我主动争取天天上夜班。晚上8点上班，早上8点下班，这样就不用参加每天两小时的革命讨论了，就有时间画画了。夜班工作是给白天的各工种准备原料，最痛苦的是和炸油条的面。50斤面粉一缸，要在滚烫的水里放上一斤二两五盐，一斤二两五碱，半斤矾。要双手伸到水里搅拌面粉，像下地狱一样的痛。口子顺着掌纹裂开，见到白肉，流血，眼里是泪水，不是哭，是生理反应。每早要和三缸面，每次要把手伸进碱水里都要先吸气，咬牙，夹紧双腿。每天夜里都不能睡觉，但是白天是我的，我自己的。全部用来跑去各个公园画画，沉浸在另一种生活中。最后，这个工作因为给了我太多的自由，被领导调换了。

我爱读书，我父亲的书柜都贴着红卫兵的封条，我也偷偷打开过，都是古文，当时我看不懂。倪初万的父亲是民主人士，家里的书柜没有被封上封条，我们就偷出来看，还在画友中间传看。无名画会的人各有各路，每个人都能弄到好书，很神奇的。有多少根本在社会上看不到的书，听也没听说过的书，竟然在我们中间流传，几年间从未间断过这种传阅。这是我们在画画之外最频繁的活动。我的生活中也只是两件事，画画、读书。当时社会上没有几本书是可以让普通人看得到的，铺天盖地的都是毛主席著作和关于他著作的著作。

每次到倪初万家拿书都是晚上。我鬼鬼祟祟地站在他们院子巨大的丁香树丛的阴影里，把上次借的书还给他，等他再拿出新的书来。他无声地溜回家里，许久不出来。他家里总是暗暗的，而且没有一点声音，那时每个家庭都是这样的夜晚。我记得最珍贵的是《傅雷家书》和《约翰·克里斯朵夫》，上面有傅雷的亲笔留言。他是倪初万父亲的好友，我那时竟然不知道他已经自杀。有一本白皮的编译参考丛书之一《海鸥—乔纳森·利文斯顿》，就在我们画友的圈子里传丢了。倪初万至今坚持说，当年丢的，不仅是这一本。

书一到手就像蚕吃桑叶一样地看，不停地看，经常一夜看完一本书。因为借给你的人催得急，我就走路看书，骑车看书。经常撞到电线杆，要不就骑在电线杆的斜拉钢缆上。这是好玩的。不好玩的是街上巡逻的工人民兵，他们想起什么就要检查你：看的是什么书？我就把书一合给他们看，封面是关于社会主义哲学的，书名不记得了，作者是新中国的哲学家，好像姓齐名字也忘了。因为这个书皮的脊够厚，很多本书我都是夹上这个书皮看。这是表面镇静，其实心里突突直跳。因为要是他们查出我看的那种书，肯定是通知单位，又是一通批判，罪名一定是“看黄色小说”。在社会低下阶层没有那么多的政治知识，“黄色”是一种能够概括很多违背当时政治规范的罪名。

当年我们喜欢听音乐，上中学时是在同学车临家听。因为他们家是民主人士，他是张自忠将军的外孙，他家就有了一个外界没有的环境。他家有个落地的黑胶片唱机，基本都是听西方的古典乐曲，那时只觉得好听，真的听不懂。当时很难找到音乐听的，普通人家里很少有磁带有唱片，更很少有唱机。几乎除了那些上流人家，大干部家，很难在一般百姓家里见到除收音机以外能出声的物件儿了。记得66年夏，我外公外婆连夜慌忙砸毁了自己家的黑胶唱片，为的是赶在红卫兵来到时有个好表现。我外公是个京戏迷。

那时街上的音乐都是些什么？一致的激昂，一致的叫喊，内容是关于热爱毛主席和他的事业。1977年之后，不记得具体时间了，不记得向谁借的唱机，只记得听的是贝多芬第五交响曲。一开机，那几个音符迸发出来，我的泪就下来了，不知勾起什么来了，百感交集。那一刻像刀一样刻在心上。

感谢那个时代。没有那种环境，那种压力，我怎么会有那么美好的深刻的感受呢。

七十、八十年代中国人的收入很少，我工作两年出师后一个月工资是21.08元。工作单位的饭费是12元一个月，每月的公车月票要5元。我只好画月票，还帮别人画。用水粉颜料，给它脱了胶，在很旧的月票底板上画上当月的小票儿。用衣纹笔画，衣纹笔细到只有几根毛，小票有两枚邮票大小，做这个事情要很耐心的。月票底板是一年换一次，贴在上边的小票是一月换一次，那就要月月画了。

最终，车站的查票人查出来我的假月票，通知了单位，批判了我一个多月。我真是少不更事，我认为使用假月票是去画画，画的画是国家文化的一部分，国家本就该支持我，我没有错。我是认真地这么想的。可想而知，党支部的人有多生气。他们心想怎么就制不服我，结果就天天开会批判我。说我画的是修正主义的花花草草，不务正业，占国家便宜可耻。我当时真是没有幽默感，认真地顶着，直到发了急性黄疸型肝炎，住了医院此事才了结。去医院是个早晨，外婆走在前头，我夹着一卷什么东西，几乎快倒下了，就觉得路这么远，好像永远走不到。街上没人注意我，那时的街上谁也不想多看谁一眼，也没什么好看的。这是我人生第一次尝到凄凉的滋味。那是1977年夏天。

有段时候，我们这个小集体几乎天天在一起画画。没有固定的时间，只是分手时谁问一句，明天去哪呀？就会有个约定。玉渊潭，紫竹院，香山，樱桃沟，八大处，颐和园，文化宫，故宫，后来有北海，什刹海，都是我们的画室。当时的公园大多都在城市的西边北边，奇怪的是很少去景山。没有几点的约定，早下班的早到，有时有的人黄昏才来。画不了画了也来，参加天黑之后的谈话，那也是这群人的重要交流。

每天下班和画友们聚集，一天的精神生活才开始。现在想起来人格是分裂的，在单位工作时人是一个样子，画友相聚时又是一个样子。很像现在国际化大公司里的白领们那种人格分裂的状况。去公园聚会，画画，谈话。因为那时的公园就是一块圈起来的荒地，在那画水树云花，理所应当。没人质疑你画什么？为什么画？在街上不行了，就有不少怀疑的目光。在公园谈话旁边耳朵也少，人迹罕见。仔细看我们的画就可以发现，随着政治形势的松动，我们画画的地点也在向城市里边移动。

当时的人是不能自由活动的。出门旅行是一种复杂而冒险的事情，到处都要“单位介绍信”。也就是说你离开你的城市去旅行，要有单位来证明你有工作需要的理由去旅行。不可能是你自己想要到哪里走走，你自己想做什么不能成为一种理由。大概是从五十年代开始的这个规矩，八十年代以前很多很多的北京市民30多年没离开过这个城市一步。全中国都是这样的。

1980年之前，我为了画画只离开北京市一次，和大家去北戴河画画。出行的那张介绍信是大年龄的画友伪造的。结果离开北戴河的时候，我离队行动，被警察扣住。原因是我回答不出我来北戴河的理由，当然我不能回答说我的小吃店派我来画画，警察非笑喷了饭不可。

公园在自己住的市区里，至少还可以想去就去。那时的公园没有现在这么人工化，我们觉得自己像是在巴比松一样，把公园当作大自然。我走进公园，面对一棵树，一朵云；我现在还记得那是一种真正成为了人的感觉。绘画温暖着我，愉悦着我，充实着我。

现在看起来，那时候我们画了那么多水树云花。好像我们只对花花草草感兴趣。其实不然。那时的社会要求每个人拿起革命的笔做武器，清除异己，清除每一个独立的人格。一天到晚火药味超极浓，人人弩张剑拔。全民皆兵，什么都叫武器：锣鼓琴键画笔，扫地的扫帚擀面的棍。什么都叫战斗：拔麦子叫夏收战斗，炸油条叫促生产战斗，几个人在一起叫战斗小组，学校的班级叫排，年级叫连。每一天都有敌人在，在哪儿你并不一定看得见。自己也是敌人，狠斗私字一闪念。社会的趋向越是这样，我们越逆反，越逆主流而行。当社会越要消灭人的独立人格，那些坚持自己的人，必然开辟一片自己的土壤，建立自己的精神世界。

水树云花，闲逸离世。逆反当时的虚夸的歌颂，意味着一种独立的精神追求。很是了得，可以令人惊慌。当时美院有一个画家就指着我的画说没有一点革命气息，我能听出他的语气中的不安，因为他是我父亲的挚友。

七十年代，你要逆行，你有何去处？不像三、四十年代，还有个延安。七十年代或是监狱劳改营，或是人迹罕见的公园。一棵树一朵云，成了我们一种必然的精神抗争，寄情人生的净土。相反要是在三十至四十年代，我们这样逆反性格的人，一定也会唾弃风花雪月鸳鸯蝴蝶，因为在那个时代，水树云花就是不同的意味了。我一定会拿起笔做刀枪，跟着鲁迅抨击黑暗，揭露民生苦痛。我肯定会投笔从戎，直接跑到延安去了。

七十年代，每个人的命运都紧紧地和政治相连。国家的政治变动影响着个人的命运。无名画会的人也不例外，经常谈政治。人人谈政治，传政治“小道消息”。1976年夏，最多的小道消息是一会儿传“老毛”快不行了，一会儿传还好着呐。记得是个下午，在玉渊潭，远处隐隐约约传来似哀乐似喊叫的声音，很不正常。大家立即静下来，不记得是谁说一定是毛主席出事了，气氛一下压抑了。我们没画完画，就收拾画箱，四散回家了。这是我们画画以来唯一一次自己中断画画，突起的狂风暴雨都没有中断过。走时好像赵文量嘱咐大家这几天一定要特别小心。

我和邵小刚没有回家，直接跑到天安门。我们站在门洞底下，面对着金水桥上一群茫然的人，他们都在看着天安门城楼发呆，突然有一个人喊道：“都给我站直喽”。他一边鞠躬一边高喊：“一鞠躬……”，桥上的人群惶惶然地跟着鞠躬。他是矮个有白发五六十岁的男人，圆圆的头，国防绿的军官制服。突然旁边有人拉了我们衣服一下，人不见了，我们明白不能站在这里。

毛主席的去世，普通老百姓要做的就是近一个月天天早晚对着他的遗像致哀。每个单位都建立他的灵堂，挂黑布，放哀乐。成为一种短期的例行公事。我们单位最厉害的是有个比我大一岁的女孩，整整一个月，天天一早一晚做极其痛苦状，可以天天哭两场，一转身又是满面春风的。我知道她的愉悦来自于她终于有机会接近自己的目标了，很快她入了党还当上党支部成员了。最显著的变化就是她不用每天炸油条了，身上也不再有菜籽油的味道。

虽然在我们的作品里没有政治性的题材。在一个个政治事件中，我们都是积极的参加者，因为我们对正义有独立的见解。随着自己的成熟，我参加每一次政治事件动机是不同的。但内心的根本动力是因为我有自己的正义感，有愤世的叛逆的情结。还有一种冯至讲的，正义冲动效应。1976年的“4.5”运动，我兴奋地在天安门广场跑了一天，晚上不敢回家，躲在孟庆国的小屋里。最深的记忆是当天入夜，街头到处是默默无声的一群群裹在黑蓝色棉大衣里的工人民兵。他们都是三条腿，有一条是从棉大衣里伸出来的一条木棍，那是铁锹的木把。一派肃杀之气。1978年，“民主墙”，我居然第一次在公众讲演，还赢得了掌声，尽管听众不过十几人。

我竟然也还清晰地记得很多当时画画时的情景：几个人，几乎一个姿势，单肩背着画箱、书包，有近十斤重，很多人都背斜了肩。一个手揣在裤兜里，散散地走着，前前后后有时拉得很长，或是一大横排。其中有一个人看到了自己想画的题材，停下了，大家就一起议论着，很快其他人就散开，各自找到自己感兴趣的题材。常有几个人画同一题材，好像没人在意这个。画画时的姿势也很相像，因为大家都用自制的无腿小画箱，大小跟一本辞海差不多。都是左手托着画箱，还拿着笔，一只手可以拿好几支笔，右手画，这样画画的样子是很少见的。

站在你的树面前，一边慢条斯理地打开画箱，一边眯起双眼观察，力图忽略那些细节概括地找到气氛。挤颜色时是很仔细的，挤得很少很齐，排列在调色盘上就像一条彩虹。我们无名画会人的调色盘、画笔在画画圈里是出名的干净。调色盘画完一定仔细地反复地擦，使调色盘像有一层玻璃一样的光亮。画笔一定用肥皂仔细地洗，把笔根留的颜色洗干净，用小纸条包上，笔毛永远是软软的齐齐的。我们是在享受这些细节，也在享受这里边含有的自尊的滋味。

赵文量画画是很天马行空的。他经常会从落在纸上的第一笔开始，就一直追寻着纸上的变化画下去，旁观的人不知他的思路从哪来的。有时他画完已经看不出画和面前的风景有多少关系，可是他还是仔细观察着面对的风景，我在一旁看得总是很奇怪。他画画出奇地慢，经常当你以为他快要画完时，他会为最后一两笔，再画上一两个到几个小时。他画画的时候很喜欢和我们散散地聊些什么。

杨雨澍画画时身边总是有围观的人，人们觉得他像外国人。他画画总是很严肃，不管他画箱里的纸有多大，他总是像做件大事一样，腰杆挺直，目不斜视，一言不发。他好像一直是站着画画，我不记得见过他坐下或蹲着画画。

王爱和总是坐着画画，不管在哪，她总是要找个地方坐下。可能是她当时身体不好，也可能她就不是一个讲究洁净的姑娘。她坐着的视角和我们站着画出来的透视差不多。她总是画得很慢，看半天，一笔才落下。她画海的时候，久久地坐在那，看着一个海浪接一个海浪，打来退去。她拿着画笔，似乎在等海浪什么时候凝固在那才画。她画画时绝不理会身边发生的任何事情，我有时站在她身边很久她也察觉不到。她平时动作也很慢，脑袋大的人动作总是慢。她有一个大脑袋，一条巨粗超黑的辫子。

杜霞也是画画很慢的人，她画画时很轻盈，总是用很少的颜色，很小心地调颜色，很小心地画。她的画平和，动作也平和。她画画很爱说话，有时自言自语。她那时少了一颗牙，说话漏风，不是很清楚。

马可鲁画画的样子气势很大、很激动。他总摆出很帅的姿势，越有人看越帅。

田淑英画画时总是收紧嘴唇，还一动一动的，很像水里的金鱼。她画画很放松，很平静，好像不是画画，是在干个什么日常的活计。经常她画完我们就说好，她总是说，什么呀，一点都不像。她是真地一直都这么认为。可能到今天她还会这么想：我画就是了，你们用不着这么鼓励我。

韦海很有特点，他怎样画画我不记得了。他唱歌的情景我记忆犹新，他可能是怕震到我们，他总是在离我们很远的地方唱，声音很大，传得很远。我不懂他唱得好不好，他歌声里总是有很激情的情绪，很感染人。

我没有注意过我自己什么样，我画画很快，像我现在吃饭。

还有好多人，我记不清他们的特点了，可能因为平时一起画画不多，来往又少。

那时的无名画会有几个人真是能人。极浓的DIY气氛：杨雨澍做的画箱、调色刀像艺术品，我们暗地里都希望得到一个；石振宇做的裤子极其专业；邵小刚用一本两寸厚的字典学会了英文，他还会做眼镜……。几乎画会里每个男人都会做木工，我也学会了做木工，学会了裁剪裤子，用缝纫机。我自己做的画箱很小，只好把画笔锯短，才能放进箱子里。我的画箱用染布的孔雀蓝染料做成湖蓝色的，好看极了。小画箱可以放在书包里，上下班时带着没人注意，可是只能画小画。自己做的带腿画箱太大了，就做了一个超大帆布书包装它，石振宇还画过一张我驼着背，背着大书包的漫画，很有趣。

我发现用鞋盒子的盖儿那样的硬纸壳做油画纸板很好用，用了好多，好些人叫它是鞋盒子画。我的第一批油画是用邵小刚的外文书里的书页，两张粘在一起涂上骨胶做的油画纸。

还有一件很有特点的事，我们几乎都是以小画幅作画，基本是 A4 纸面大小。尤其是开始那几年，大家很一致。现在大家留下的小画幅作品总和就有几千张。你要是没看到那些画，一定会想，A4，那么小的地方能画出什么来。回想起当年画这些小画，似乎没有感到过局促，没有感到过地方小得转不开身。方寸之间，竟容得下我们那么丰富的感受。方寸之间，可以风起云涌，可以如醉如痴。记得有时没有了感受可画，笔也是空洞的。一张小纸怎么也画不满，填不完。就像中国人说的“室雅何须大”。在那个时代，我们的感受与外部世界差别是那么巨大，使得倾吐这些感受变得很迫切，表达的机会也很珍贵。自然，画中的精神世界就饱满起来，这就是有所感而发。画中一但充满精神世界就突破物理的大小了。

这些小画成了无名画会的特点，也成了那个时代的特点了。我一进入无名画会的圈子，他们就在画小画，我就开始跟着他们画小画，也不知是从谁开始的这种形式。那个物质匮乏，人民匮乏的时代，我们每一个人都不能免于匮乏。我们又是被排斥在主流之外的“业余画画的”，政府是丝毫不会给我们提供绘画资料的。我们只有画小画，节约得来不易的材料。正好也使我们缩小目标，不引人注目。因为“业余画画的”就是意味着你不是被政府认可的画家，这个称谓带有一定的非法的含义。这是很重要的一个画小画的客观原因。

看看我们画幅的尺寸，它也是在变化的。基本上是和政治解冻同步地逐渐地画幅变大了起来。

几乎每次在外边画画都能遇到好奇的人，你画多久他站你旁边看多久。好像北京人至今还是那么好闲，好围观。最好玩的是有人会站在你的正前面，挡住你的视线，他还会看看你的脸看看画，问，你画哪儿呐？还有人会站你一旁合影留念，使你觉得自己象颐和园的铜牛。那时的人是很无聊的，去公园里溜的人更是因为无聊。看画的人最多的品评就是画得像不像。要是正赶上我们中间谁的心情不好就麻烦了，一定会引起口角。赶上谁的心情好就拿那品评的人开心，你一言我一语可好玩了。

那时我们就很有“环保”意识，只要画完画，一定要把地上擦笔纸拾起来，一点不留痕迹。我们有几个人淘气，包括我，有时把调废了的颜色抹在地上、树上，赵文量会马上制止。现在的人很难猜出我们当时的想法，我们当时想的是：如果把环卫工人惹烦了，就会告诉他们领导，我们再来画画就会困难了。我们是在保护自己画画的环境。至今我拍片，还一定跟制片反复强调搞好扫尾工作，别让人家怕了摄制组。

赵文量跟每一个人说不要把图钉扎在画面上，要侧着按在边上。不要用手摸画，就像不要用手摸自己的眼球。现在仔细看，很多无名画会人的画上都在四角上留有图钉的痕迹。一定是半圆的地方没有颜色，那是图钉帽压在画上挡住了画笔涂不上颜色；但没有钉子扎的孔。

画是我们存在的意义，是我们生命的证明。我有一段流浪在北京，搬了十几次家，至今什么都没有留下，连我的朋友出国时托我保管的一箱物品都丢了。当年的画没丢，而且像新画的一样。杜霞放在我这儿的画，二十几年后交还给她时也都是完好无缺。今天的社会，谁有钱就尊重谁。当时的社会没有谁尊重谁。全民尊重毛主席，人与人之间相互没有尊重可言。在这个集体里那种尊重艺术的氛围衍生成一种自尊人格，它影响了我的后半生。

我沉浸在这个小集体里，它成了我生活的主要部分。我依然要面对我的工作单位、社会。我渐渐长大了，我变成单位里的“老大难”。因为我读书，画画，成长，我有自己的人格，有自己的好恶，自己的观点，又是一个天生淘气的人，我总是有意无意地触犯当时的政治规范，单位规章。我成了单位党支部的对立面，“坏分子”的典型。但我没有那些低级卑劣的毛病，领导抓不住给我治罪之处。我倒是经常在那些无知的政治讨论会上与领导争辩，使领导威风扫地。

1977年之后，打压、吓唬、写检查、告家长的办法对我失效了。他们只好用“流放”的办法让我远离群众，我被安排到郊区和一个老师傅看砖。两年砖用完了，我又被安排去看楼。又和另外一个老师傅在一起。不知为什么，一座楼空空的几年没人住。我很快乐，我有大把时间玩，画画。我很怀念一同看砖的老师傅，我还画了他的像。忘了他姓什么，记得他是涿鹿县的人，不知道他现在还在不在人间了。他讲了好多我不知道的事情，他告诉我许多抗日时好玩的事。告诉我一看人的鞋就知道他老了没有，他的鞋尖烂了就是老了。因为他撒尿时没力气了，尿总是洒在鞋尖上就容易烂。那时的人都穿布鞋。后来我才明白，人老了，走路抬不起脚，就容易把鞋尖踢烂。幸好他的话党支部不知道，否则他一定惨了，至少是属于黄色事件。

领导想要让我失去尊严感，就安排我到百货大楼广场前卖冰棍。那是当年北京仅有的三个消费中心之一，也是最出名的一个，经常人山人海的。别人家单位都是老太太去卖，我在那里边一定是很搞笑的样子。但我不觉得这样的我就失去尊严了。我依旧快乐，我行我素。这样我反而就不用回单位参加革命的讨论。前一段，我居然在《中国CHUNG KUO》这部电影里看到当年百货大楼前卖冰棍的情景，可惜拍摄的时候我还没有那份工作。

我很清楚地知道我的尊严来自于绘画，那是我的精神家园，我生命意义在于我有精神生活。

1979年后，我们这个小团体渐渐来往得不是那么紧密了。其实在我进来这个小团体时起，交往的过程中渐渐地自然形成了两三个更亲密的朋友小圈。这些小圈接触更多，交往更深。要是以无名画会所有成员而论，我和大多数的人之间相互是很不了解的。他们的家庭，他们的工作，他们的社会情况，他们的私生活，相互几乎完全不了解。我们大家的交往基本上是保持在公园里小饭馆里，活动基本是画画聊天。我是很少去别人家里，只是赵文量、王爱和、杜霞的家去得很多，因为我们来往得很密切。我和203的那圈朋友来往得很少。203是文化部宿舍的门牌号，成了一圈人的简称。

1949年新中国成立到八十年代初新时期之前，中国是物质匮乏的时代。个人财富早已被革命剥夺了，人之间财富差距很小，富有抑或贫穷不能在人们之间划分阶级。但是人们的生活中有明显的阶级，不是地富反坏右与所有非地富反坏两个敌对阶级，而是统治阶级和被统治阶级。统治阶级就是当政阶级。“革命干部”是其代称。填写家庭出身时就可以把“革干”当成阶级成分来填。“高干”是这个阶级上层的代称。高干有自己的学校、购物场所等等，我妈妈所在的“北京男八中”就是高干子弟学校之一。东华门附近有个食物“特供点”专供应高干们，他们甚至独占接触文化的特权。这些特权完全可以显示不同阶级的身份。与之相对应的下层阶级被统称作“小市民”，虽然当时宣扬“革命没有高低贵贱之分，只有分工不同”。“革干”和“小市民”阶级这两个阶级有很深的矛盾，这点明显地反映在“文革”初“走资派”遭到的惨痛的境遇上。就连温和的杨绛写的“文革”回忆里都可以看到这一点。机关大院里的孩子就属于这类干部子弟。因为他们分享着这个阶级的“天赋优越权”，自然生出优越意识。我很反感这种优越意识，所以跟他们来往很少。也不是所有的干部子弟都有这种优越意识，冯国东的父亲是个将军，他自己却没有这种优越意识。

无名画会成员的组合不是偶然的，每一个人都是有社会属性的人。细细想来，无名画会的成员们，基本是来自于社会的中层阶级，相当于现在的中产阶级。我们中间有些年长的成员，他们的家庭在旧社会里也是属于资产阶级或中产阶级。我们这些生在新中国的年轻的成员，大多数家庭都来自知识分子、干部家庭，属于新中国统治阶级的中层。我们至少不像那些低层阶级的孩子们那样的经济拮据，要负担家庭生计。这使我们处在一种共同的社会位置，我们的品味、语境、价值观就有了一种沟通的基础。这也是我们之间有人来自被政权迫害者的家庭，有人来自政权的得利者的家庭，为什么还会形成一个团体的原因之一。

在那个时代中，我们没有也不可能跳出那个时代的影响。尽管我们当时的行为是在挑战当局，挑战社会。我们属于那个时代的叛逆者之一。

无名画会的艺术局限不在于画幅的大小，而在于我们当年的视野小，精神境界就小。我至今天还是存在这个问题。在我们当年的艺术中是避世的态度，所以我们着力地关心着自己的感受、关怀着自己。自然，视野就小。除个别一两个人外，无名画会的作品里少有对众生的关怀和追问。我不知这是不是一种自私，至少今天我们对艺术的观点已经很不同了。今天，资讯发达，新闻解禁，我们了解那么多生命存在的状态，那么多自然的、社会的摧残，那么多的无助。我们不能无视他们的存在，我们的艺术不能只关注着自我那点微小的痛痒，那样的艺术又有什么意义。无名画会的艺术在境界中有一种深层的民族性，独特性。它是发端于中国文人画中那种乱世修身的个人境界。但是，今天的我看来，只是养眼极好。我不能满足自己停留在那么局限的境界里，因为我通过影像艺术认识了更多的艺术大师，窥见了他们展示出来的宏大的精神世界，宽厚的关怀。

我们之间的分歧是存在的，我关心的少，不是太了解。有些争执、分歧很无意义。我记得在1979年筹办第一次“无名画会”展览时，关于谁排在什么位置，在哪个展室，是争执最多的。甚至关于我的画应该不应该放在进门左手画展的最尾位置也有争论。反而我不记得我们中间有哪个曾经为自己的艺术观点争得面红耳赤。或者我们之间谁为了不同的艺术见解而分裂的。有时我能感觉到有人在对什么有意见，我不明白为什么事情，也不想明白。也经常听到几个人背后批评一个人或是他的艺术，却几乎没有见过当面的批评。我不知道他们是不够坦荡，还是对自己不自信。背后议论或批评几乎形成画会里共有的习惯，背后的谈论批评可以不计言辞的伤害，甚至可以对自己的言词不负任何责任。至少这是一个让人必须改正的习惯吧。

有一次在紫竹院，下大雨，我画一棵在雨中的柳树，我也站在雨中。调色板上的颜色在雨中，油水混合，变得泥泞了，画笔都拉不动了。而且超级冷，身体直抖。现在看来画面还有颜色粘粘的样子，画得并不算好。走到街上，行人匆匆跑过，好像下的不是雨是硫酸。我慢慢地走着，心里想，这些庸人，碌碌无为。我觉得我是画画的人，是最有价值的人。自己心中有一种孤傲的英雄感泛起。莫名的自大。这种感觉是来自于画会里的影响，也来自充斥着社会的英雄主义教育的影响。

我们从小受的是革命英雄主义教育——具有牺牲精神，以死去的英雄做榜样，为了党的事业贡献自己的生命。每个人陷入一种正义感的陶醉之中。我小的时候，几乎每个孩子都能流利地背出一大串革命烈士的名字，而能背出水浒“一百单八将”名字的孩子要少得多。我到现在还记得不少烈士的名字。我小的时候特别想从事的职业就是烈士，我以为那是一个崇高的职业。

在我们逆反的社会里盛行的英雄主义，其实也作用在我们这些逆反者身上。八十年代之前高压政治的社会告诉我们，自由无望。我们这些与主流社会流逆行的人，必然产生一种自我流放的感觉。对自由的绝望是带有悲剧色彩的。大家自然下意识地给自我涂上一层崇高的，英雄的，悲剧的色彩，下意识地在自我高化。至今我还有一种自我边缘化的潜意愿，享受着给这种状态抹上淡淡的悲剧色彩的高化的感觉。我们这一代人至今也依然习惯性地自我崇高、自我高化。就是我在写这篇文章时，我可能就在自我高化，我无法避免这样的现象发生。我毕竟是那个时代长大的。没有人真正地可以特立独行。这些社会特性在你成熟期会渗浸你的性格，成为你性格的一部分。甚至到现在，在那个时代成长起来的人的嘴里，悲剧这个词还带有浓浓的褒义。比如研究无名画会的一本书，名《……一个悲剧的前卫……》。我想了很久也不明白，无名画会的“悲剧”究竟发生在哪里？因为写书的人和我们是同时代的人，他可能下意识地在高化我们而已。前一段见一个同画会的朋友还在说“……我们是悲剧英雄……。”

我们无名画会这个圈子里有一种崇拜氛围也是很有时代特点的。七十年代，社会里充斥的个人崇拜情结并不是1968年突发的，也不是1964年林彪才开始制造的，它由来已久。它使人们忽略个人价值，就像现在社会刺激崇拜明星情结，可以产生极大的获利点。于是当今社会就有了宠物一般娇贵的明星和红卫兵一般热情的“粉丝”。个人崇拜情结一直就是有意识地被使用的工具。崇拜心理有时是随着青春期发育而产生的生理现象。青年人希望尝试自我价值而去模仿他人，这种模仿很容易被利用，或是自行衍生成崇拜情结。模仿和崇拜之间一纸之隔。

我知道自己在青春期时很长的时间里都有着一种崇拜情结。我当时很崇拜画会里的年长成员。我有一段时间一下了班就往有位年长成员家里跑，我外婆说我长在他家了。他家盖小房，我就回我们大院里，拉上公家的木材要给他送去。我妈妈阻止我，我竟然和她大吵，还骂她。我认为他是伟大的艺术家，政府不帮他，我帮，没错。他的妈妈做手术在家养病，我和另一个朋友轮流看护。我觉得为他做事我愿意。凡是他们需要帮忙的，我都希望能帮上忙。有一阵差不多他们走到哪我就跟到哪。我现在看来，当时我有不少的画、行为都在模仿他们。当时的我和现在追捧周杰伦、周笔畅的“粉丝”们有什么区别？因为我们都年轻过。

当时，我们抵制着外边社会里的崇拜情结对个人的压力，顽强地培育、维护着自己的独立人格。奇怪的是，同时我们的小团体中间却也在生成着崇拜氛围。当时我们画会里不少人认为世界上画得最好的艺术家就是我们画会里的谁了。我们中间有多少人在暗中模仿某人。大家对绘画大师，崇敬如神。记得刚结识唐平钢时，他对我们素常崇敬的大师信口批评，我都惊了。我们传看着安徒生的《光荣的荆棘路》，它已经不是童话了，它是圣徒的赞美诗。“文如其人”也是当时常常引用的一种褒义评价，其实它只是用于催化着人们的崇拜情结。我一直到很大了才明白，基本没有“文如其人”这回事的。这种崇敬的氛围就是崇拜氛围。至少当时没有人站出来告诉大家，我们应该警惕这种崇拜情结在我们小团体里的蔓延。我们正经历着“文革”后期，外面社会的状况时刻在教育着我们。

不知道我们有意还是无意地在营造着小团体里的崇拜氛围。大家都在树立崇敬目标，追随共性，弱化个性差异，就容易凸现一个中心人物、一个流派了？当年，尽管无名画会整体风格和其他团体的绘画风格之间有很大差异，陌生的眼睛一下就可以发现我们作品之间的风格、题材、趣味是很近似的。后来渐渐不少画友离开了，若干年之后他们的作品里却出现了新的个人风格，在这套画册中是可以看到这个过程的。

我们尽管多年自觉地在与当时的主流意识抗争，我们毕竟是在那个政治意识下完成的教育与自我教育。你常常是和你反对的东西有思维方式上相像之处。无名画会里的氛围是在当时其它小团体里不多见的。甚至至今，依然有这种氛围弥漫在我们某些人身上。在当年，也是这种氛围成就了我们这个小团体。她产生一种凝聚力，这种力量使我们坚持下来，举办展览，把自己公布于世。很多在当年的一些画画的小团体，最后不了了之，就证明了我们这个小团体的凝聚力。也正是这种氛围，使得我们这个小团体解散了。这个分散是必然的。也是生命现象的折射。我们在这个小团体里度过自己的青春期，人总要长大，实践自己的独立人格。之后有人讲，分散就是离开的人有负于谁，伤害了谁，是没有良心的。这种议论就已经证明我上述的氛围是确有其事。

在我们几十年后再相聚时，有一种争论：我们画会有没有灵魂人物。有灵魂就有肉体，就有价值差别，就可以导致个人崇拜。就会弱化一些人的价值，夸张一些人的价值。我们知道这种价值差别对每一个独立人格的损害。坚持人是平等的民主观点是一个地下自由团体当然持有的观点。时值今天，我们这个小团体里还是要争论它，这是很有意思的现象。无名画会要是当年解散之后，没有2006年7月的重新聚合；没有七十，八十年代的我们和2000年代的我们同时展现出来；今天研究无名画会就只局限在一个狭小的范围里。因为在无名画会贯穿了我们生命的过程时，在我们身上看到了时代的变迁和个体生命的衍化的相互作用。我们就具有了生命样本的意义。七十年代，2000年代，只是我们生命旅途的两个车站，连接这两站之间那二十几年的轨道，弯曲而漫长地画出人生的弧线。从我们看到了人。

二十几年前，也是丁香盛放的时节，我们一心埋头画画，心清如水。自命不凡，白眼看青天。我们在抗争着什么？我们在建树着什么？我们为什么画画？艺术给了我们什么？我们得到了什么？

今天，同样是丁香盛放。主流社会关注了我们，挖掘我们的过去，为它赋予不平凡的意义。我们似乎知道、又似乎不知道，今天的主流社会为什么要突然青睐我们。我们不深究，大家兴致勃勃，配合主流，齐唱高调。我们还一心画画吗？还心清如水吗？我们在抗争着什么？我们在建树着什么？我们为什么画画？艺术给了我们什么？我们得到了什么？

我们一心希望无名画会声扬四海，在中国现代绘画史上占有一席之地。无名画会出名了，有人或多、有人或少地就会有所斩获的。有人期待走进绘画史，成为“圣人”；有人期待为自己艺术家的身份加码，为绘画这个饭碗镀金。

但是我们大家都不如20年前真实了。

因为我们知道，推广需要有卖点，大家心照不宣。我们看到了机会。我们情不自禁地积极营造、推动各种活动。一边诉说着当年为艺术自甘寂寞，一边兴致勃勃地参加着每一个出名的机会。塑造着自己可敬的人格，重彩浓描着一段段历史，不乏神化自己的成分。演说讨论，真真假假。不惜说出不算谎言至少不够真实的话语。私底下暗中相互指摘，公众场合相互搭台。

如果有一天“无名画会”也名声显赫，就证明列农 John Lennon 说的是真话：“我跟你讲，你必须变成大浑蛋才能成功，这是事实。而 Beatles 就是世界上最大的浑蛋，我不是在开玩笑。……如果你成功了，你就是浑蛋。”（《列侬回忆 Lennon Remembers》p.111，列侬和杨-温纳 J.S.Wenner 的谈话）

我有幸见过不少“成功人士”，我相信列侬不是信口雌黄。他语言很糙，但深入本质。这不是坏事好事的问题。这说明社会变化对每个人的影响。我们有幸经历了两个截然不同的社会，社会巨变了，价值观巨变了，个人面临的压力巨变了。这些巨变实际是作用在每一个人身上的。催化人的衍化。我们这些无名画会的人，最有趣的就是在自己的身上明显地反映出这种衍化。

我看过关于美国那个扫地工亨利-达吉 Henry Darger 的纪录电影——《不真实的国度 In The Realms of The Unreal》。介绍他一生扫大街，只是在扫地之余，默默埋头画着自己的世界。他从不出家门，没人知道他，他也从没寻求过人们的认同。直到他死去，人们进入他的房间，发现了他的艺术，绘画、小说把房间塞得满满的。

艺术，我们为之付出一生的那个东西到底对我自己意味着什么？

艺术真的会使我感到人能成其为人吗？

1979年，夏，画会成立了，展出了。这个小集体开始散开了。大约从那时起，陆续有人就不再出现了。两三年的时间之后，就只有我们四五个人经常来往了。

我是1983，或84年离开了，是年轻人里最后一个离开的。之后和同学徐海林一起画画。和冯国东、孙大力成了好朋友，在一起画画。结交了不少新朋友。和老冯一起梦想挣笔钱，一天到晚只是画画，喝酒。我们一起打零工，做灯箱，生存。有一段我们流浪在北京，自我边缘化。这段时期画画很少，也不知道画什么了。不知为什么突然写了一段诗。因为解决穷困干上电影，因为电影被拉进广告圈，因为喜欢做主就喜欢上广告。爱上影像艺术之后，做起影像艺术。

在一次次的错误中，一次次的追求中，改变着自己的人生轨迹。那是一段段故事。故事连着故事，每人都在用自己的一生上演着一部电影。

回首望去，我的“无名画会”那些年，真的是酿花天气参冷暖，半晴阴。

在“无名画会”那些年代的不少画，被我撕了或在上面重新画了。

撕了，重新画了，原来的就看不见了。

人生可不是画儿。人走过的必留痕迹。

这个痕迹今天还在自己的身上看得到。

2007-11　2008-7

王爱和删节

The Budding Season: In Memory of the Days of the *Wuming* Group

Liu Shi

"It's at times cold and at times warm, when willows are shedding leaves; it's at times sunny and at times cloudy, when flower buds are forming."

This is the first line of a poem in the classical style that my father wrote in 1978. I'm seated now to write about the story of my coming of age. It feels like a fruit looking back on its own budding season. The past is like a distant romance. One moment it seems to be moving, and another to be standing still.

I matured quite late. Youngsters in those days all matured later than youngsters today. My case is even more special, probably because I lacked the nutrients and hormones that are plentiful nowadays. At the end of 1971, I graduated from the No. 65 Middle School, not knowing what the future held. Life in middle school consisted of three years of labor in the countryside, factories or military camps, not to mention the happy times when we were demolishing old city walls, making bricks, and digging air-raid shelters. I have no memory of learning anything, but my memories of the many blackboard newspapers and Chairman Mao's portraits that we painted are still fresh. That was the beginning of my painting career.

My so-called painting of Chairman Mao's portraits was actually copying. There were different versions of his portraits available. Usually I would choose the woodcut kind. I copied them on blackboards, walls, big-character-posters and cross-stitch embroidery. When my works resembled the originals, a strong sense of achievement would fill my heart. It seemed that in my class only Xu Linhai and I could do the copying well. Xu was better than I. The blackboard newspaper was replaced every week or so and each new edition required a new portrait of Chairman Mao. We would wait until the girls finished writing the articles before we started to copy a portrait on the blank space they saved for us. That gave us a sense of being "big shots."

I spent most of my time hanging out in the residential quarters of the government office where my father worked, in what used to be the living quarters of a princess from the Qing Dynasty, a daughter of Emperor Qianlong. During the May 4th Movement in 1919, these quarters also served as the Science College of Peking University. The whole area was a huge labyrinth, with office buildings in the front and living quarters at the back and in the west.

My parents were sent to the countryside, and so were my elder brother and sister soon after. I didn't know where my parents went, just that it was a cadre school. I was left alone at home with my grandma, who had come to stay with me and take care of the house. All the parents in the residential quarters had been sent to the countryside, leaving behind a bunch of old grannies and children.

An army of children my age ruled the compound. We seldom ventured past the high walls. Housing over a hundred families, the compound seemed too big for us to cover in one day. Inside was our colony, while outside was the battlefield of adults. You have to bear this in mind: I lived in my grandma's pokey courtyard during the six years I was in primary school and was never allowed to go outside. The patch of sky I could see was a few dozen square meters big, with branches of an old jujube tree lying against it.

The high walls sheltered us from the chaos outside. Inside the compound was a joyful scene. Every family had pet animals, from common livestock to more creative creatures like silkworms, snakes, mice, crows, swallows, and hedgehogs. Strangely, no one kept dogs. Around the houses were garden plots, some no bigger than a pillow. One family grew Portulaca Sundial in handled chamber pots and lined them up in front of their house. We planted a great variety of flowers and vegetables, many of which are hard to find nowadays, like magnificent magenta broad beans, one-meter-long snake gourds, grenade-like bitter squashes. We fertilized the fields with our own piss and shit.

We ate almost everything available: the honey bags from the bellies of bees, the tiny shrimps from moats around the city, and the mushroom called "moss of dog pee" under the big old pagoda tree. Boy, we drove the old ladies mad!

Our playgrounds were everywhere. We played on the roof of the huge palace, which reached over ten meters high; we played in the dusty secret chamber of the old Western-style building; we even played in the long dark air-raid shelters. What surprised me most was that the armed guards at the gate had no bullets in their bullet belts. They were filled with cotton!

That was about all I did during the three years of my middle school. As I graduated and started to work, most parents and elder siblings returned home one after another, bringing back with them a depressing atmosphere as well. Our idyllic life was gone.

At the age of sixteen, I was assigned by the government to a job at a small restaurant called "Shanghai Snacks," on Taijichang Street across from City Hall. The street was mostly lined with government offices and visitors were rare.

It was a cold winter in early 1972. A man with a big face and a big belly came on his tricycle to pick me up at the Food and Drink Company where I had registered. Two other new students and I sat in silence on his greasy tricycle, which dragged slowly through the small alleys. The sky was a deep blue and silver sunshine shone down on the empty streets. The man riding the tricycle used to be a well-known chef roasting Peking ducks and was now the Assistant Secretary of the Party branch of the company.

That was how I plunged into society, alone and unaware, like a sleep-walking man. Compared to what I am now, at that time I was just like a person who hadn't woken up yet. I had no idea what was going on around me. Nor did I have a clue about what I wanted to do or what I was doing.

Some said that we graduates of 1971 were lucky since we escaped being sent to the countryside. But I didn't feel that way. My work was boring and depressing. I felt I was doing something that had no connection with me. All those unreasonable and endless compulsory discussions after work on revolution were simply torture for me. I lived as if under a pot lid, suffocated to death.

Since I had experience in painting Chairman Mao's portraits, I became the artist in my workplace. Whenever there was a festival of some sort, May Day or National Day, I'd be sent to the park to prepare for the celebration. I'd paint slogans on huge boards in yellow or white. I'd also paint Van Gogh-like sunflowers on a red background, which at the time symbolized political loyalty. On some boards I painted workers, farmers, and soldiers beaming with smiles. They smiled because it was a festival. Otherwise if the paintings had a political purpose, they would have looked fierce and agonized; we'd make their eyebrows look like the Nike logo to indicate anger, we'd make their eye corners tilt upward and their mouth corners tilt downward. Their faces were always radiant with red, because red was the color of a good person.

We also had some odd jobs to do. For example, we would twist crepe paper of various colors and tighten them into colorful decorations to hang in the trees to create a festive atmosphere. When I traveled to North Korea in 2005, the way they prepared their National Day celebrations looked very familiar.

Around 1973 or 1974, I met Shao Xiaogang and Ma Kelu when we were all preparing for the National Day celebrations. Ma Kelu could paint images of workers, farmers, and soldiers on huge billboards, which impressed me deeply. At the beginning, he took us to Dongjiao Minxiang and Xijiao Minxiang several times. There we'd practice sketching the Western-style embassy buildings built at the end of the Qing Dynasty. Our sketching style at that time was not much different from the mainstream academic style of the former Soviet Union.

By 1973 or 1974, my father was able to travel back and forth to Beijing. Seeing that I was always drawing, he introduced me to one of his former classmates who was an artist in the Central Academy of Fine Arts and asked him to teach me painting. As you can imagine, this man's studios were filled with paintings depicting the illusory and depressing revolution. It was more than I could bear and six months later I left.

One afternoon in 1974, Ma Kelu took Shao Xiaogang and me to Yuyuantan Park. Few people would visit the park in those days. As we walked deeper into the park, the tranquil lake and its earthen shore came into sight. Far away were a few people, scattered in the desolate woods. Like most people at that time, they were wearing blue or grey Mao-style uniforms and ordinary hairstyles. They were all drawing scenes they had chosen. No one uttered a sound. As it got dark, they actually cheered up and started to talk and sing in loud voices, as if nobody were watching. Some people stared at them and as they approached the streets, they muffled their voices and became cautious. My days with the painting group had begun.

These were in fact members of the *Wuming* Group, as they became known later on. We were just a circle of painting friends, but we were very close, closer than the colleagues we worked with every day. We spent almost all our free time together. Today my family has forgotten the names of my former colleagues, but they still remember those of my painting friends. In the 1970s, the circle was basically our only social world.

China in the 1970s was just like an enormous pot, with six hundred million people stewing in it like six hundred million potatoes. The Party was determined to overcook the potatoes so that they could make obedient mashed potatoes. They wanted everyone to lose his or her original identity and independent personality. However, there would always be a bunch of hard cores who refused to get mashed in with the rest.

I could feel that there were quite a few hard-core "potatoes" around me, but I couldn't tell them apart. Everyone was wrapped in a disguise. The principle was that when there was a stranger around, a person with original views had to wrap himself up, faking cries and laughs and telling lies.

In 1972, the Italian filmmaker Michelangelo Antonioni shot a documentary about China entitled *Beyond the Clouds*. It was rumored he'd been invited to make the documentary by Chairman Mao's wife, Jiang Qing. The problem was, he didn't have the slightest idea how things worked in China, so he just recorded what he actually witnessed. He focused his affectionate eyes on the most underprivileged people. When Jiang Qing didn't see rosy pictures and praise for the revolutionary era, she became angry and called on the whole country to denounce Antonioni. As a matter of fact, none of us knew who he was, let alone had seen the movie entitled "*Chung Kuo* China." Everybody talked nonsense at the denunciation rallies. We said ugly things about Antonioni and beautiful things about Chairman Mao. There were even people who faked tears of indignation. It really didn't matter much who Antonioni was. Our greatest concern was to protect ourselves. As a Chinese saying goes, those who follow my way will thrive; those who go against it will perish. Discussions of this sort lasted two hours after work every day. The topics were baffling and kept changing. Such scenes were included in Antonioni's film.

In the 1970s, the Red Guards were no longer making trouble. Homes were no longer being ransacked. Old people were no longer seen kneeling down on the streets, being rebuked and beaten up. The evil spirit in human nature that had been fired up gradually died down. Chairman Mao was no longer giving puzzling instructions, which had once driven us to the streets in the middle of the night yelling madly. It seemed that Chairman Mao and the whole nation were suddenly at sea. Everyone was experiencing a profound sense of *ennui*. When all the passion was consumed, apathy hit. Yet the country was still being ruled with an iron hand. Only one voice was allowed. Any divergent idea was regarded as dissent and the offender harshly punished, either denounced, put in jail, or even executed according to the degree of the offense. Newspapers and radio—the only media we had access to at the time—asked the same question over and over again: Are you loyal to Chairman Mao? Are you loyal to his Maoism, his cause, and his country? Wherever there were people, this was their sole topic of conversation.

I remember a trip my friends and I took to Beidaihe to paint the sea. Despite having a fever, I kept painting on the beach. I wasn't trying to work through a problem with perseverance; I was just enjoying the breeze and the sunshine, and especially the freedom of doing whatever I wanted to do. What a great pleasure that was! Though I was feeling terribly hurt because I was being pushed aside by one or two members of the group, it didn't seem to matter much at the moment. In this little community, my rebelliousness and restlessness, my longing to seek knowledge, my eager pursuit of art were all unleashed. Compared to the outside world, our community was actually a free land.

During those years, the *Wuming* Group was made up of very special people with character, confidence, and passion that other people at the time lacked. They sang Western songs that no one heard in the outside world. They talked about mysterious foreign movies that no ordinary people could see. They discussed modern Western artists—the Impressionists, Fauvists, and Cubists—artists I'd never heard of before. They painted pictures in styles that were never found in the official media or the Central Academy of Fine Arts.

The first thing I did after I met my girlfriend was to introduce her to our little painting circle. I showed her paintings and taught her how to paint. Later on she became one of our group. She was very special. The world in her paintings was so innocent yet so complicated. I had a close friend in my workplace called Meng Guoqing. He had a troubled family but painted well. When we became good friends, I happily introduced him to my painting group. Later on, I brought more of my good friends to this group, including Yin Xiaolin, Xu Hailin, Zhao Feng, Meng Jian, and Little Ju.

In the 1970s, the underground artistic atmosphere was quite strong. Apart from us, there were many other small circles of artists, estimated at more than ten in the city of Beijing. Artists from different groups knew one another. There were also groups devoted to literature, photography, and so on.

Very few people would paint alone during those days. On the one hand, resources were scarce. On the other hand, one could barely endure the great political pressure alone. When several people came together to paint, there would exist some sort of spiritual support among them. It was like primitive humans nakedly facing nature; only in tribes could they survive.

Painting in those days was not completely banned. Nobody could stop you since there were no written regulations in this respect. No one could claim that painting was an act of disrespect for Chairman Mao. However, it was quite a scene for a small group of people to paint together. There were vigilant and suspicious eyes around you and you had to be prudent. And the most important thing was that you couldn't make people feel that your group had any notion of opposing the government. If you were caught saying a few words those revolutionaries considered counter-revolutionary, you would be readily branded as an "active anti-revolutionary." Once branded, you'd get a taste of the might of "the dictatorship of the proletariat." Not only would you suffer miserably, but the rest of the group would be affected as well. It was no joke.

When young art lovers gathered spontaneously, the older ones, who were more experienced and seasoned, dealt with the outside world. They naturally became the center of the circle. Many small circles had one or two such central figures. They were always offering useful advice to the younger ones. The *Wuming* Group was able to pull through those hard years largely owing to the experience and the vigilance of the older members. Just like a pack of animals in the wilderness, the older ones were always positioned on the outer edge of the group, watching carefully for possible dangers. They made sure those who ran away or tended to get in trouble came back to the pack.

As Feng Guodong told me long ago, art is not a profession; it's an addiction. What he said was a true reflection of the state of mind of those young artists. I was obsessed with painting, regardless of what else might happen to me. It seemed that there was a spirit in my heart that was out of my control. I didn't paint to entertain myself or to improve my condition. I painted because I felt this was the only way to make myself live as a real human being, to be an artist who left behind long-lasting works of art.

To make time for painting, I asked to work on night shifts, from 8 p.m. to 8 a.m., so that I could avoid the two-hour discussions on revolution that followed the day shift. My job on night shifts was to prepare the ingredients for the next day. The toughest thing was making the dough for deep-fried twisted dough sticks. In a huge vat were 25 kilos of flour and boiling hot water. I had to pour in 600g of salt, 600g of soda and 500g of alum and stir everything with two bare hands. There were cuts along my palm lines, my hands were bleeding. My eyes stung and shed tears. I wasn't crying. It was only a physical response. Every morning I had to knead three vats of dough. Each time before I put my hands into the mixture, I'd take a deep breath, clench my teeth and tighten my legs to brace myself for action. I couldn't sleep every night, but the days were mine. I spent all of them painting in the parks, completely immersed in another kind of life. In the end, I was moved to another job since my boss noticed that the old one allowed me too much freedom.

I loved reading. I even secretly peeked into my father's bookcases, though at that time they had all been sealed up with paper strips by the Red Guards. I couldn't understand the ancient Chinese prose in those books. My friend Ni Chuwan's father was a non-Party democrat with some influence, so his bookcases were not sealed. We took some of his books out and passed them around among our group. Amazingly, in this way almost all of the members of our group managed to read a few really good books. Many of the ones we passed around were unknown outside our circle. This went on for several years. Reading was something we did almost as frequently as painting. My life was composed of two things: painting and reading. During those years, the whole country was flooded by works written by or about Chairman Mao. Average people didn't have much access to other kinds of books.

Visits to Ni Chuwan's house all took place in the evening. I'd hide in the shadow of the huge lilac tree in his yard, waiting to exchange the books he'd lent me with new ones. He'd tiptoe into their house and remain there for a long time. Inside his house, it was always dark and silent, like every other house in those years. I remember my favorite books were Fu Lei's *Home Letters* and *John Christopher*, which had been autographed by Fu Lei, since Fu Lei was a good friend of Ni Chuwan's father. I didn't know then that the author had already committed suicide. Some books we borrowed were lost, the white-covered edited and translated version of *Jonathan Livingston Seagull* being one of them. Even today, Ni Chuwan insists that more than one book was lost at that time.

Whenever I got a book, I'd devour it, like a silkworm eating a mulberry leaf. Quite often I'd finish reading a book overnight, since the lender was always pushing you. I read as I walked or rode a bike and often bumped into electricity poles or the supporting steel cables. This was no fun at all because there were workers and militia patrolling on the streets. All of a sudden they'd be scrutinizing me. I would then close the book and show them the cover. It was the cover of a book on Socialist Philosophy. I don't remember the name of the book now, but the author was a philosopher of the new China. I hid many of my favorite books in this thick book cover to avoid trouble. I looked calm but my heart was beating rapidly. If they found that I was reading banned books, they'd surely notify my workplace. Then I'd be charged with reading "pornographic books" and a series of criticisms would befall. The average people at that time didn't really have much political sense. The term "pornographic" was used for many offenses against political regulations.

We were fond of music at that time. When I was in middle school I'd go to my classmate Che Lin's house to hear music. As his family were non-Party democrats and he was the grandson of General Zhang Zizhong, he enjoyed a freedom very few people had. They had a standing gramophone at home. We listened to classical Western music, which sounded beautiful but was really beyond our understanding. Music was hard to get in those days. Few ordinary families had cassette tapes or records. Even fewer had a record player. Outside of upper-class families and cadres of the CCP, it was rare for anyone to own anything more than a radio. And what was the popular music of the day? Unified fever, unified yelling, all about Chairman Mao and his cause. As a matter of fact, music of the Party was no more than the flame under the big pot that was cooking the mashed potatoes.

At some point after 1977, I was able to borrow a record-player. I don't remember exactly when or from whom, but I do remember the record I played—Beethoven's fifth symphony. As the first notes rang out, I couldn't hold back my tears. I don't know what the music reminded me of, but I was so overwhelmed by complicated emotions that the moment is carved into my heart.

In a way, I'm grateful for those tough times; without such an environment and such stress, how could I have had such beautiful deep feelings?

The wages of Chinese people in the 70s and 80s were very low; two years after I finished my apprenticeship, my salary was 21.08 yuan a month. Twelve yuan went for my meals at work and five yuan went for a bus pass. To save money I started forging the monthly bus pass for myself and others. I used watercolors. First, I unglued the used monthly ticket from the yearly pass card. Then I drew a new ticket on the pass card. The brush point was extremely fine with only a few hairs. The monthly ticket was the size of two stamps. It took great patience to paint one. The pass card was changed once a year but the pass ticket was replaced every month. So each month I had to paint a new one.

Unfortunately, the conductors finally caught me and informed my workplace. I refused to admit I was wrong and I wasn't kidding. I thought forging a monthly ticket was almost like practicing my painting. Besides, I was just painting part of the national culture and I thought the government should support me. I really was too naive at that age. You can imagine how mad the people from the Party were. They couldn't believe that they couldn't convince me I was wrong so they held daily meetings to criticize me. They said I was painting "flowers and grass of revisionism" and doing things unrelated to my own work. They said it was shameful of me to take advantage of the nation. My punishment lasted over a month. I really didn't have any sense of humor at that time and I single-mindedly stood my ground. My resistance finally ended when I contracted a bad case of hepatitis and had to be admitted into hospital.

I had to walk to the hospital. It was a summer morning and my grandma was walking ahead of me. I was carrying something under my arm and was close to falling over. I felt as if the hospital was too far away and I'd never reach it. Nobody paid any attention to me. During those years no one took much notice of others as there wasn't much to see. This was the first time I had a taste of desolation. The summer of 1977.

For a while our small circle got together almost every day to paint. All it took was for someone to ask, "Where are we going tomorrow?" Yuyuantan, Zizhuyuan, the Fragrant Hills, Yingtaogou, the Eight Great Sites, the Summer Palace, the Cultural Palace, the Forbidden City, and later Beihai Park, Shishahai—they all became our studios. Most of the parks were in the west or north of the city. Strangely, we rarely went to Jingshan Park. We never set a fixed time. Those who got off work early would come early. People sometimes came after dusk, even though it was too dark to paint; they'd still join in the discussion, an important part of the group's communication.

Our spiritual life wouldn't start until the circle came together after work each day. It seemed that we had split personalities as we behaved one way at work and another at our gatherings, just like today's corporate white-collar workers. We felt free to meet, paint and talk in the parks since in those days parks were deserted spaces. It was interesting to paint the water, trees, clouds, and flowers in there. No one would question what or why you were painting. It was different on the street, you'd be surrounded by suspicious eyes. But in the parks, it was safe to talk as there were few people about. But if you look carefully at our paintings during those years, you'll find that as the political atmosphere relaxed, our painting sites gradually moved towards the city center.

People didn't have much freedom to move around. If you wanted to travel outside the city, you needed a "letter of reference" from your workplace certifying that you were traveling on business. This practice started in the 1950s. By 1980, the vast majority of Beijing citizens hadn't set foot outside the city in thirty years. As a matter of fact, the whole country was alike in this respect—for thirty years the Chinese people had been confined to their own city or town.

Prior to 1980, I had been out of Beijing only once to paint. We travelled to Beidaihe (about 200 km. from Beijing). Just before heading back to Beijing, I went out alone to paint and ended up getting detained by the police because I couldn't tell them why I'd come to Beidaihe. Certainly I couldn't have told them that my snack store had sent me here to paint. They would have died laughing.

It's good to have parks in the city where you live. At least you can go there whenever you wish. Parks back then were not as artificial as today. I felt like I was in Barbizon or Paris, where parks are just part of nature. When I walked into a park with trees and clouds in sight, I felt like a real human being. Painting gave me warmth and joy, giving my life purpose.

Looking back, it may seem that we painted so much water, so many trees, clouds, and flowers that they were our only interests. But that's not the case. Society at that time demanded that everyone pick up their pens and brushes as weapons to help Chairman Mao eliminate his enemies. This destroyed everyone's independent personality—and the more society demanded conformity, the more we fought against the mainstream. When society wants to ruin the independent personality of the people, those who resist and hold on to their ideas will surely open up a world of their own as their spiritual home.

We painted rivers, trees, clouds, and flowers, staying far away from the everyday. Such tributes to rebellion and romanticism denoted an independent spiritual pursuit and were so overwhelming it would make people panic. One artist from the Central Academy of Fine Arts remarked that my paintings did not strike the approved revolutionary tone. I could sense the uneasiness in his voice, all the more so since he was my father's best friend.

Where could you go if you ran against the tide in the 1970s? In the 1940s there had been Yan'an (the endpoint of the Long March), but in the 1970s, you went either to prison or to deserted parks. A tree or a cloud was destined to become the canvas for our spiritual struggle and reflections on life. Had we lived in the 1930s or 40s, people like us who tended to be rebellious would surely have foresworn sentimentality or romanticism; back then, rivers, trees, clouds, and flowers had a different context and different meanings. I too would have followed Lu Xun and used my pen as a weapon to expose the miserable sufferings of the common people. I would even have cast aside the pen, joined the army, and gone to Yan'an.

During the 1970s, everyone's life was interwoven with politics, and any political change would affect the fate of every individual. Politics was a daily topic for all. Our group, *Wuming*, was no exception; like everyone, we talked about politics and repeated political "gossip". In the summer of 1976, the most common gossip was about "Old Mao's" health; one minute he was on the brink of death, the next he was hale and hearty. It happened one afternoon when we were in Yuyuantan Park. We heard cries like a dirge wafting from the distance. Soon the cries quieted down, people near us fell silent. Someone shouted that something must have happened to Chairman Mao. A repressive tension swept the atmosphere. We packed up our painting boxes and scattered. That was the only time we stopped painting voluntarily. Even sudden rainstorms wouldn't stop us. As we left, Zhao Wenliang warned us to be especially careful during the next few days.

Shao Xiaogang and I didn't go home. Instead, we ran straight to Tiananmen Square. We stood under a doorway, facing an expressionless crowd standing on the Golden Water Bridge. They were staring at the Tiananmen Rostrum blankly when all of a sudden a man's voice yelled, "Stand straight!" He shouted, "First bow ..." as he bowed down. The crowd followed suit out of fright. The man was in his 50s or 60s. He was short, wearing an army uniform, with a round head and grey hair. Suddenly someone tugged at our clothes and was gone. We realized we were standing in the wrong place.

After Chairman Mao died, all the common people had to mourn before his portrait every morning and every evening for nearly a month. Every workplace had a mourning hall, which was decorated with black cloth and filled with funereal music. It became a routine for a short period. A girl in my work unit by the name of Zhang, who was one year older than I, would put on a painful face every morning and night, crying twice daily. However, what struck me was, the moment she stepped out of the mourning hall, she was lively and cheerful again. I understood that her happiness derived from the fact that she was moving closer to her goal. Sure enough, she was soon admitted into the Party and was even appointed member of the Party branch. The most striking change to her life was that she no longer had to deep-fry dough sticks and would never again be bothered again by the smell of rapeseed oil.

Though our paintings were never political, we were active participants in every political event because we had our independent views about justice. As I matured, my purpose changed each time I took part in a political event. Nevertheless, a sense of justice and a complex of cynical rebellion were my inner drive—or as Feng Zhi put it, a justice and impulse effect. When the April 5th Movement happened in 1976, I spent the whole day running around Tiananmen Square with excitement. Afraid to go home at night, I hid myself in Meng Qingguo's little house. I remember clearly the streets packed with crowds of silent workers and militia wrapped in black and blue cotton coats. Every one of them had "three legs" sticking out of their coat—the third leg being a wooden shovel handle. Dreariness blanketed our world. During the Democracy Wall Movement in 1978, I even made a speech and was applauded by a small audience of less than 20 people. During the June 4th Movement, I fought one whole night with three of my friends. "Fight" is not a political word, but a word for war. On the West Street of Qiansanmen were endless rows of shiny steel helmets and bayonets, undulating like ripples under the moonlight. The soldiers walked toward us, stooping and shoulder-to-shoulder. Only the steady tromping of their footsteps could be heard. For one moment, all of us were frozen. Though the silence barely lasted a few minutes, it was engraved in my heart.

I wonder how I can still remember clearly each instance we painted as a group: a bunch of us, walking almost in unison, each with a painting box and bag weighing almost five kilos slung over our shoulder. Many of us had our shoulders deformed by the heavy load. We would walk at a leisurely pace, with one hand in our pants pocket. Sometimes we'd be far apart from each other, sometimes we'd form a row. When one of us stopped after spotting something he'd like to paint, we'd have a discussion and then scatter around, looking for subjects that caught our eye.

On several occasions, a group of us would paint the same subject and nobody would mind. Even the gestures we made while painting were the same; since everyone used the same home-made legless painting box as big as a dictionary, we'd all hold the box and brushes in our left hand while we painted with our right.

Standing in front of trees we had chosen as our subject, we would take our time opening the painting boxes, taking in the trees with eyes half-closed, trying to get a general impression while ignoring the details. We were careful not to squeeze too much color onto our palette and to keep the paint in little neat gobs. The array of colors on the palette resembled a rainbow. As a matter of fact, the *Wuming* Group was known for the tidiness of our palettes and brushes in the circle. We thoroughly cleaned our palettes after each session, making them shine like glass. We carefully washed the brushes with soap, leaving no colors stuck to the bristles. Then we'd wrap the brushes in strips of paper so the bristles were always soft and tidy. It was as if we were savoring these details and the self-esteem they embodied.

Zhao Wenliang painted with wild imagination. He would start with a first stroke then chase the changes on the paper. Casual observers would be puzzled where his inspiration came from, for sometimes when he finished a painting, you wouldn't know how it was connected to the scenery in front of him, even though he was still observing it with great intensity. This always left me wondering. He painted extremely slowly. Often when you thought he was about to finish, he would spend one or more hours on the last one or two strokes. While he was painting, he'd enjoy chatting with us.

When Yang Yushu painted, he would always draw a crowd. People thought he looked like a foreigner. He was always serious while painting. Despite the size of the papers in his box, he acted like he was doing something really great and large-scale, silent with his eyes fixed and his body held straight up. It seems he always stood up when he painted; I don't remember him ever sitting down or squatting.

Wang Aihe preferred to sit when she painted, no matter where she was, maybe because she wasn't in good health, or because she didn't care much about hygiene. However, her perspective was close to ours when we were standing. She was really slow and would only paint after long observations. When she painted the sea, she would sit there for a long time, watching the waves come and go. She held the brush in her hand, as if waiting for the waves to freeze. She would ignore everything around her. Sometimes she wouldn't even sense that I was standing next to her. She was slow in her daily life too. As is said, people with big heads are slow. She had a big head and a super big black braid.

Du Xia also painted slowly, but she had a light style. She used very little color, mixing the colors cautiously and painting carefully. Her paintings were as mild as her movements. She liked to talk while painting, sometimes to herself. As she had a tooth missing, she couldn't speak clearly.

Ma Kelu was full of momentum and excitement while painting. He was always striking a cool pose. The more people watched him, the cooler he would look.

When Tian Shuying painted, she would purse her lips and move them like a goldfish in the water. She was quite relaxed and calm, as if she were doing daily chores instead of painting. When we complimented one of her paintings, she'd just say it wasn't good at all—and she really meant it. Maybe she was thinking, "You don't have to say things like that to comfort me. I'll paint anyway."

Wei Hai was quite unique. I don't remember how he painted, but the way he sang is still in my memory. Maybe because he was afraid of startling us, he'd stay away from us and sing in a loud penetrating voice. I don't know if he sang well or not, but he did have something in his voice that was passionate enough to touch your heart.

I didn't notice how I myself painted. Anyway, I painted fast, the same way I eat today.

There are still many others whose characteristics I don't remember, but only because I didn't spend much time with them.

Quite a few people in our group were talented do-it-yourselfers. Painting tool kits and palette knives made by Yang Yushu were in themselves works of art; all of us secretly craved one. Pants made by Shi Zhenyu were of professional quality. Shao Xiaogang picked up English using a dictionary no thicker than two inches. He even learned to make eyeglasses. Like almost every man in the group, I could do some woodwork. I also learned to cut pants and sew with a sewing machine. I made a very small tool kit and had to cut my brushes short to fit. My tool kit was dyed using a beautiful indigo, which was also used to dye cloth. I would fit my kit into a school bag so that nobody would notice it on my way to and from work. I could only use it to draw small pictures. The other tool kit with legs was too big and I had to make a very big canvas bag to hold it. Shi Zhenyu once drew a funny cartoon of me carrying the big bag with a hunched back.

I figured out that the cardboard from shoeboxes was ideal for oil paintings, so I used a lot of it. Many people called my paintings shoebox paintings. My first oil paintings were painted on the pages of Shao Xiaogang's foreign language books; two pages glued together with bone glue made good paper for oil painting.

Another thing special was that when we started out, most of us painted small-format pictures about the size of A4 paper. Now, years later, we have thousands of small paintings. If you haven't seen them, you might wonder what can possibly be drawn on such a small rectangle of space. Looking back on the years of small paintings, it seems that we never felt constrained. We never felt the space was too little for us to wield our brushes over. It was amazing that such a small piece of paper could hold our rich feelings, could captivate us and allow our imagination to run wild. Sometimes when we weren't in the mood, our brushes would feel hollow and couldn't fill even the tiniest piece of paper. As the Chinese saying goes, the elegance of a house doesn't rest in its size. In those years, there was a huge gap between our inner feelings and the outside world, making it urgent for us to let our feelings out yet difficult to find outlets. Naturally, our spiritual world exhibited in our paintings kept growing as these were feelings that rose from the bottom of our heart. As long as the spiritual world in the paintings was rich, the size of the paintings never mattered much.

These small-sized paintings have become the trademark of the *Wuming* Group and also of that era. When I joined the group, they were already painting on small-format papers, so I just followed along. Nobody knows who started the style. During those years when everything was scarce, everyone was poor. Besides, since we'd been rejected by the mainstream as "amateurs", we couldn't get any painting materials from the government. We had no choice but to paint in small format to conserve what hard-earned materials we had. On the other hand, the small format didn't attract too much attention and helped us maintain a much-needed low profile—"amateur" meant we weren't recognized by the government and were de facto illegal. This alone was an important reason to paint small pictures. And if you track the size of our paintings over time, you'll find that they grew larger in step with the thawing of the country's political climate.

We were often the object of much curiosity when we painted. We always had company, no matter how long we worked on a painting. It seems Beijingers have a lot of free time on their hands and enjoy rubber-necking, even nowadays. The funniest thing was when someone would stand right in front of you, blocking your view, and look from your face to the painting, as if wondering what you were painting. Sometimes people would stand next to you for a photo, as if you were one of the bronze bulls in the Summer Palace. Most people at that time were bored, especially those you saw strolling in the park. These bystanders mostly commented on whether our painting accurately depicted our chosen subject, unwelcome comments when we were in a bad mood. Inevitably, one bystander would ridicule another's artistic judgment, setting off an argument. It was great fun to listen to their running commentary.

Even at that time we were quite eco-friendly. When we finished painting, we'd collect all the waste paper around us. But some of us misbehaved and smeared the leftover colors from our palette on the ground and trees. Zhao Wenliang would stop us at once. It's hard to imagine what we might've been thinking at that time—maybe we thought we were simply marking our territory. We weren't thinking that if we annoyed the cleaners, they'd report us to their supervisor who'd banish us from the park. Since then, when I shoot a film, I emphasize to my crew the importance of cleaning up so people won't get annoyed at us.

We got a lot of practical advice from Zhao Wenliang. For example, he advised us not to make holes in our paintings by pinning the paper to the wood backing when we were painting. Instead he told us to put the pin next to the paper and let the overlapping pinhead hold the paper in place. If you look at the paintings today, you'll see small unpainted half-circles in the four corners marking the placement of the pinheads. However you won't see any holes. As Zhao Wenliang told us, never touch the paintings with your hands, as you never touch your eyeballs with your fingers.

Painting is what we lived for. Painting is the proof of our life. For a time I led a vagabond life in Beijing, moving from house to house a dozen times, keeping nothing, not even a box of belongings my friends had entrusted to me when they went abroad. The only things I kept were paintings: mine are all still with me, as new and fresh as the day I painted them; even the paintings Du Xia had entrusted to me were returned to her in perfect condition twenty years later. In today's world, people with money are respected, but in the time of the Cultural Revolution, nobody was respected. Nobody except Chairman Mao. There was literally no respect among ordinary people. The respect our small circle had for art developed into a self-esteem that played a significant role in the rest of my life.

Though our group had become the major part of my life and absorbed most of my energies, I still needed to face my work unit and society. As time went on, I became a problem for the work unit; never mind that I was born incorrigible, as I matured I developed my own personality, I read and painted, I had my own likes and dislikes, my own point of view. I stood in opposition to the Party branch. I was always challenging the political regulations and rules of the work unit. I often argued with the leaders at those meaningless political discussions, cutting them down to size. I was the model of "the corrupted." But because I'd never done anything low or despicable, the leaders could never find fault with me.

After 1977, such measures as suppression, threats, writing self-criticism, reporting to parents all lost their effectiveness on me. They had to "exile" me to isolate me from the others. I was sent to the suburbs to keep watch over a stockpile of bricks with an old man. When the bricks were used up two years later, I was assigned to work as a janitor in an empty apartment building with another old man. For some reason the building had been abandoned for several years. That suited me fine—I had lots of time to relax and paint. I painted a portrait of the old man from the brickyard. He was from Zhuolu County in Hebei Province. I don't remember his family name. I'm not even sure if he's still alive. I miss that old man. He told me many things I didn't know, funny things that happened during the Anti-Japanese War. He said you could tell if a man was old or not from his shoes. If a man's shoes had holes on the front, it meant he was old, because he was too weak to keep his piss from dribbling on the tips of his shoes so they wore out sooner. People at that time wore cloth shoes. I accepted what the old man told me until I realized later that when people grow old, they drag their feet and that might be why the tips of their shoes wear out. Luckily for the old man, the Party branch didn't hear what he told me, otherwise they might've charged him with indecency.

In a final effort to humiliate me, I was sent to sell popsicles in the square in front of the best-known and busiest department store in Beijing. Other work units had old women selling popsicles there, and it must've looked odd to see me working alongside them. Nonetheless, I didn't feel ashamed. I was still cheerful and doing as I wished. I had a clear picture in my mind that my dignity came from painting, my spiritual home. The meaning of my life lay in my spiritual life—not to mention the fact that I didn't have to go back to my workplace and participate in the political discussions anymore. Not long ago, I saw a scene in Antonioni's film of people selling popsicles in front of the department store. Pity that I hadn't gotten the job yet when the movie was shot.

I knew clearly that my dignity came from painting, and that was my spiritual home, and the meaning of my life rested on the spiritual life I had.

After 1979, our painting group began to drift apart. In fact, small circles of two or three friends had naturally formed over the years, and there was more communication and deeper relationships inside those small circles. I myself had little knowledge about most of the other members of the group. I knew almost nothing about their families, jobs, social status, or private lives. Our activities were confined basically to painting or chatting in parks and small restaurants. I rarely visited anyone at their home except Zhao Wenliang, Wang Aihe, and Du Xia, with whom I had closer ties. I seldom had any dealings with friends living at 203. 203 was a door number in one dorm building of the Ministry of Culture and it became the shorthand for that circle of people.

During the period from 1949 to the 1980s, China was poor. But people were clearly classified. I'm not referring to the two opposing classes defined by the Party—the class of the land-owning, rich, anti-revolutionary, bad, and right-wing at one end of the spectrum, and the opposite class at the other end. I mean the divisions within the latter class—the ruling class and the ruled class. The ruling class was the class in power in the new times. "Revolutionary cadres" was the actual name of that class. When you filled out a form, you put in "Revolutionary cadre" as your class. "Senior cadres" meant the upper part of that class. They had their own schools, shopping centers, and so on. Beijing No. 8 Boys' School, where my mother worked, was one of the privileged schools in Beijing. A "special food store" near Donghuamen was set up for senior cadres. They even had the privilege of being exposed to knowledge. During the Cultural Revolution, a special Red Guard unit called *liandong* was made up of children of senior cadres. This kind of material privilege surely underscores their identity as a separate and entitled class.

The lower class was generally called "petty townspeople." The government of the time advocated that everyone—outside the class of the land-owning, rich, anti-revolutionary, bad, and right-wing—was equal. As was said, "there were no classes in revolution, only people with different jobs." "Revolutionary cadres" and "the proletariat" were deeply at odds, which was apparently reflected by the miserable suffering of the "capitalist-roaders" at the beginning of the Great Cultural Revolution, and could be sensed even in the memoirs written by Yang Jiang, an uncontroversial writer. Children who lived in the government buildings belonged to the elite class. They shared the privileges of the class and naturally developed a superiority complex. But not all children of Party cadres shared that attitude. Feng Guodong was one of these, despite the fact that his father was a general—a result, I believe, from having benefited from an intact family education. But I sensed that those members of our painting group who lived in 203 had this superiority complex, which I loathed. As a consequence, I didn't have much communication with them.

Members of our painting group didn't come together by accident. Every one of us had some social advantage. Most of us came from middle-class families, which are akin to today's middle-class. Some of the older ones came from the capitalist class or middle class in the old China. We younger artists born in the new China mostly came from intellectuals' or cadres' families. We were the middle stratum of China's ruling class. At least we weren't as wanting as those from the lower classes, who had their families to support. That's why most of us had similar social status and thus shared tastes, environment, and values, making it possible for us to communicate. That was also why even though some of us came from families persecuted by the government while others came from families benefiting from the government, we could all still form one group.

Disputes arose among us; I didn't care much or know much about them. Some were petty. When we were organizing the first exhibition of the *Wuming* Group, we couldn't agree on whose paintings should go in which exhibition hall, or whether my paintings should be placed at the end of the hall to the left of the gate. But I don't have any memories of arguments or divisions arising from our views on art. We all seemed to agree on the basics; and as proof, there's been no drastic change in anyone's painting style after we went our separate ways.

Still, I sometimes felt that people were dissatisfied. I didn't understand why, nor did I want to figure it out. Often I'd hear people criticize a certain person or his art, but I never heard any face-to-face criticism. In fact, this kind of criticism behind a person's back became almost a habit in our group. I don't know if it's because people weren't frank enough or confident enough, or maybe because this way, if no verbal harm could be remembered, no responsibility would have to be taken. Whatever the reason, this bad habit must be corrected.

Even though we were rebels in those days, even though we challenged the government and society, it was impossible to escape unscathed from the Party's influence. Let me explain what I mean.

Our art wasn't limited by the size of the paintings but by the limited horizons of our spiritual world. The problem still haunts me today; in those turbulent years, we embraced escapism and became too pre-occupied with our own emotions, which in turn naturally restricted our horizons. With one or two exceptions, the work of our group lacked sympathy for the common people and made no attempt to reach out to them. I wonder if we acted out of a kind of selfishness. In any event, it's true the world we depicted was small. At least, it was quite different from our current views on art, especially today when news bans have largely been lifted and we have easy access to all sorts of information. We are more aware of what's happening in the world, more aware of how the rest of the world lives, of how many helpless people suffer at the hands of society and nature. We can't possibly ignore their existence. Our art shouldn't only look at our own petty ailments. What's the point of that kind of art? Of what use would it be to the world?

The art of the *Wuming* Group had a deeper meaning by virtue of its nationality and uniqueness. It originated from the personal feelings of Chinese artists when their world was in chaos. However, when I look at the paintings today, they're pleasing only to my eyes. I'm not content because the work was limited to such a small realm. My career in the visual arts has acquainted me with more masters of the form and allowed me a glimpse of a grander and passionately depicted spiritual world.

Once when I was in Zizhuyuan Park painting a willow, the rain started coming down. I kept painting, even though I was soaked, even though the colors on my palette were a wet mess and my brush wouldn't move. It was freezing cold and I was shivering. The resulting painting wasn't very good. Still, when I went home and saw people on the street running for shelter as if it were raining sulfuric acid, I walked slowly, thinking how mediocre these people were with nothing achieved, while I was an artist, the most valuable person. A sense of heroism arose in my heart—nameless egoism, which reflected not only the influence of the painting group but also the cult of heroism instilled by the Party.

From the years of Yan'an to his death, Chairman Mao always required his followers to sacrifice. He required people to sacrifice themselves for the sake of their cause. The Party made role models out of those who died in extremely tragic ways, as religions use saints as their idols. And they purposefully gave these figures a touch of tragedy to make their cause more righteous, carrying people away with a sense of righteousness. That is Revolutionary Heroism Education. When I was little, almost every kid could recite a string of names of the martyrs of the Revolution while many fewer kids could recite the names of the 108 heroes in *Outlaws of the Marsh*. Today I can still remember the names of many martyrs. As a child, my ideal was to become a martyr; I thought it was a noble career. This yearning for heroic self-sacrifice, which was in fashion in a society against which we were rebelling, actually acted upon us rebels.

The coercion in 1980 told us there was no hope for freedom and that the reign of the Communist Party—the reign over the spiritual world—would last forever. People like us felt like we were in exile within our own country. Despair deriving from a hopeless yearning for freedom was tragic. Thus I was regarded as noble, heroic, and tragic. I was lifted on high by circumstances beyond my control. Even today I have the subconscious feeling of isolating myself, of enjoying an exalted state with a touch of tragedy. Our generation still habitually tries to glorify itself today. As I write this article, I might be exalting myself, which I can't possibly avoid. After all, I grew up in that special age and was marked deeply by the pathologies of that age. Nobody can be absolutely independent in thinking and action. These social pathologies will penetrate into your character and become part of it. Up to now, the term tragedy sounds highly complimentary in the eyes of our generation. For example, one book about our painting group was entitled "... A Tragic Vanguard ..." After thinking for a long time, I still wonder where the "tragedy" of our painting group lies. Since the author of the book was about my age, he might have unwittingly sanctified us. Not long ago, when I met with one friend from the group, he said, "... we were tragic heroes ..."

In our circle there was an atmosphere of personality cult, which was also a characteristic of that age. The cult of personality, which permeated the 1970s, didn't just break out suddenly in 1968. Nor was it created by Lin Biao in 1964. It was nurtured painstakingly by the Party over many years. The Party started to create cults of personality at the time of Yan'an for the sake of loyalty education. This kind of education made people ignore their personal value but could win steady support for the Party. It was just like today's society promoting worship for pop stars, which is extremely profitable. Thus there are stars as helpless as pets and fans as enthusiastic as Red Guards. The cult of personality has always been exploited as a tool. The psyche of adulation may develop naturally as children grow up. Teenagers tend to imitate others in their attempts to realize their self-worth. This imitation is apt to develop into an adulatory mindset on its own. Imitation and adulation are close cousins.

I know I had a worship complex for a long time in my youth. I looked up to the elder artists in the painting group, like a teenager of today, unable to hide his or her great enthusiasm for stars. At one time I visited an older artist whenever I was off work. My grandma said I was literally living in his house. Once he was building a small extension to his house. I went to our compound and loaded a cart with state-owned wood to take back to his house. When my mother tried to stop me, I quarreled with her. I said he was a great artist, and if the government didn't want to help him, I would. It was the right thing to do. When his mother was lying in bed after an operation, I took turns taking care of her with another friend. I was totally dedicated to this artist. Whatever he wanted me to help with, I'd do my best. For a period of time, I followed him everywhere. Now I understand, I was imitating him in my painting and behavior. What's the formal difference between me at that time and today's fans of Jay Chou or Zhou Bichang? We were all young once.

At that time, we fought hard against the pressure exerted upon us by the worship complex in the outside world, tenaciously nurturing and protecting our own independent personality. Strangely, there was an atmosphere of worship within our own small group. Many in our painting group thought the best artist on earth had to be one of us. Quite a few of us were secretly imitating someone. We admired masters of art. When I first met Tang Pinggang, I was shocked by his casual criticism of the masters we revered. We passed around Andersen's *The Thorny Road of Honor*, which was no longer a fairy tale in our eyes. It was simply hymns for saints. "Like author, like book" was a favorable comment we often quoted. In fact, it was only used to encourage people's worship complex. I didn't realize that there was basically no such a thing as "Like author, like book" until I grew up to be an adult. The atmosphere of admiration was the atmosphere of adulation. It wasn't that we didn't know about the worship complex and its function; we were experiencing the late period of the Great Cultural Revolution and things that happened in the outside world had simply been affecting us.

I don't know if we were creating the worship atmosphere in the small group deliberately or not. Everyone was setting goals. Would there be a central figure or a school if we emphasized what we shared in common while ignoring our differences? Despite the great differences between our general style and those of other groups, we didn't encourage artistic individualism within our own group. Outsiders found that our styles, subjects, and interests were similar. As time went on, some artists left the group and their works years later exhibited new personal styles, as you can see by this collection.

Though we fought against the mainstream ideology all through the years, we completed our education and self-education under the circumstances ruled by that political ideology. Usually, you share some ways of thinking with what you oppose. It was this atmosphere that made our small group in those years, that generated cohesion and made it possible for us to hold out and become known through exhibitions. Many other painting groups broke up in the end, which was proof of how strong the cohesion in our small group had been. However, it was that same atmosphere that led our group to break up—an inevitable reflection of life. Our adolescent years were spent in the small group. One must grow up and realize his independent personality. Someone blamed the breakup on those who left. They said that they should feel guilty for hurting people and accused them of having no conscience. This kind of accusation proved that the atmosphere I spoke of above surely had done its work.

Decades later when we gathered again, a dispute arose: Is there a soul figure in our painting group? If there's a soul, there's flesh and a difference of value, which lead to a cult of personality. The value of some people will be ignored, while the value of others will be exaggerated. As we know, the disparity of value does harm to every independent personality. A secret freedom society should hold on to the democratic belief that everyone is equal. Nevertheless, the funny thing is that our group is still arguing about it today. If there had been no reunion in July 2006, if our lives of the 70s, 80s, and 2000s had not been displayed at the same time, the study of the *Wuming* Group would be restricted to a narrow scope, because the painting group lived through our lives. The changes wrought by time and individual destinies, by the give-and-take of life, have all left marks on our lives and on our work. The 1970s and 2000s were just two stops in our life journey. The time track of over 30 years connecting the two stops wound its way, drawing a curving long arc of life. You see human life in us.

Thirty years ago, when the lilacs were in full bloom, we buried ourselves in painting, with nothing else on our minds. We were pompous and arrogant, never taking anything seriously. What had we been fighting for? What had we been trying to establish? Why were we painting? What had art given us? What had we harvested?

Today, the lilacs are again in full bloom. We have been noticed by mainstream society. They are digging out our past and imbuing it with special significance. We seem to know and not to know why all of a sudden we are given so much attention. But we are not delving into it. Everyone is cheerful, cooperating with the mainstream, and singing high praise together. Are we still focusing on painting? Do we still have a pure heart? What are we fighting for? What are we establishing? Why are we painting? What has art given us? What have we harvested?

We hoped that our painting group would be famous one day, making history in Chinese modern painting. Now the group is famous. People are harvesting more or less. Someone wants to be written into painting history and be "sanctified". Someone expects to add weight to their title and gild their rice bowl of painting.

But we are not as pure and truthful as thirty years ago.

As everyone knows, promotion takes marketing. Now that we've found opportunities, we can't help creating and pushing all kinds of marketing. As we pour out the resigned loneliness of those years, we take every opportunity to make ourselves famous. We build respectable personalities for ourselves, we depict our history in bright colors. We are deifying ourselves in a way. We make speeches and hold discussions, whether what we say is true or false. We don't hesitate to say things that might not be the truth. We rebuke each other in private, but support each other in public.

If one day the *Wuming* Group were renowned, it would prove that what John Lennon said was true, "You have to be a bastard to make it, and that's a fact. And the Beatles are the biggest bastards on earth ... I'm not kidding ... if you make it, you are a bastard." (*Lennon Remembers*, p. 111, dialogue between John Lennon and J.S. Wenner)

This is neither a good nor a bad thing. This is the impact the changes in our society have had on every individual. We're lucky to have experienced two completely different and diametrically opposed societies. Society has changed greatly, and so has the pressure each one of us faces. These huge changes are in fact acting upon everyone, catalyzing mutations of human behavior. What's funniest about our group is that those radical social changes are obviously reflected in our own lives.

I've seen the documentary about the American janitor Henry Darger, *In the Realms of the Unreal*. By day, Darger cleaned buildings in Chicago, but after he finished work, he would bury himself in painting his own world. He never left his house. Nobody knew him. He never sought recognition of others. When he died, people went into his boarding-house room and found his art—paintings and novels that filled his small room.

What does art, to which we devoted our lives, really mean to us?

Can art really make me feel fulfilled?

In the summer of 1978, the *Wuming* Group was set up and went on display. From that time on, our little group started to scatter. After two or three years, only about four or five of us remained.

I left in 1983 or 1984 as the last youth in the group. After that I painted with my former classmate Xu Hailin and made friends with Feng Guodong and Sun Dali. We painted together. I also made many new friends. I dreamed with Lao Feng of making a large sum of money. We painted and drank all day long. We did part-time jobs, making lamp housings, to support ourselves. At one time we wandered in Beijing, resigned to stay away from the majority. We painted very little during that period, as we didn't know what to paint. I wrote poems for no reason and took up movie-making for the sake of money. And because of movie-making I was persuaded to shoot ads. Since I love to be my own master, I enjoyed making ads. I loved film, so I took it up.

My life track keeps changing while making mistakes and pursuing my goals one after another. They are all stories, one after another. Everyone is making a movie with their life.

Looking back on the years I spent in the *Wuming* Group, I really have mixed feelings, like the weather, warm and cold, sunny and cloudy.

I tore up or painted over many paintings I did during those years.

Torn and covered. The original paintings are gone.

However, life is not a painting. You leave marks wherever you go.

The marks can still be seen on me today.

November 2007 & July 2008

Translated by Hu Yafei, Deng Xiaorong, Loretta Law

Translation editing by René Balcer

历史照片
HISTORICAL PHOTOGRAPHS

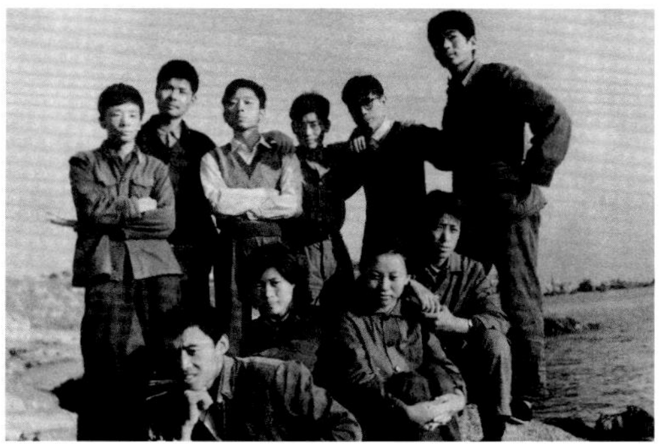
1

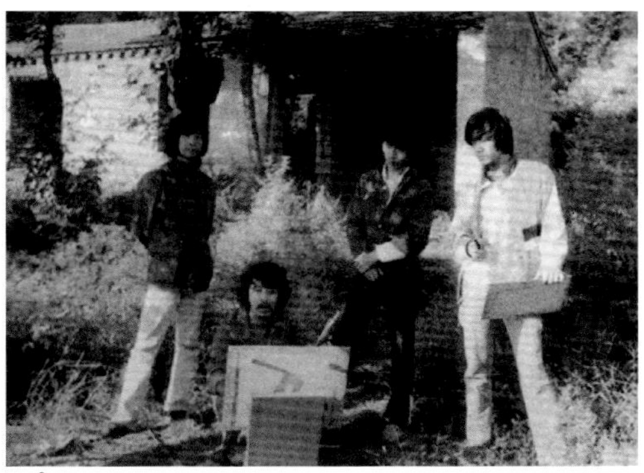
2

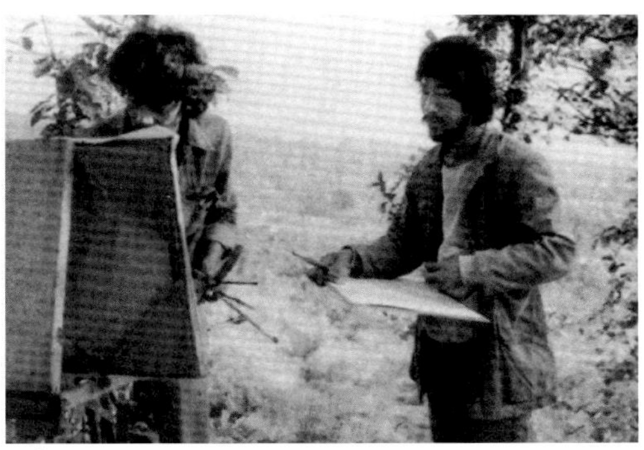
3

1 无名画会成员在北戴河。前排左起：张伟、李珊、王爱和、郑子燕，后排左起：刘是、邵小刚、韦海、史习习、马可鲁、赵汝刚，1975年秋（郑子燕提供）
Wuming members at Beidaihe. Front from left: Zhang Wei, Li Shan, Wang Aihe, Zheng Ziyan; back from left: Liu Shi, Shao Xiaogang, Wei Hai, Shi Xixi, Ma Kelu, Zhao Rugang, autumn 1975 (photo provided by Zheng Ziyan)

2 冯健、刘是、鞠保华、赵峰（左起）在西山写生，1984
Feng Jian, Liu Shi, Ju Baohua and Zhao Feng (from left) painting at the Western Hills, Beijing, 1984

3 刘是（左）、冯国东在写生，1985
Liu Shi (left) and Feng Guodong, 1985

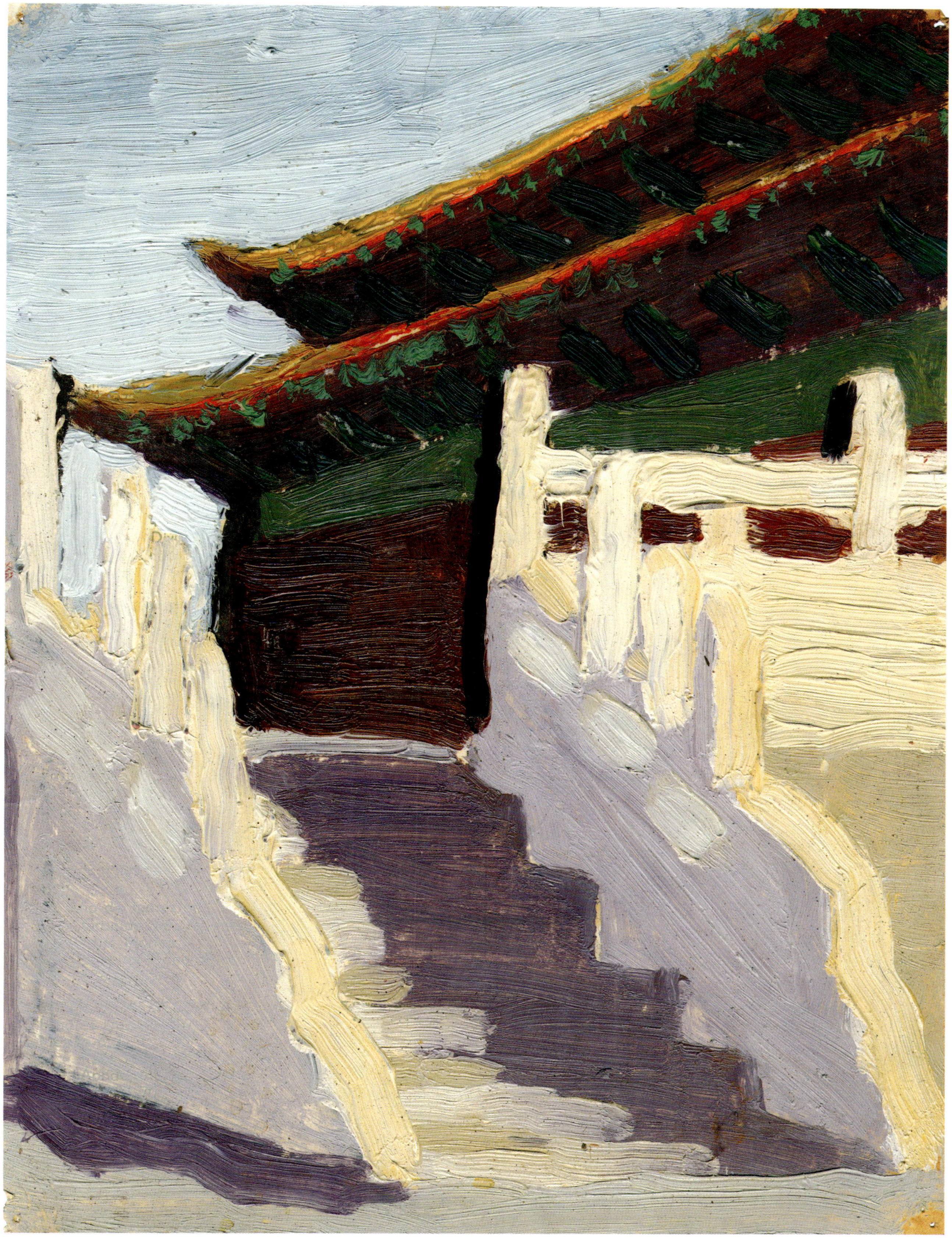

1 台阶 *1974 26.8cm × 20.7cm* **Steps**

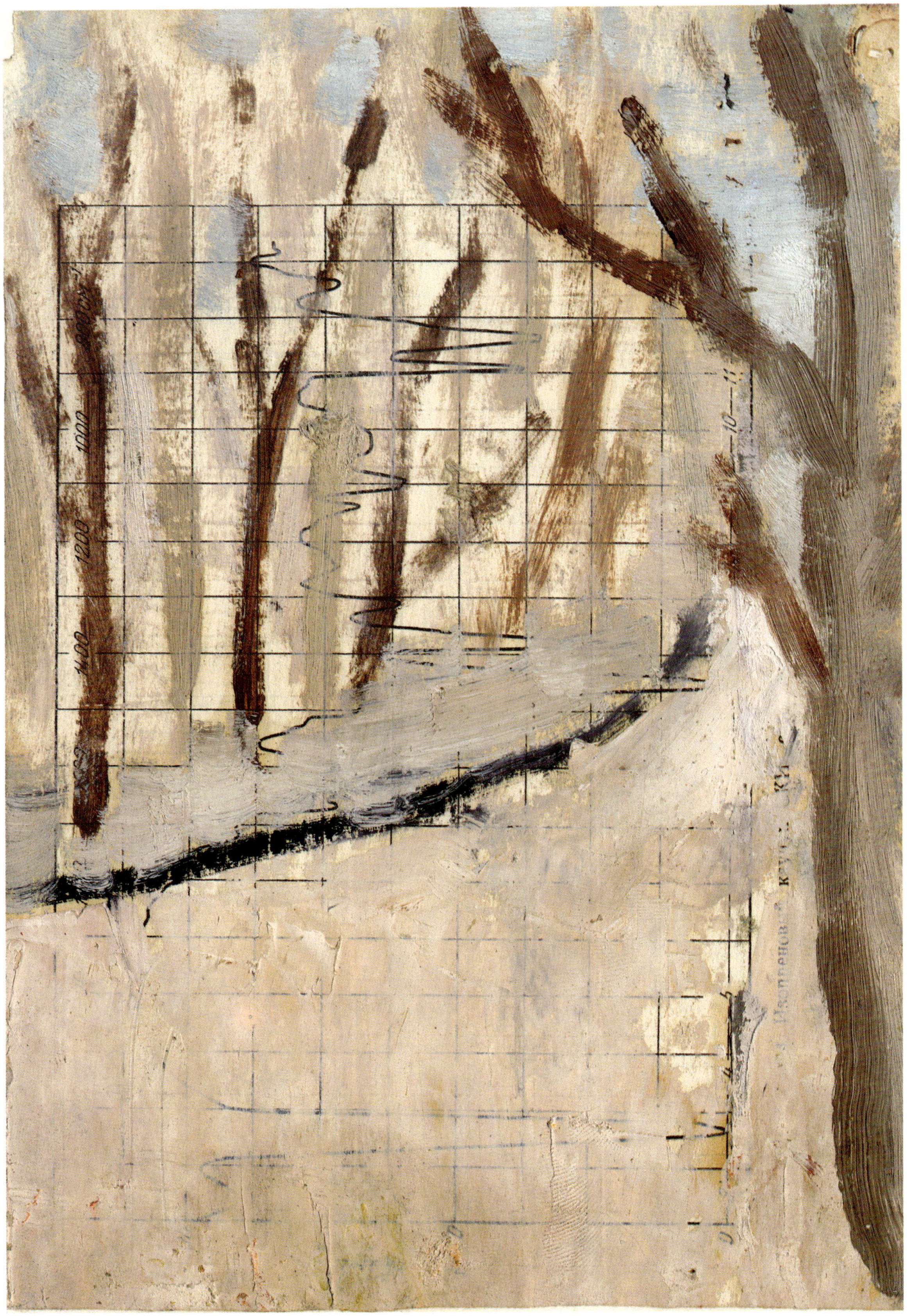

2 写生-001 *1973 19.1cm × 14.4cm* **Painting from Life No. 001**

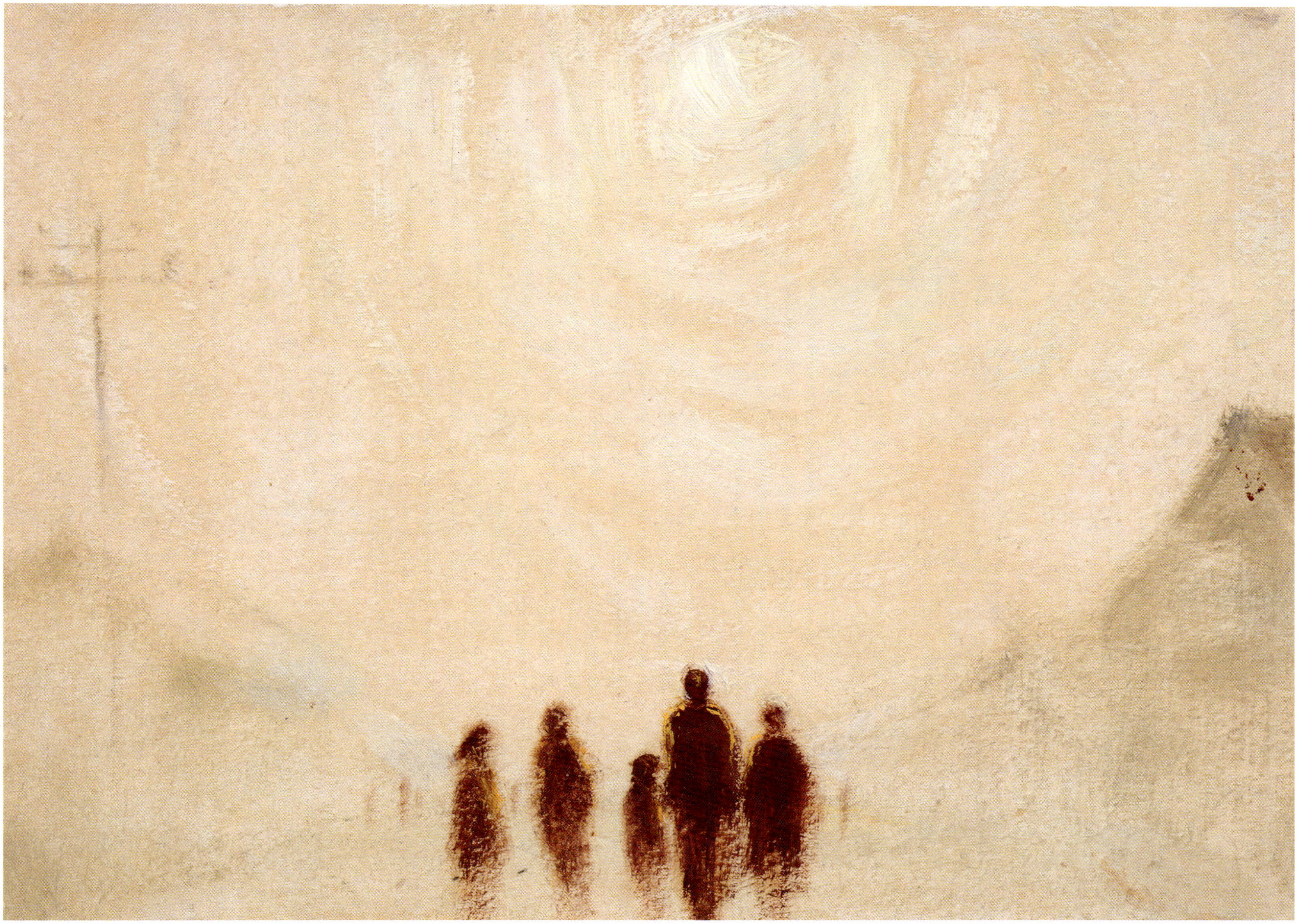

3 希望 *1975-1976 20.5cm × 24cm* **Hope**

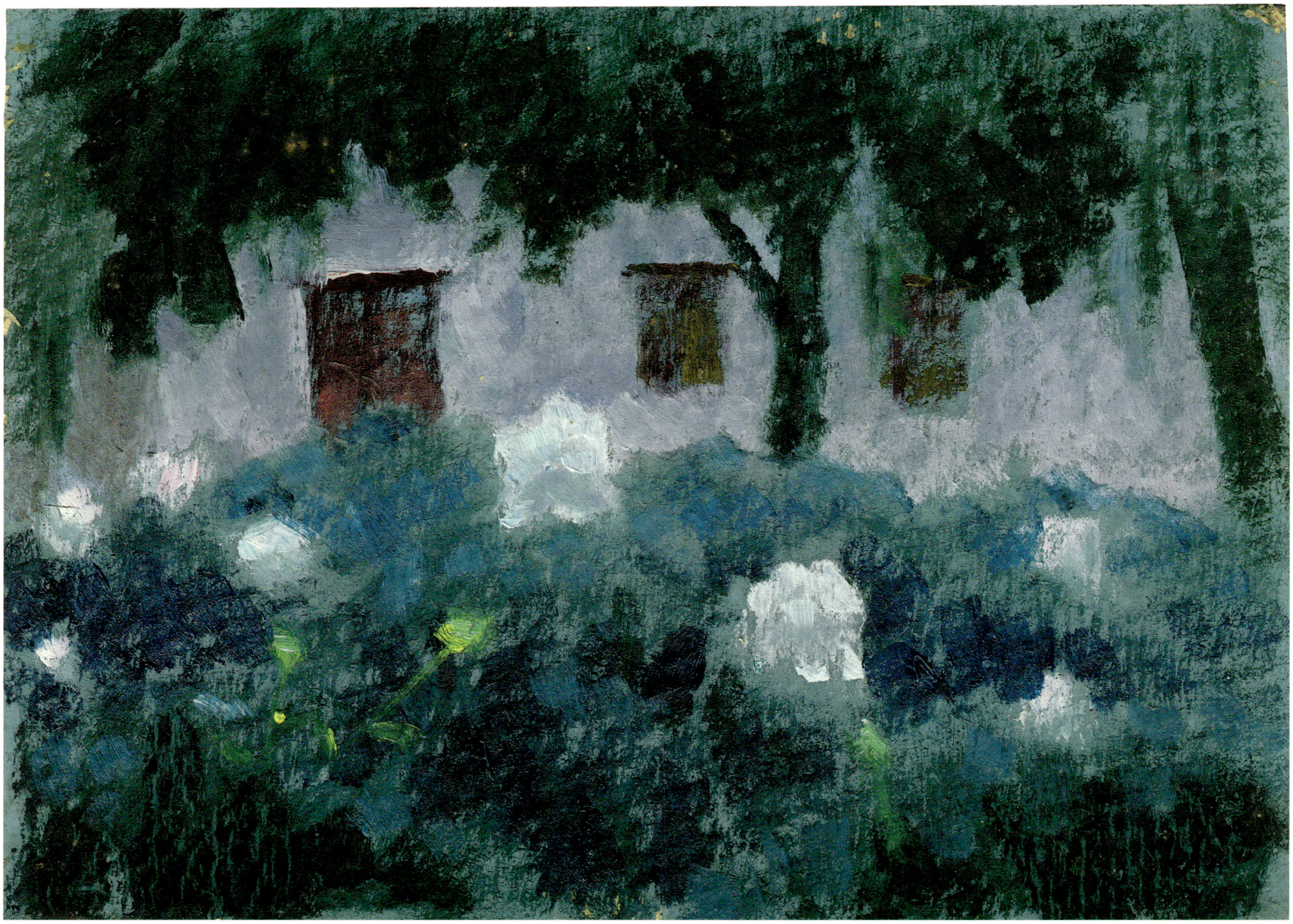

4 芍药 *1975-1976 12.7cm × 17.8cm* **Peony**

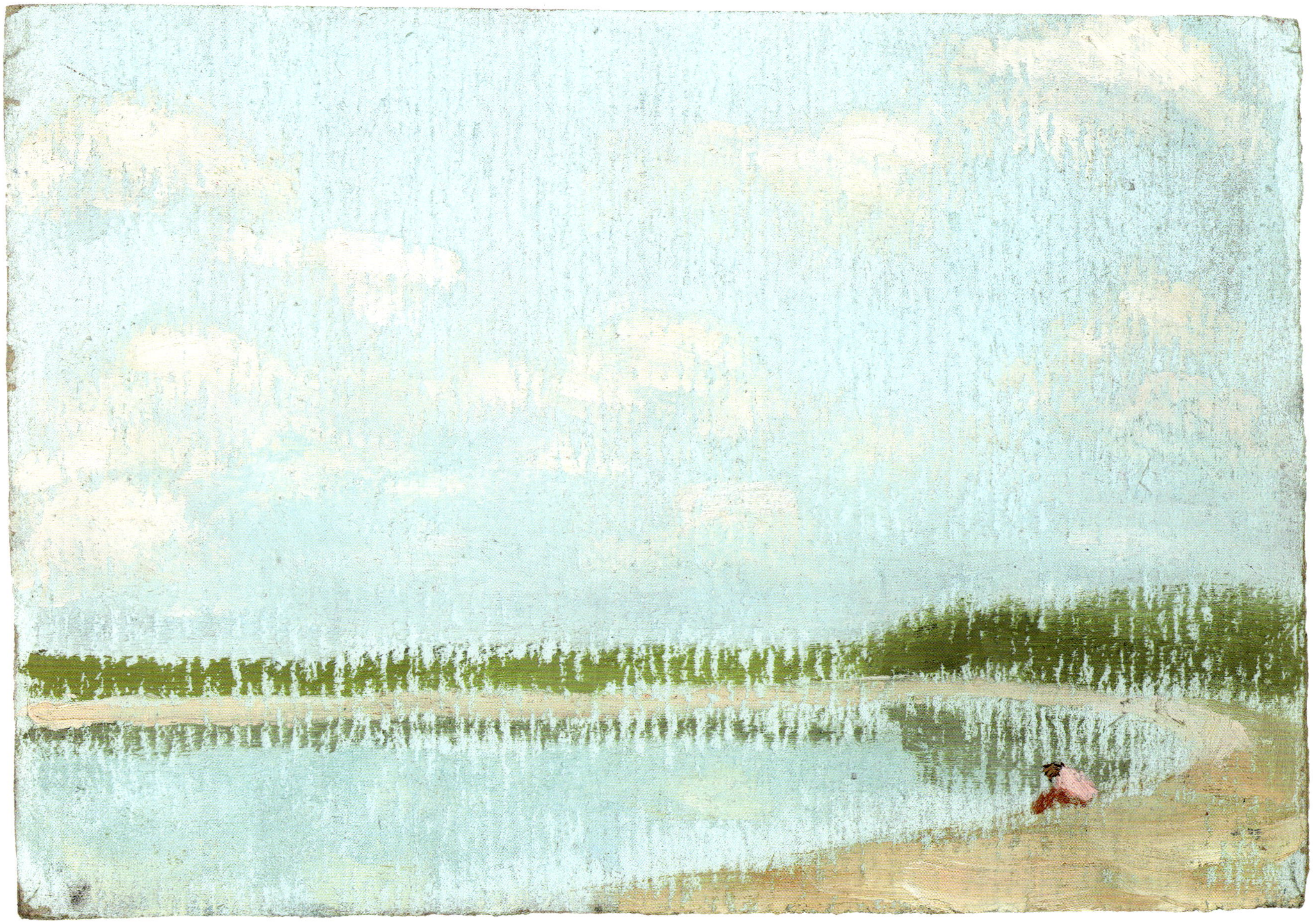

5　河边的人 *1975-1976* *13cm × 18.5cm* **Figure by the River**

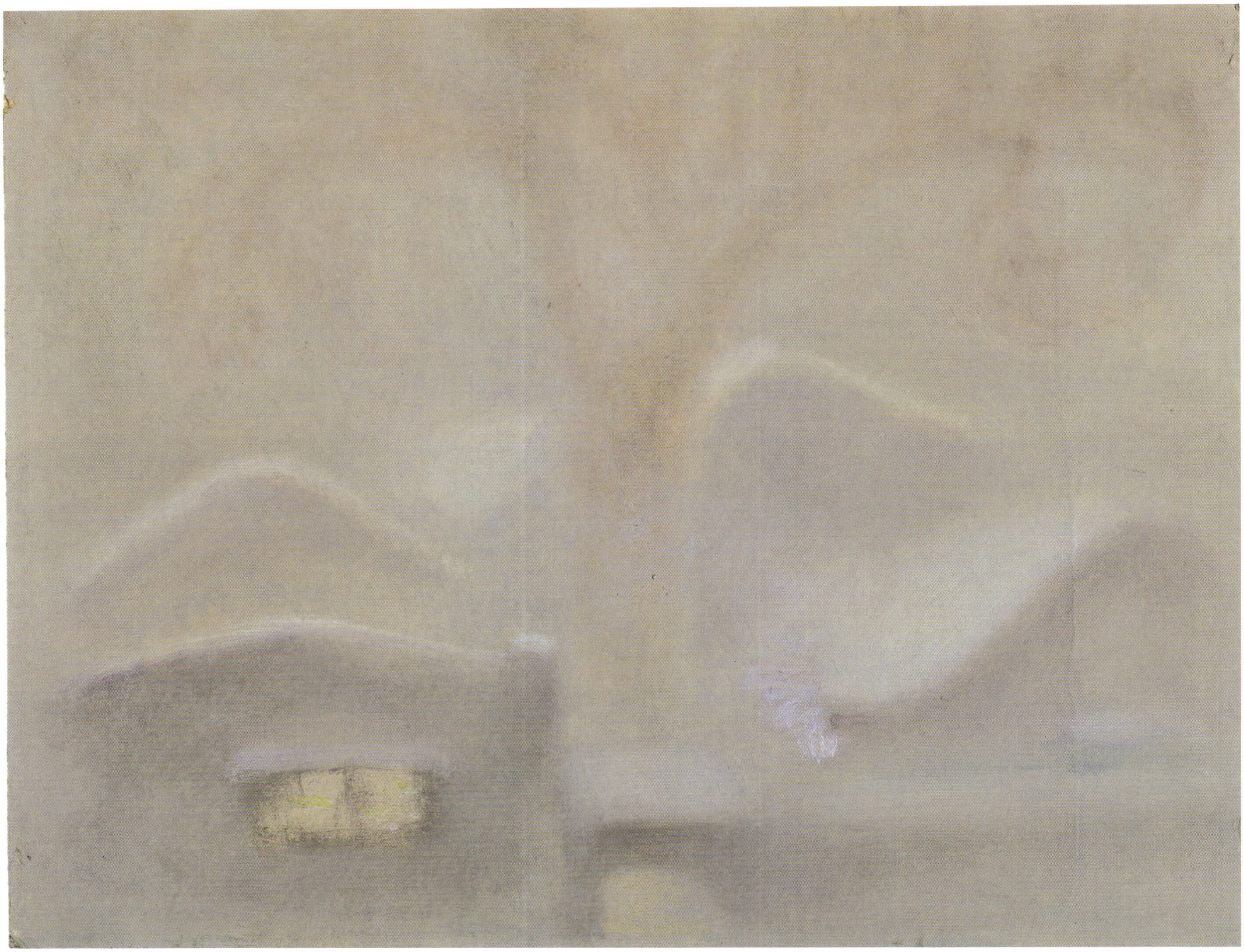

6 四川营胡同之雾 *1976-1978 20.2cm × 26.7cm* **Sichuan Camp Alley in the Mist**

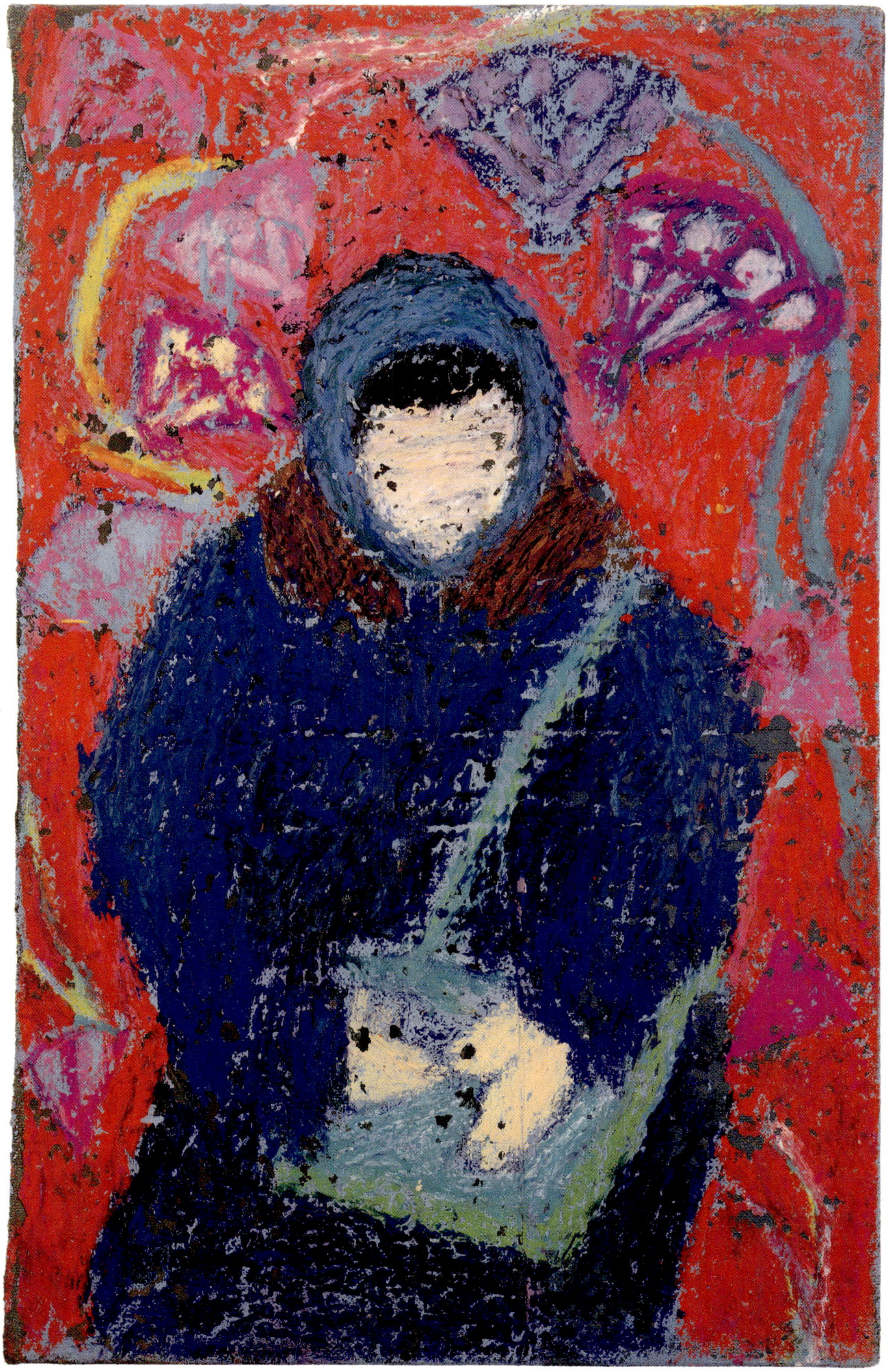

7 女孩 *1976 22cm × 14cm* **Girl**

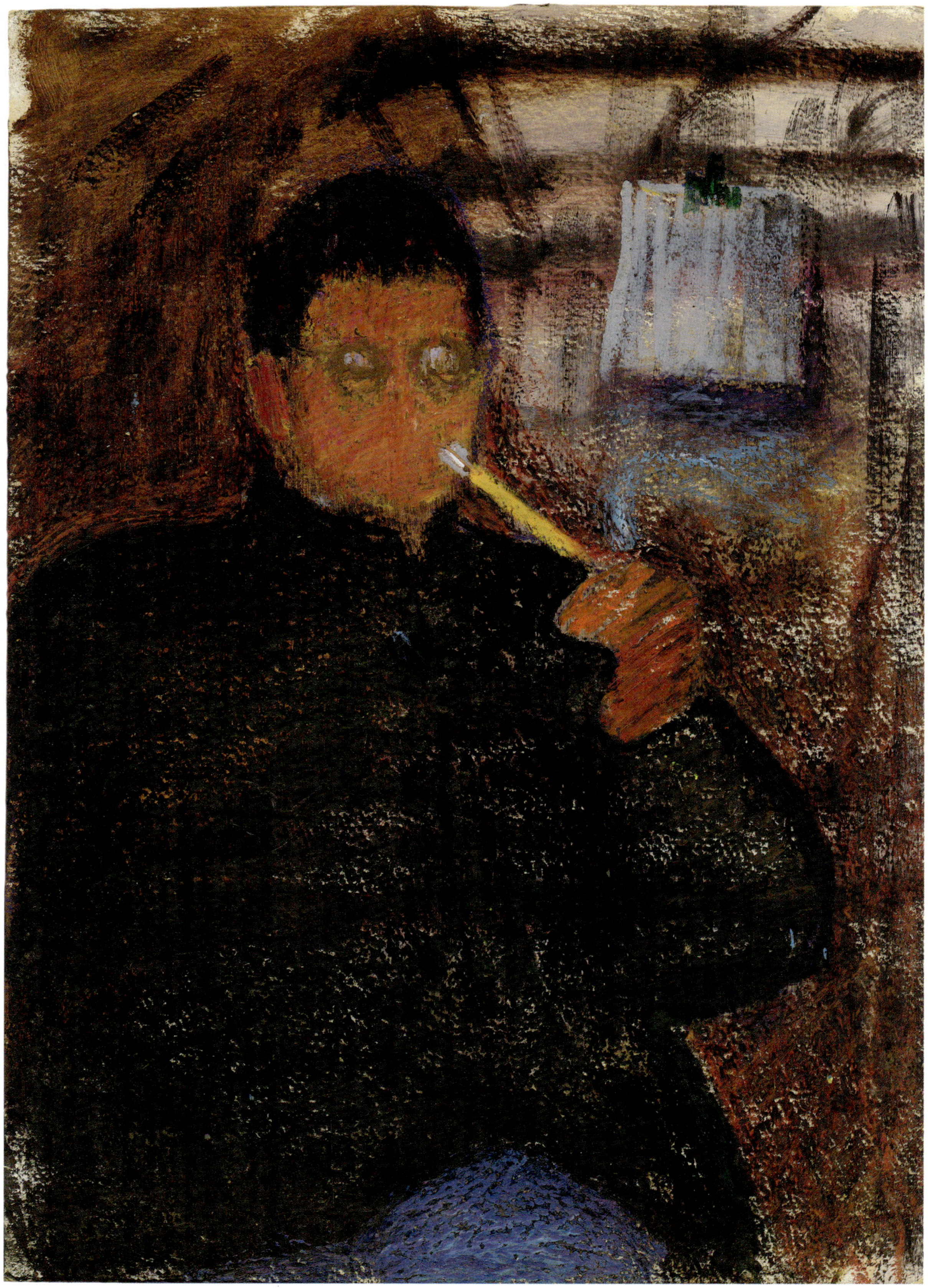

8 师傅 *1976-1977 25.7cm × 18.6cm* **Master**

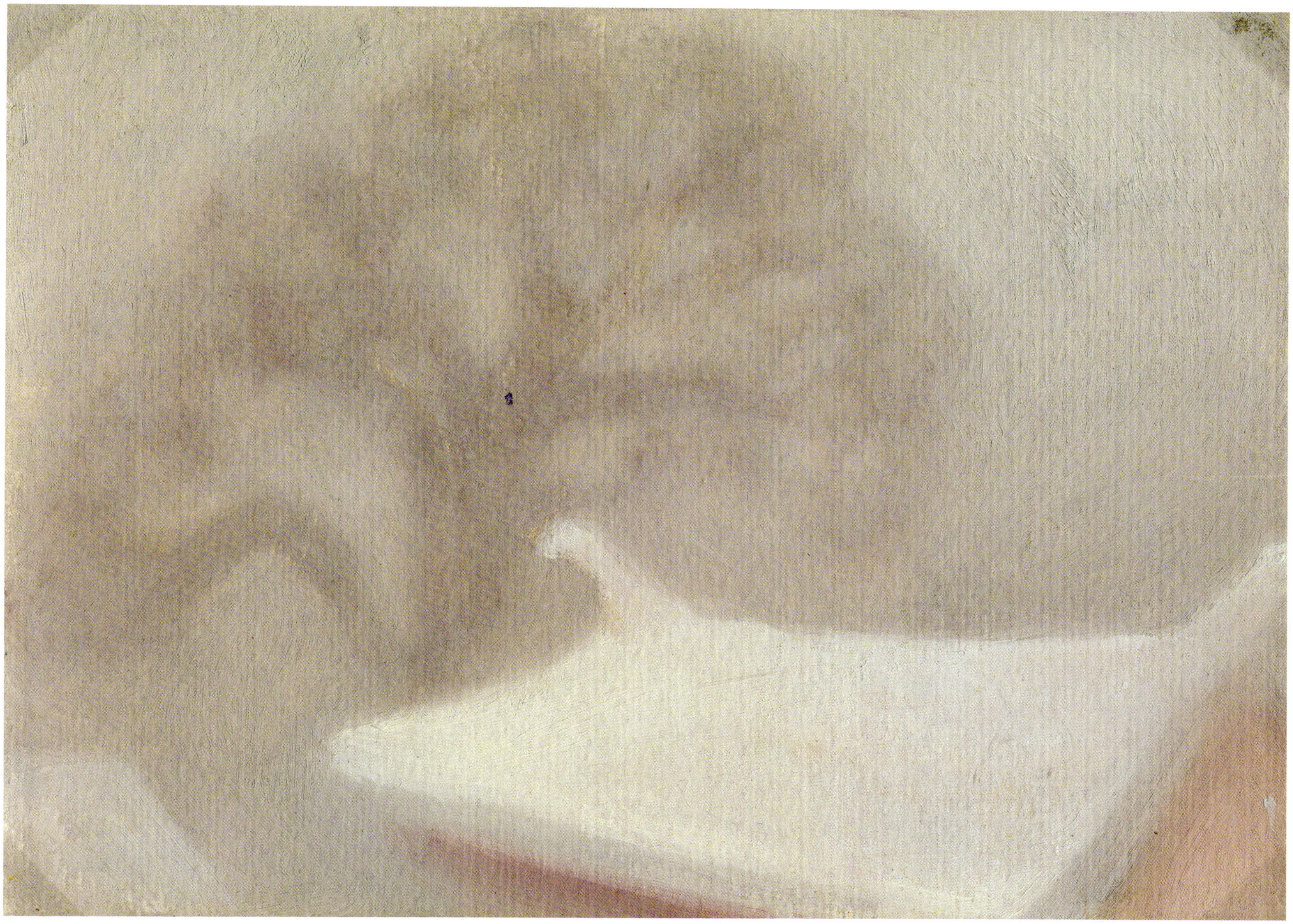

9 雪房顶 *1976-1977* *13cm × 18.4cm* **Snow-Capped Roof**

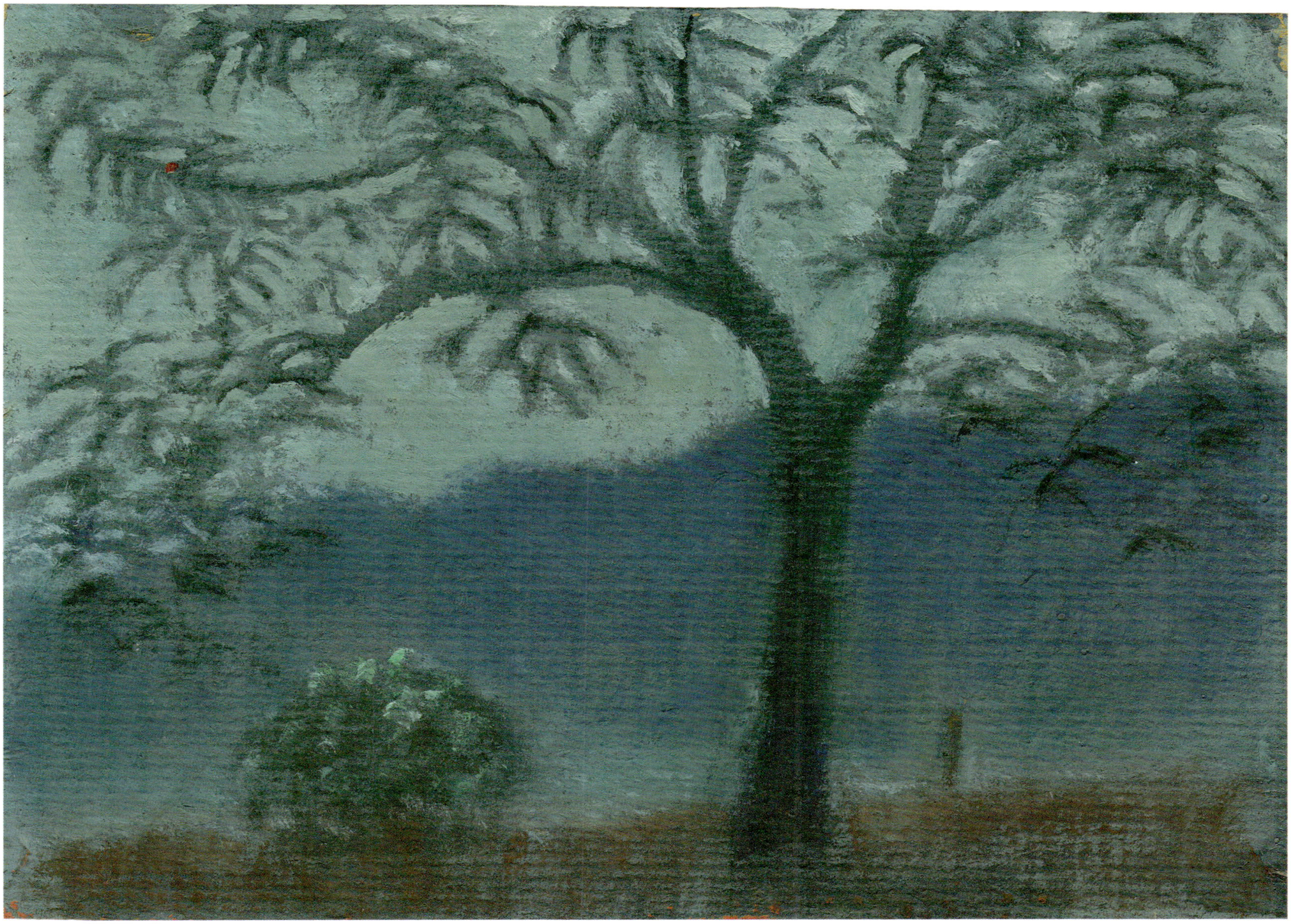

10 合欢树 1 *1976-1977 12.6cm × 17.8cm* **Silk Tree No. 1**

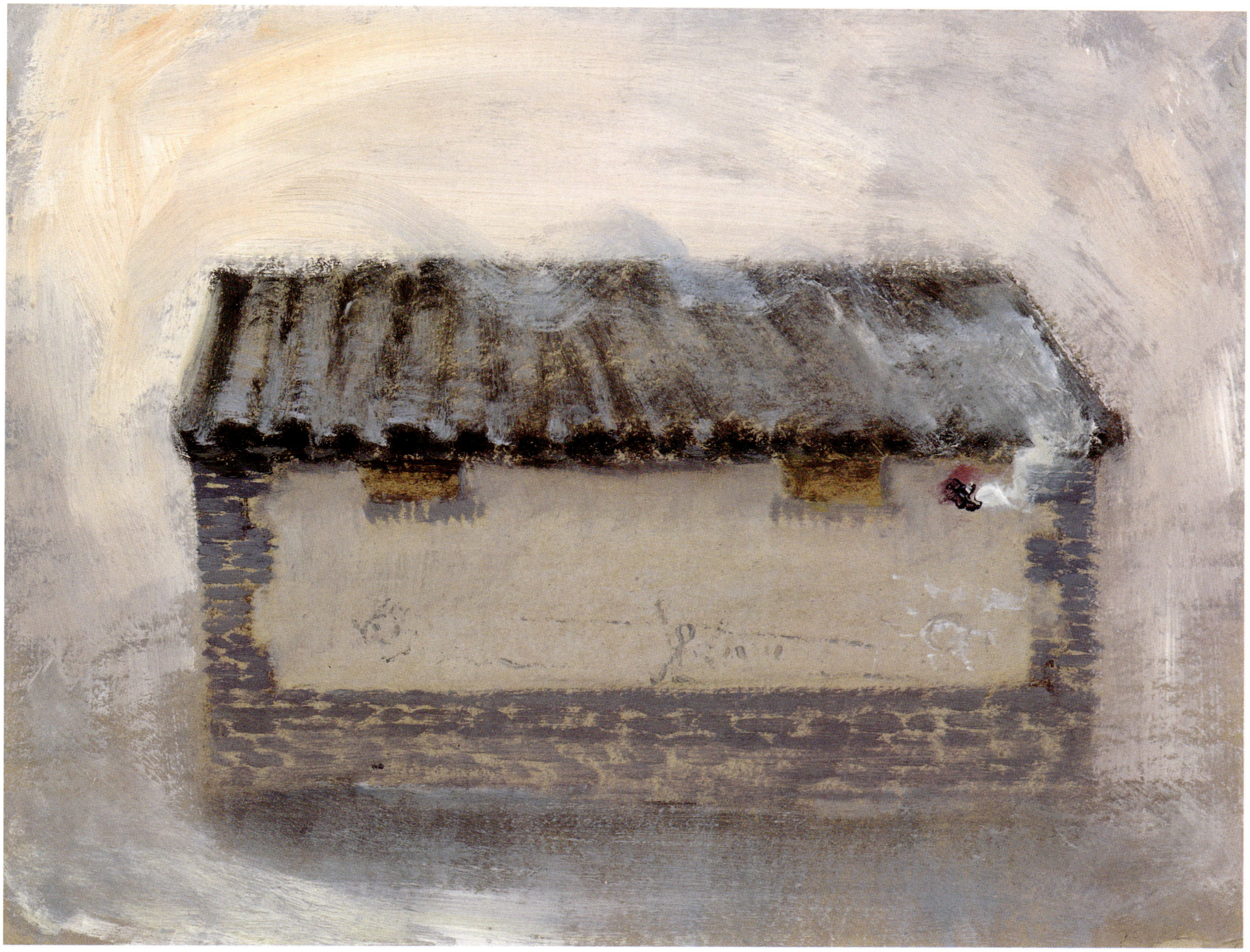

11　房子的冬天 *1976-1977 20cm × 27cm* **House in Winter**

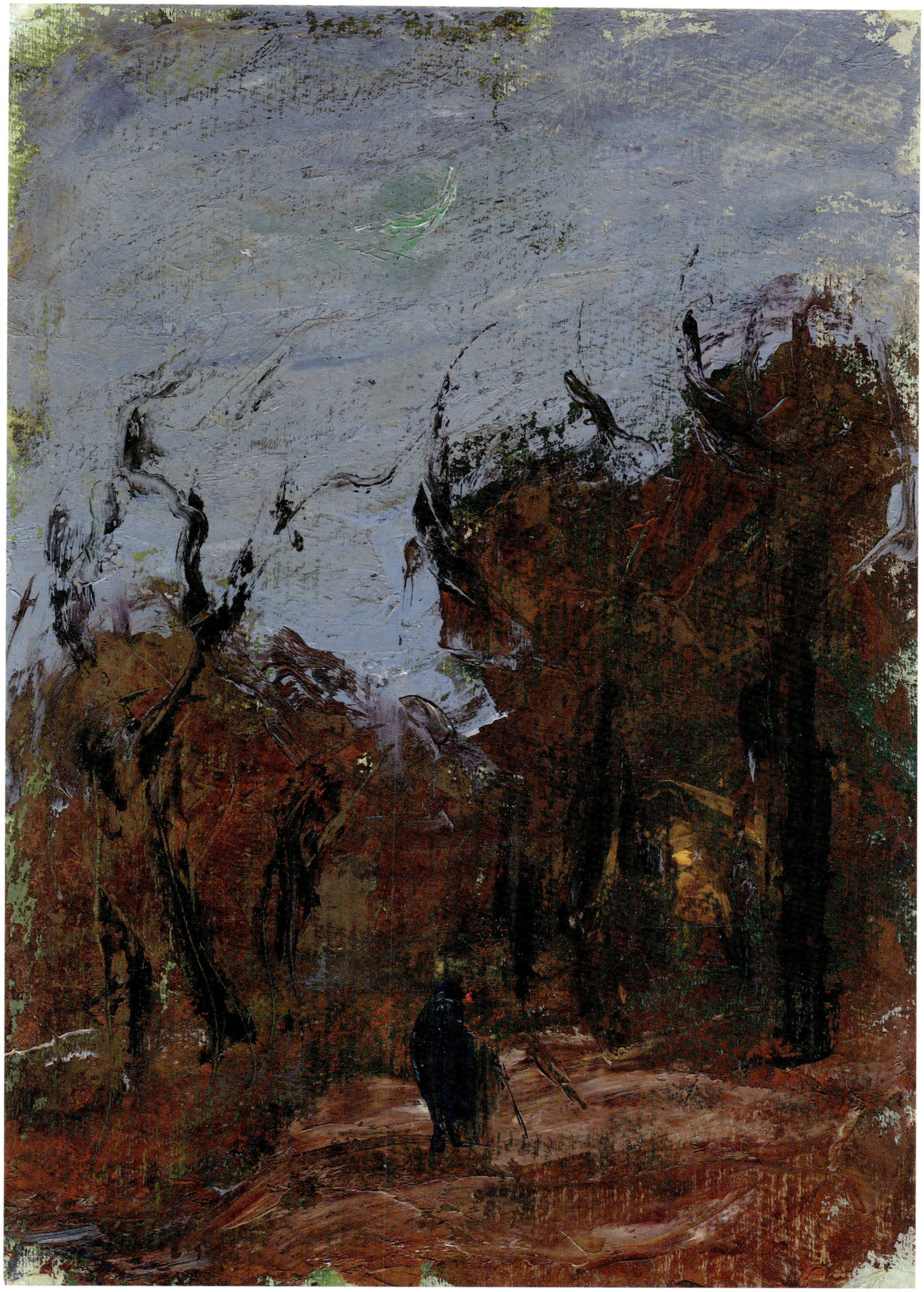

12 回家 *1977-1978 27.1cm × 19.4cm* **Going Home**

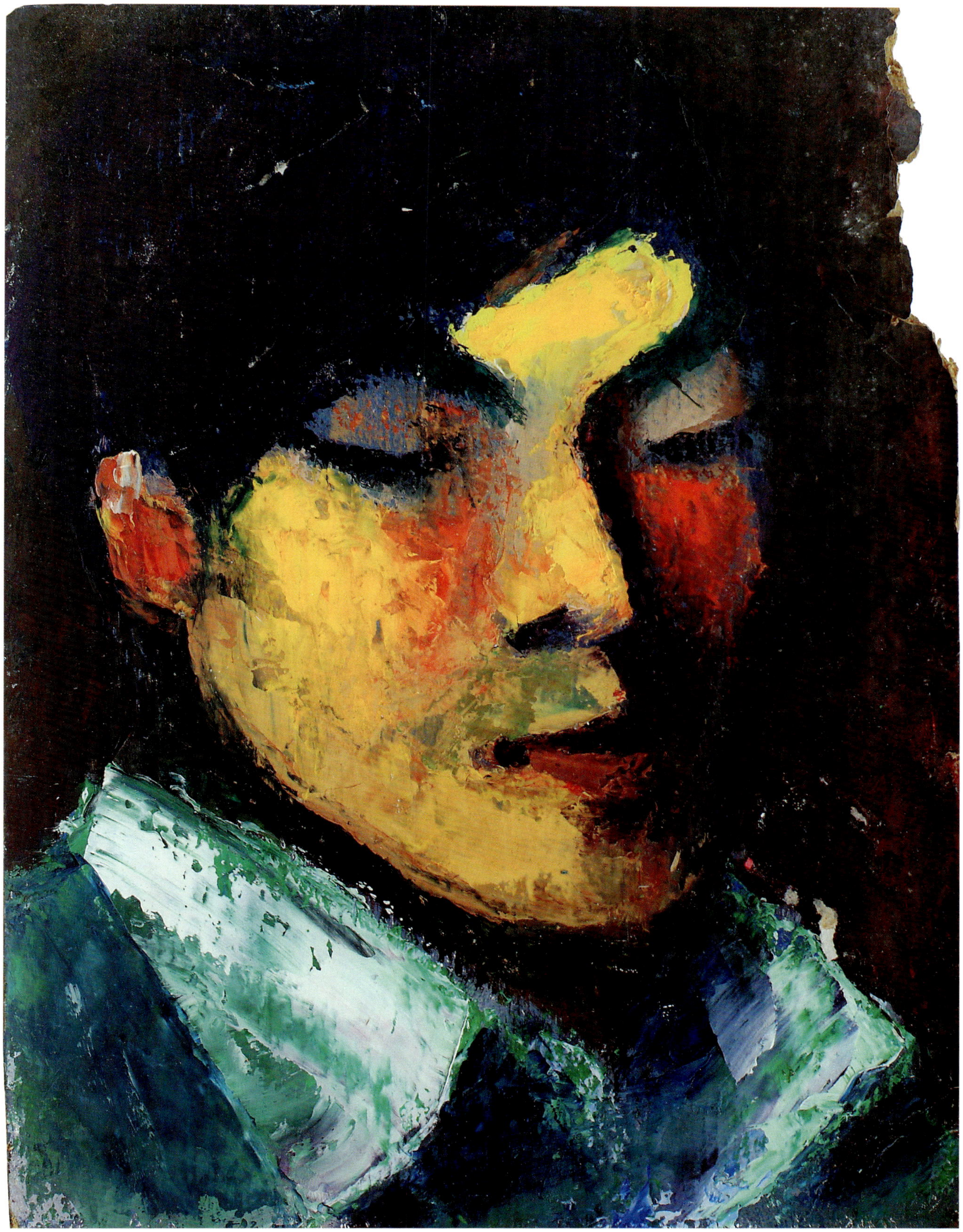

13 常顺儿 *1978-1979 32cm × 25cm* **Chang Shunr**

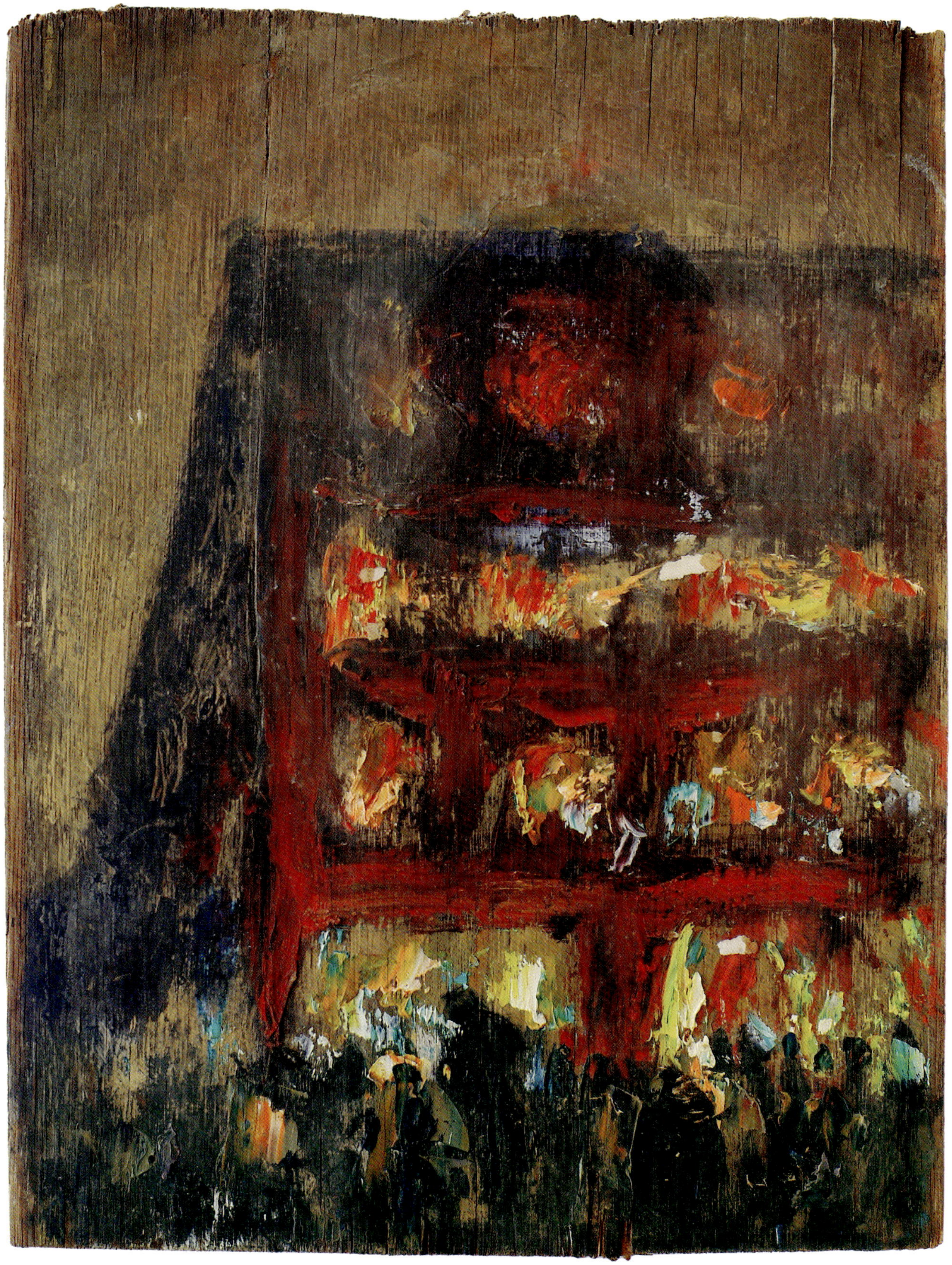

14 百货大楼之夜 *1977-1978* *40cm × 30.5cm* **Department Store at Night**

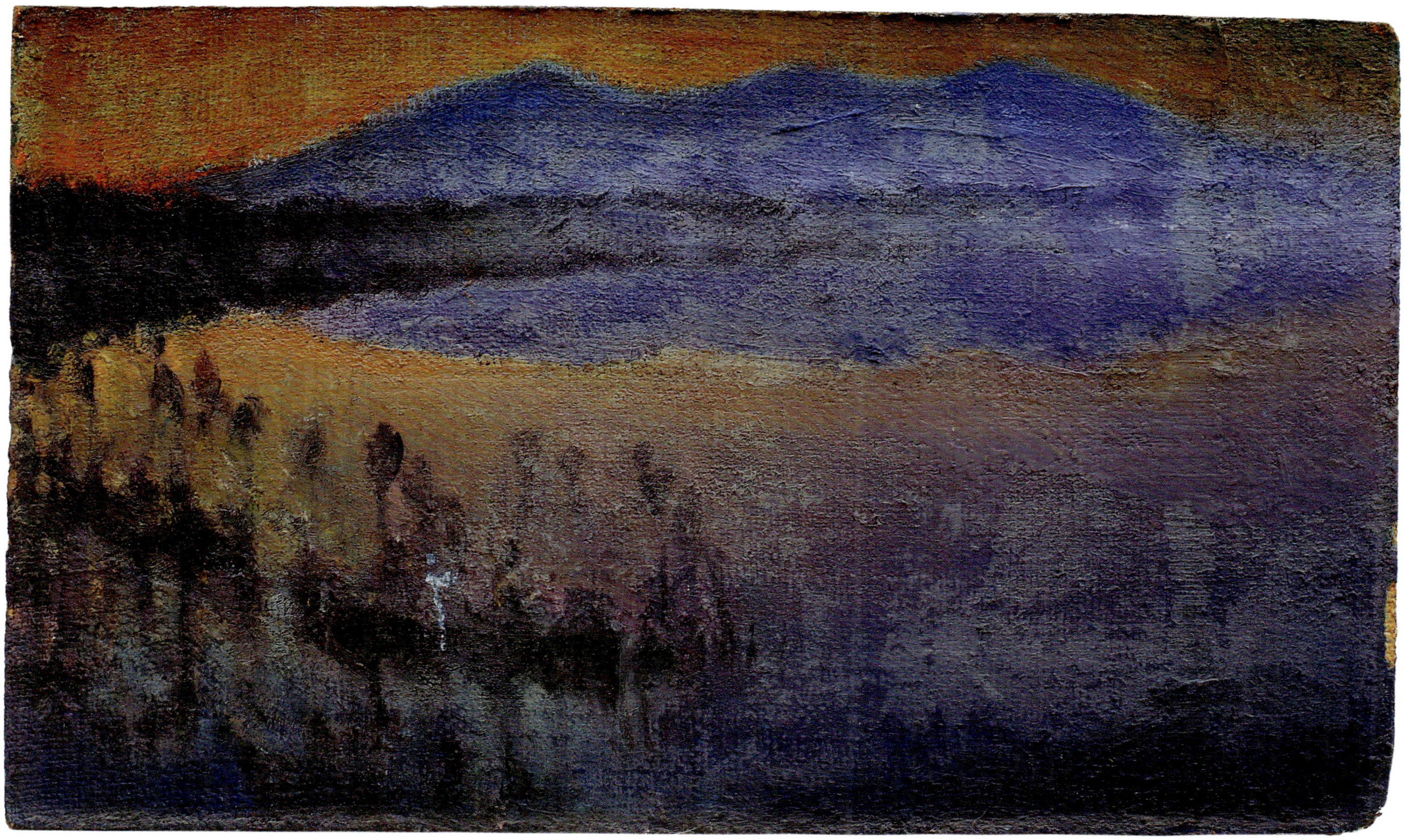

15 嘴唇山 *1978-1979* 规格不详 *dimensions unknown* **Zuichun Hills**

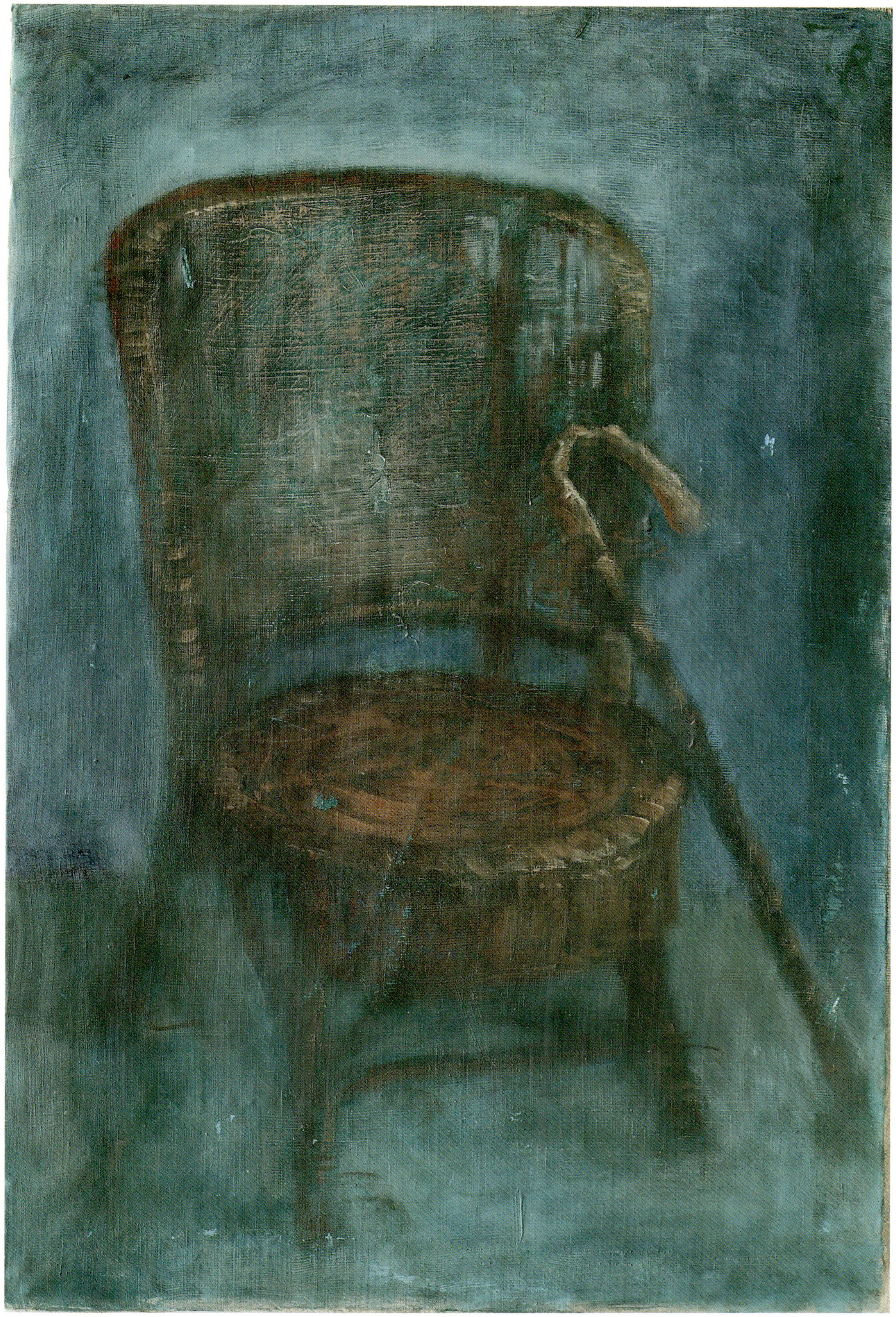

16　外祖父 *1978 73cm × 50cm* **Grandfather**

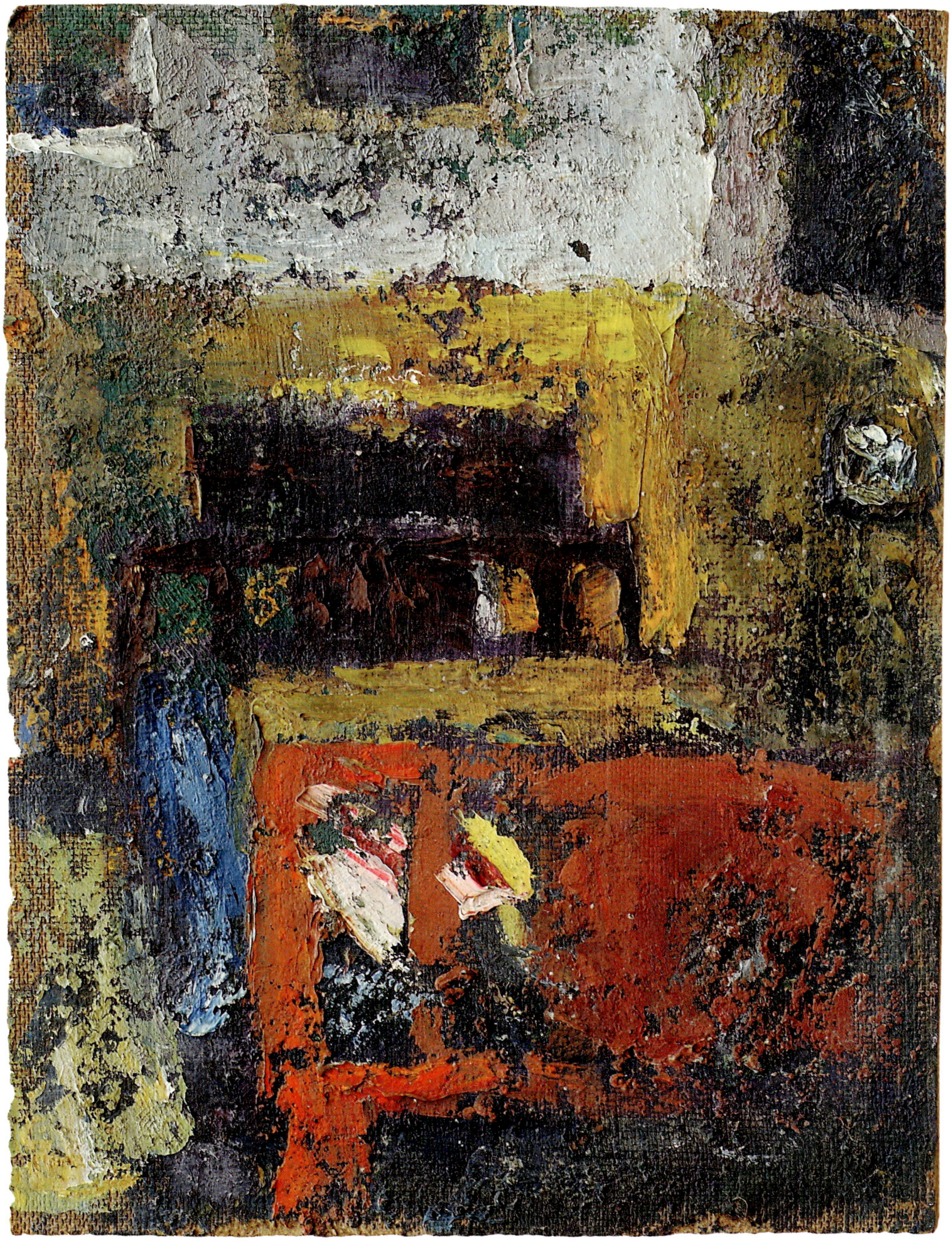

17　单人床　*1977-1979*　规格不详 *dimensions unknown*　**Single Bed**

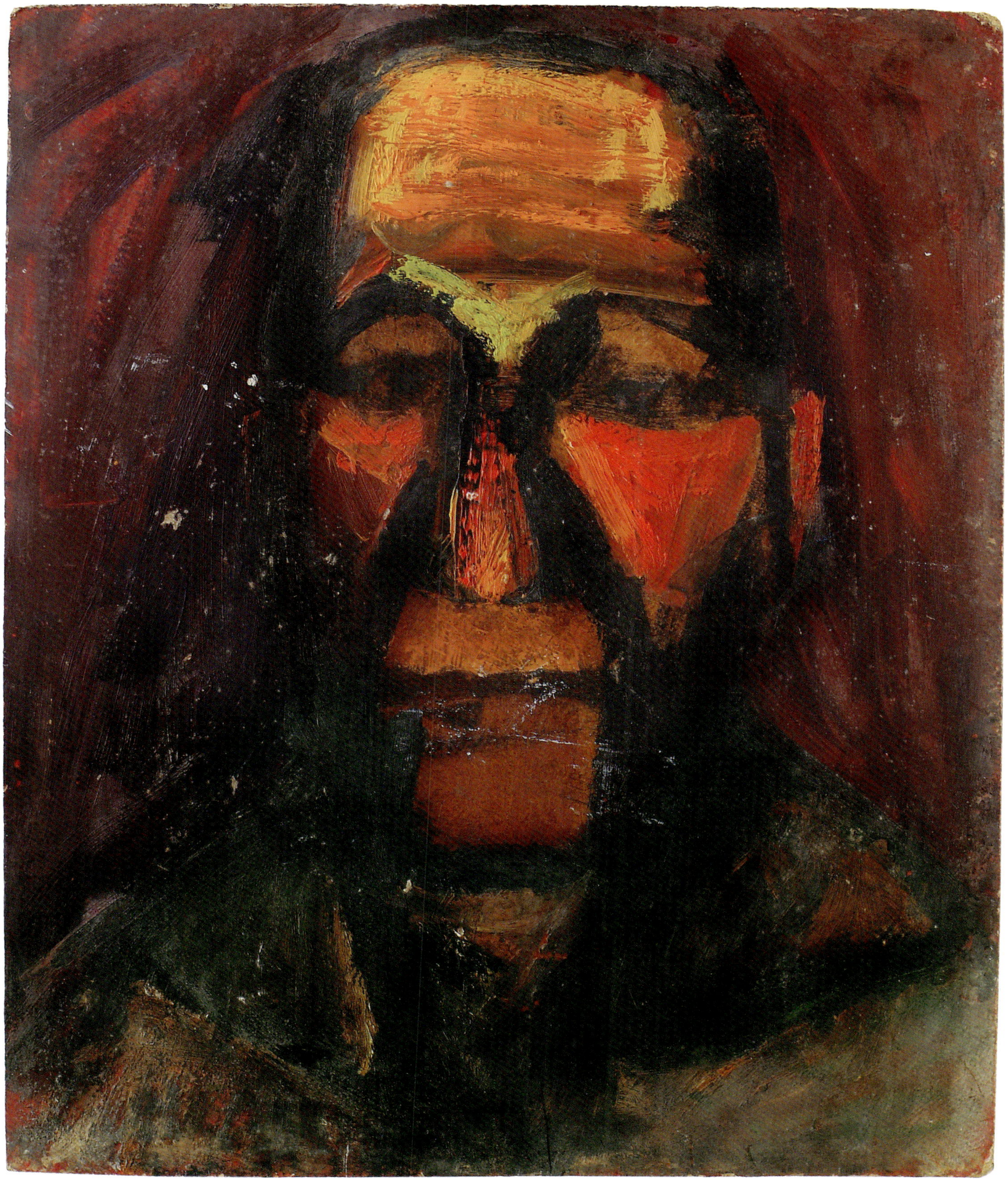

18 火夫 *1978-1979* *45cm × 39.5cm* **Stoker**

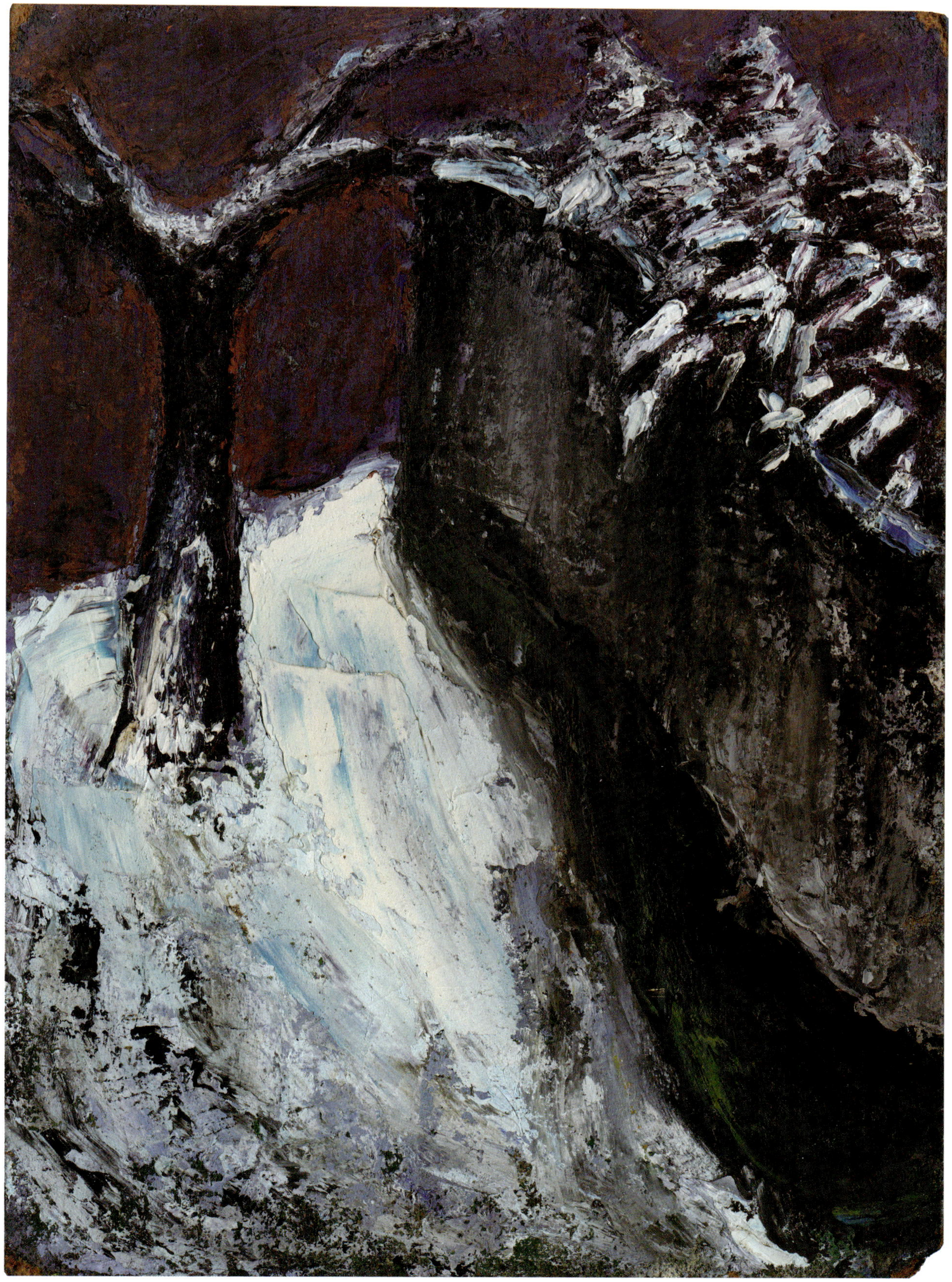

19 雪竹 1 *1978-1979* *36.8cm × 27.3cm* **Bamboo in Snow No. 1**

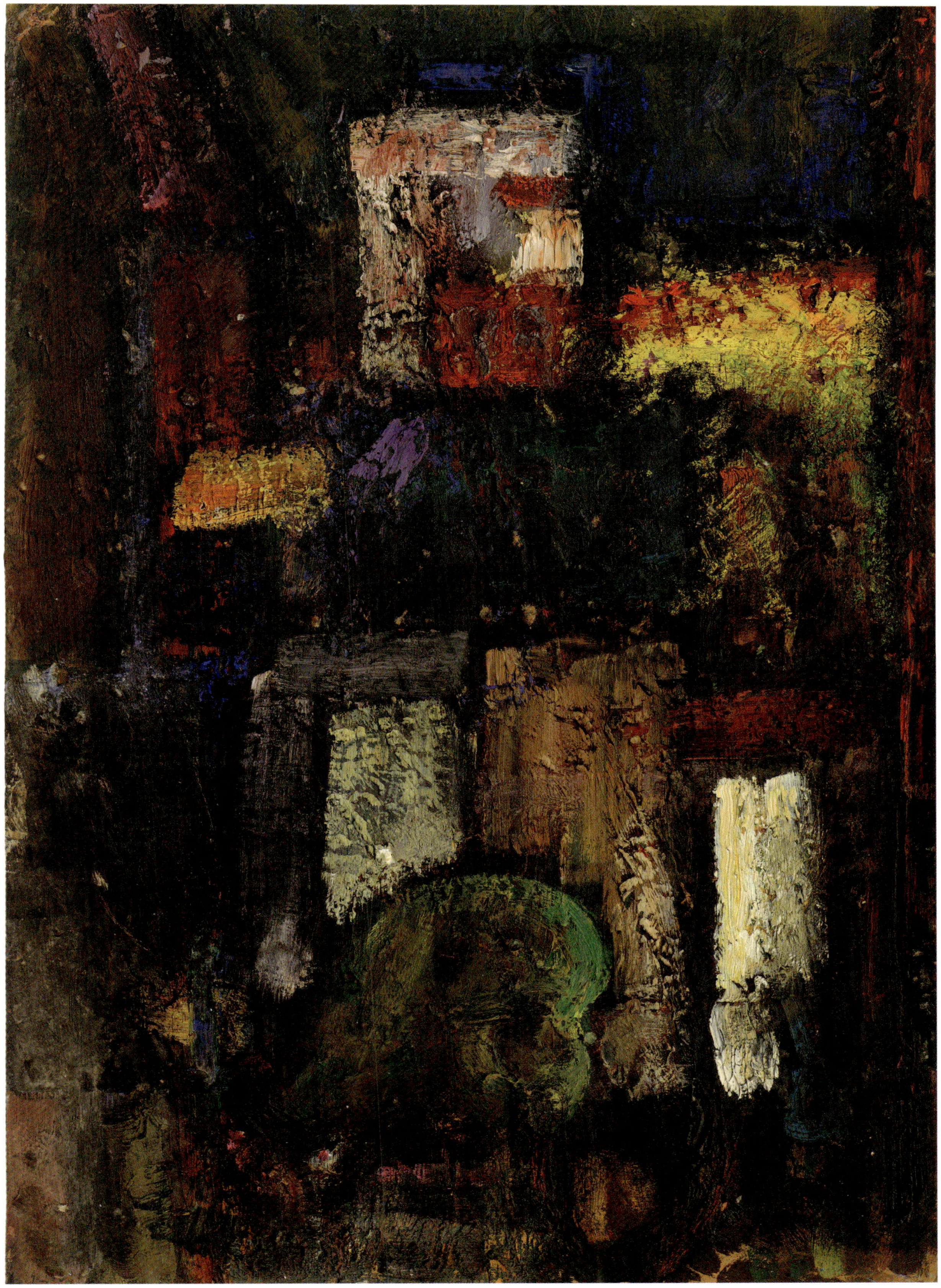

20　画板 4 *1978-1979 38.8cm × 28.4cm* **Drawing Board No. 4**

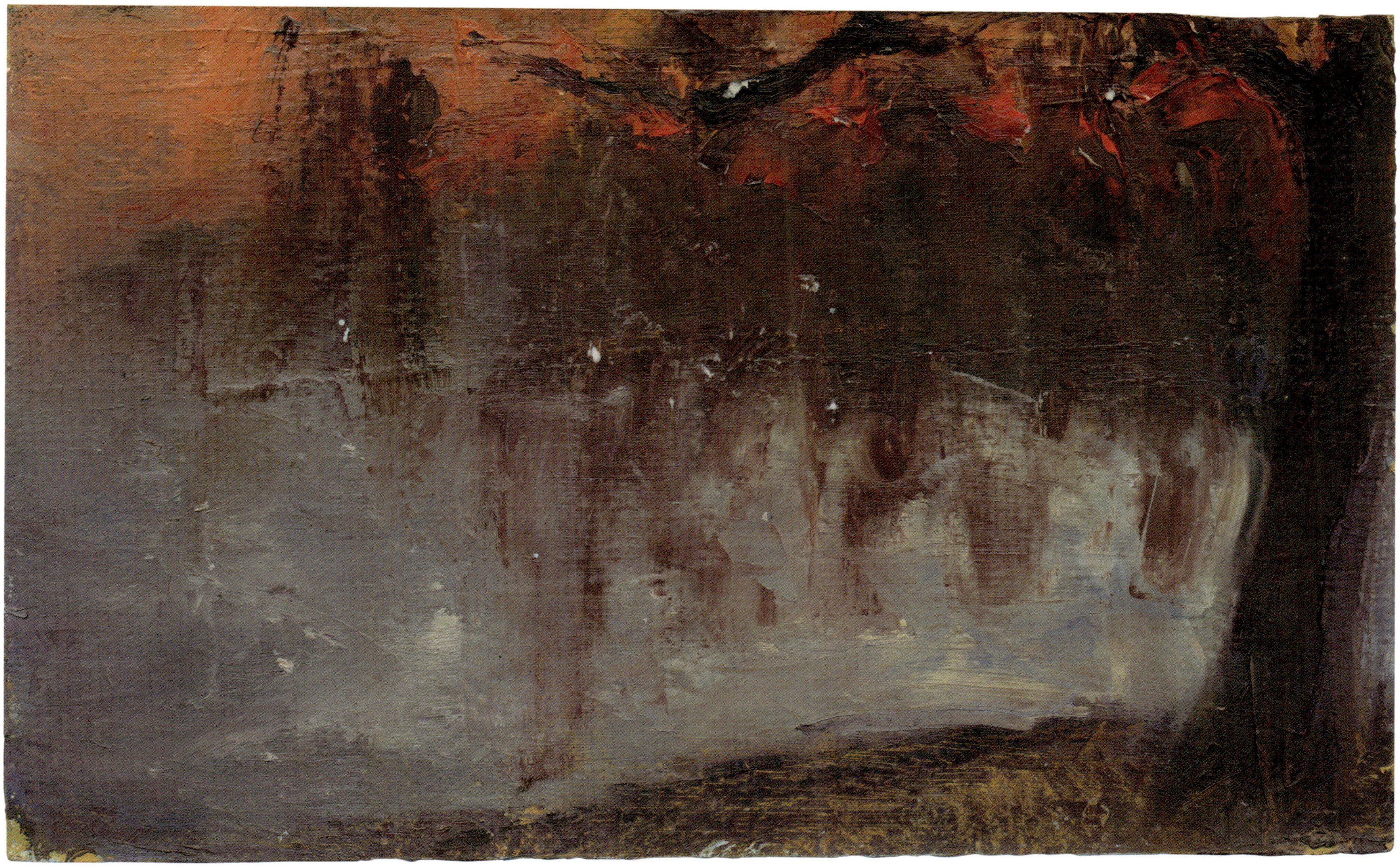

21 柳的落日 2 *1978 23.7cm × 38.8cm* **Sunset and Willow No. 2**

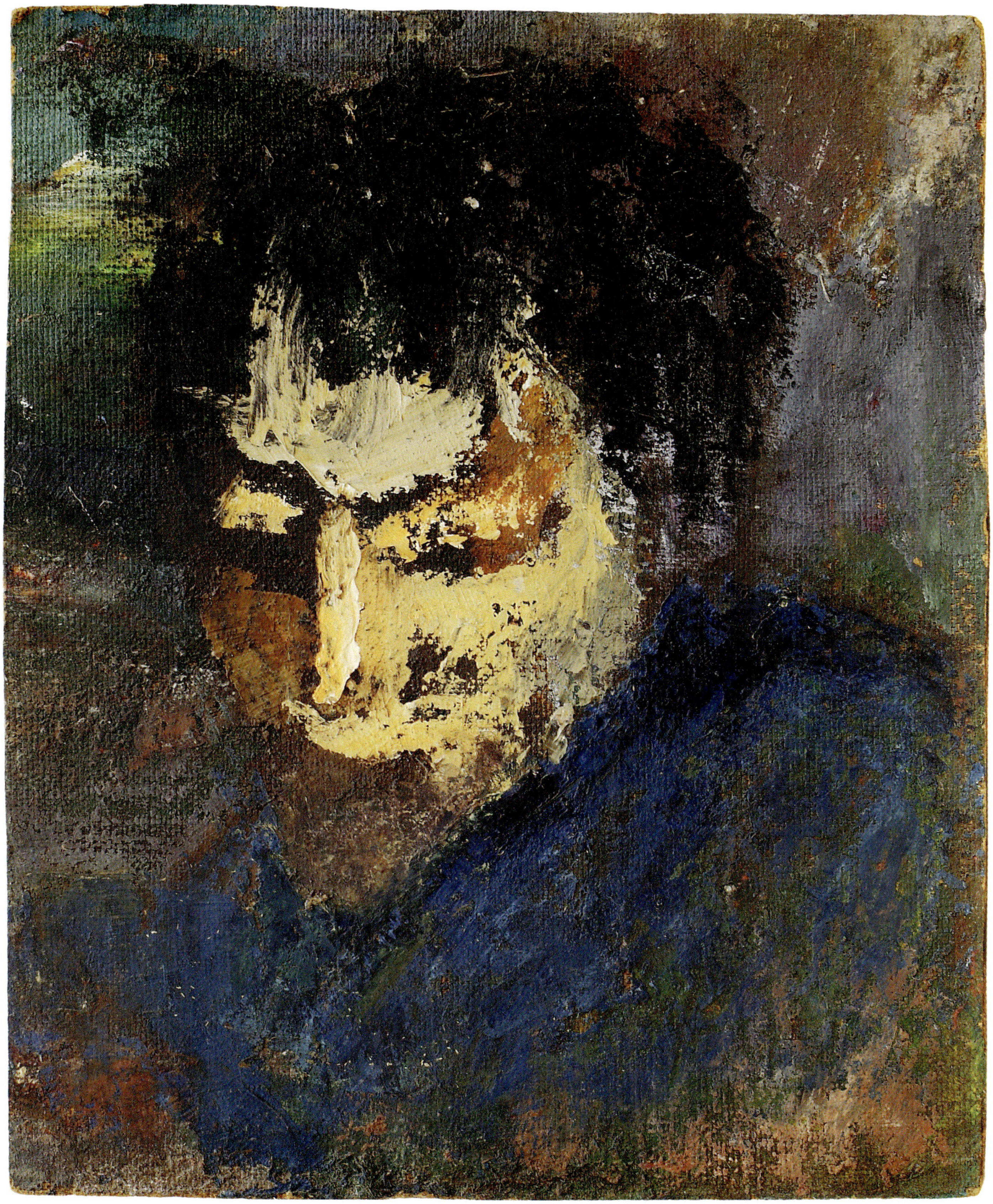

22 同学 2 *1979-1980 44.5cm × 37cm* **Schoolmate No. 2**

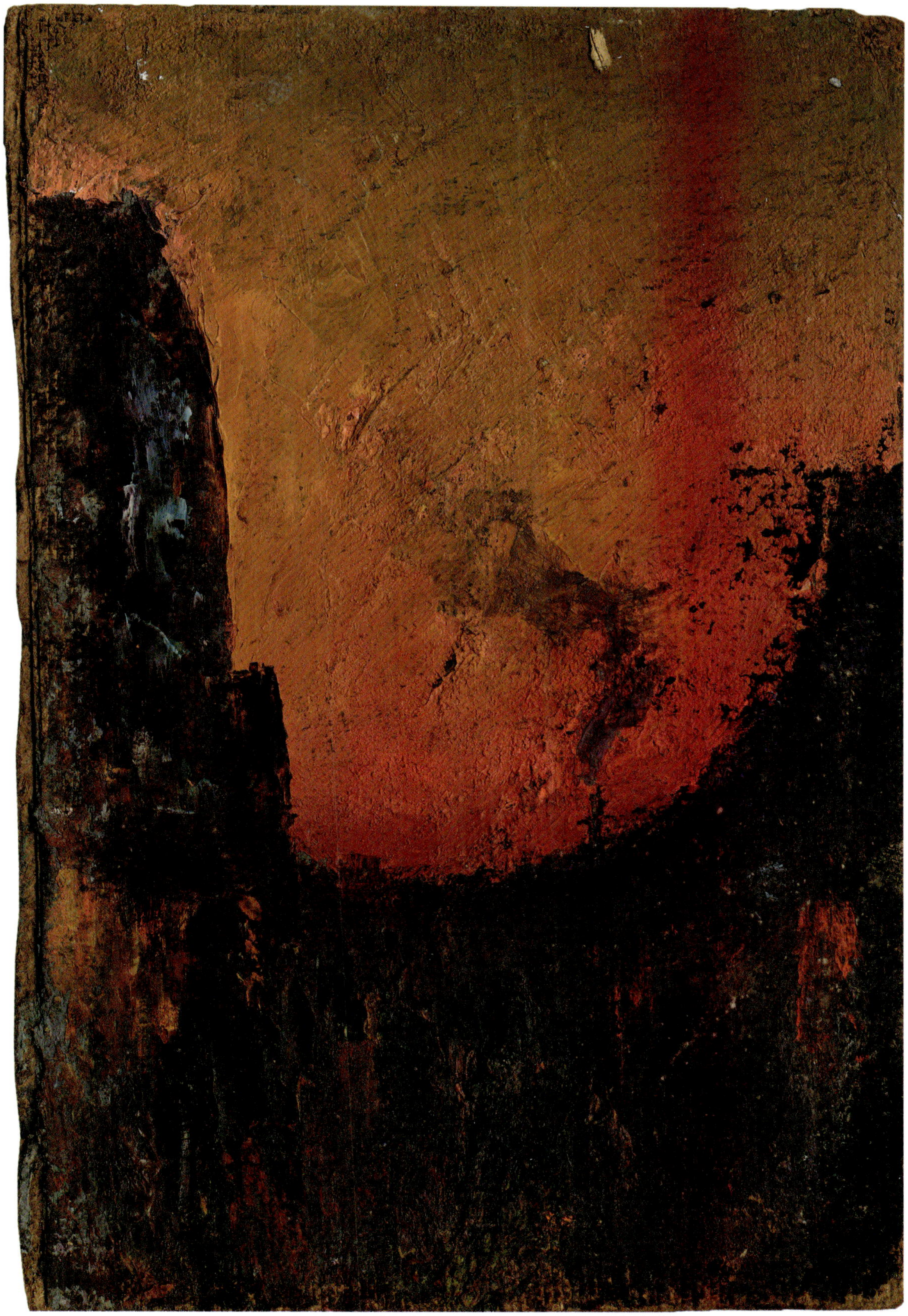

23　甜水井胡同黎明 *1979-1980 33.2cm × 23.1cm* **Tianshuijing Alley at Dawn**

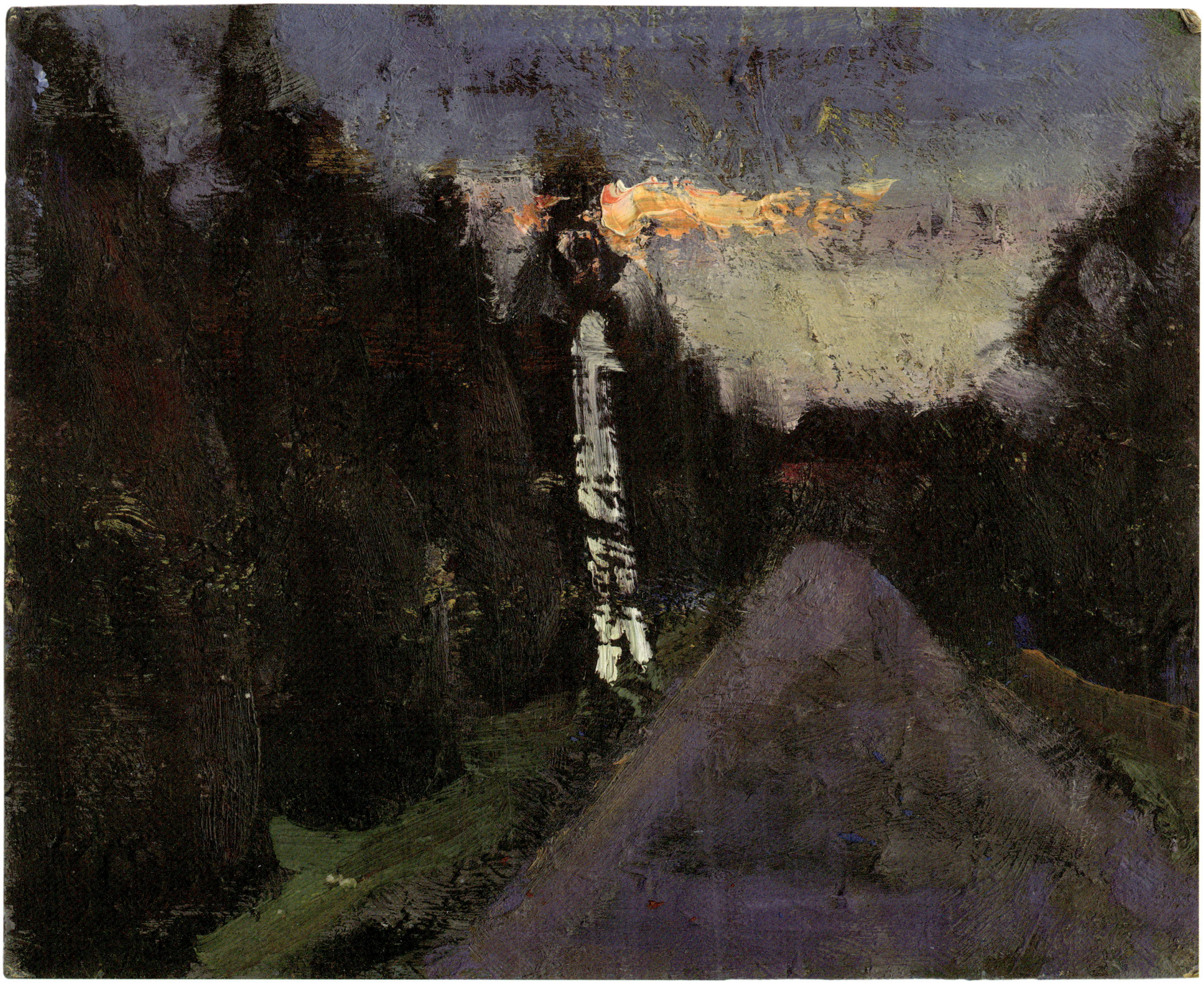

24　夕阳 *1977-1978 20.5cm × 25.3cm* **Sunset**

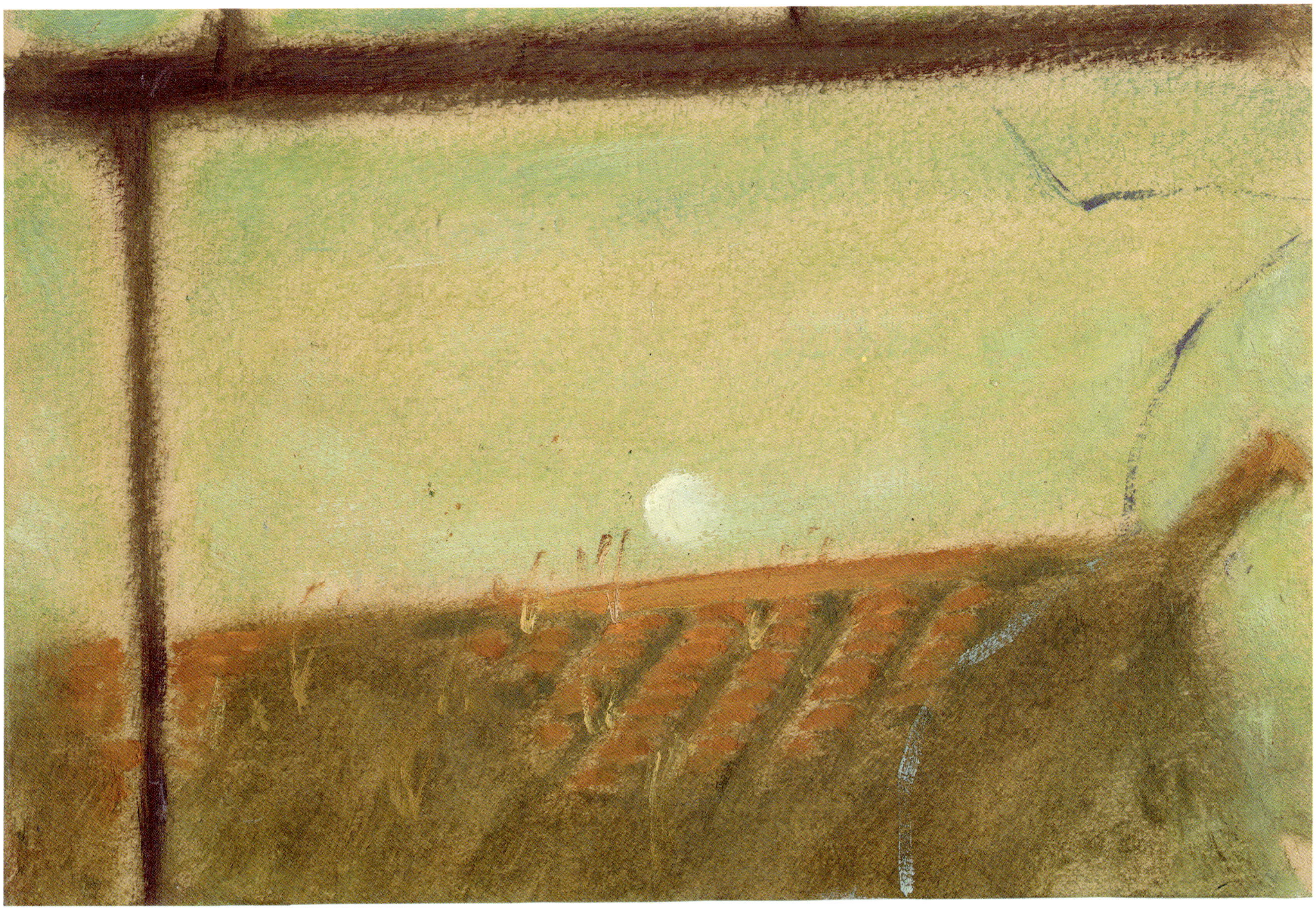

25 满月 *1979* *14.3cm × 20.9cm* **Full Moon**

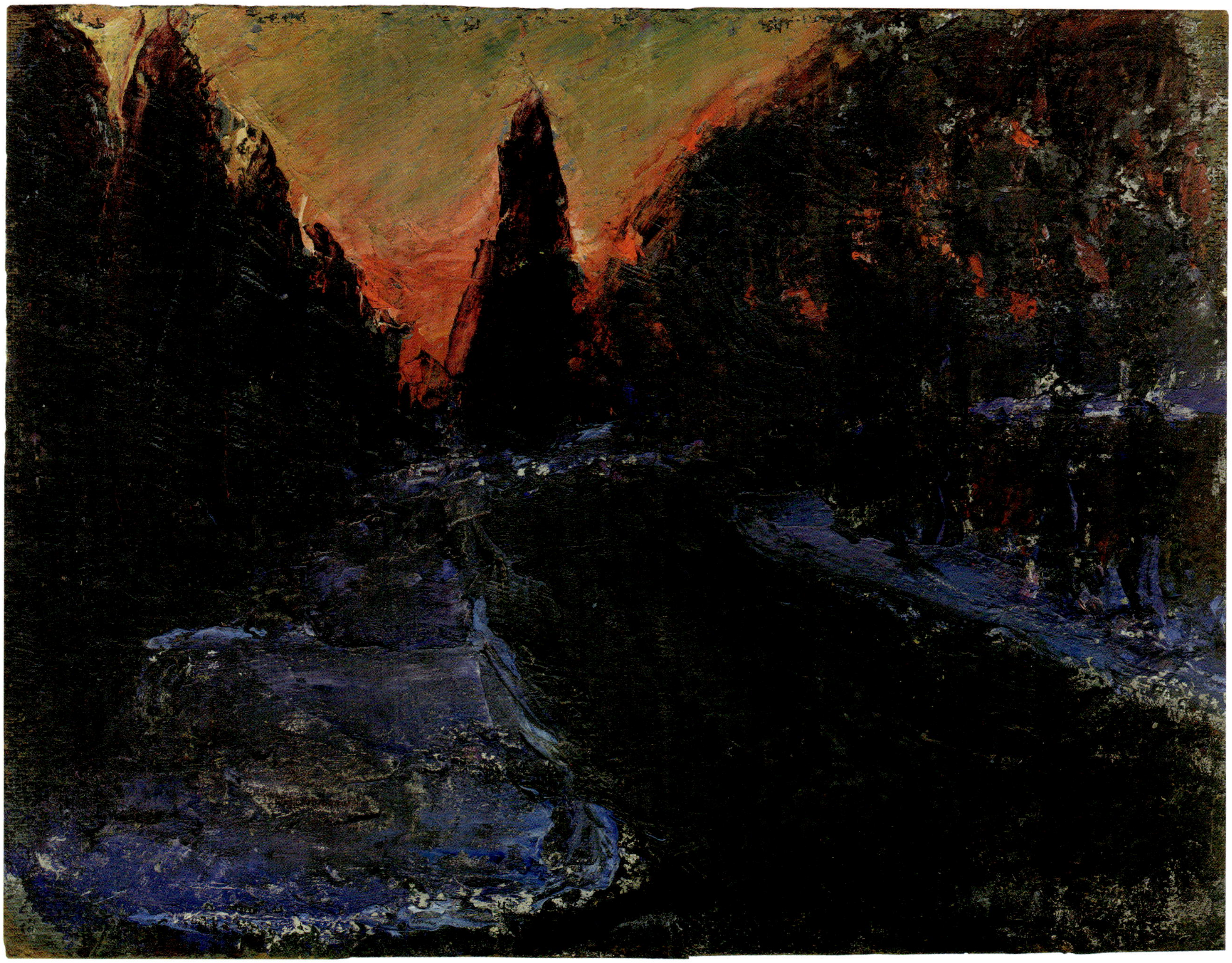

26　雪路 *1980-1981 31.6cm × 40.7cm* **Snowy Road**

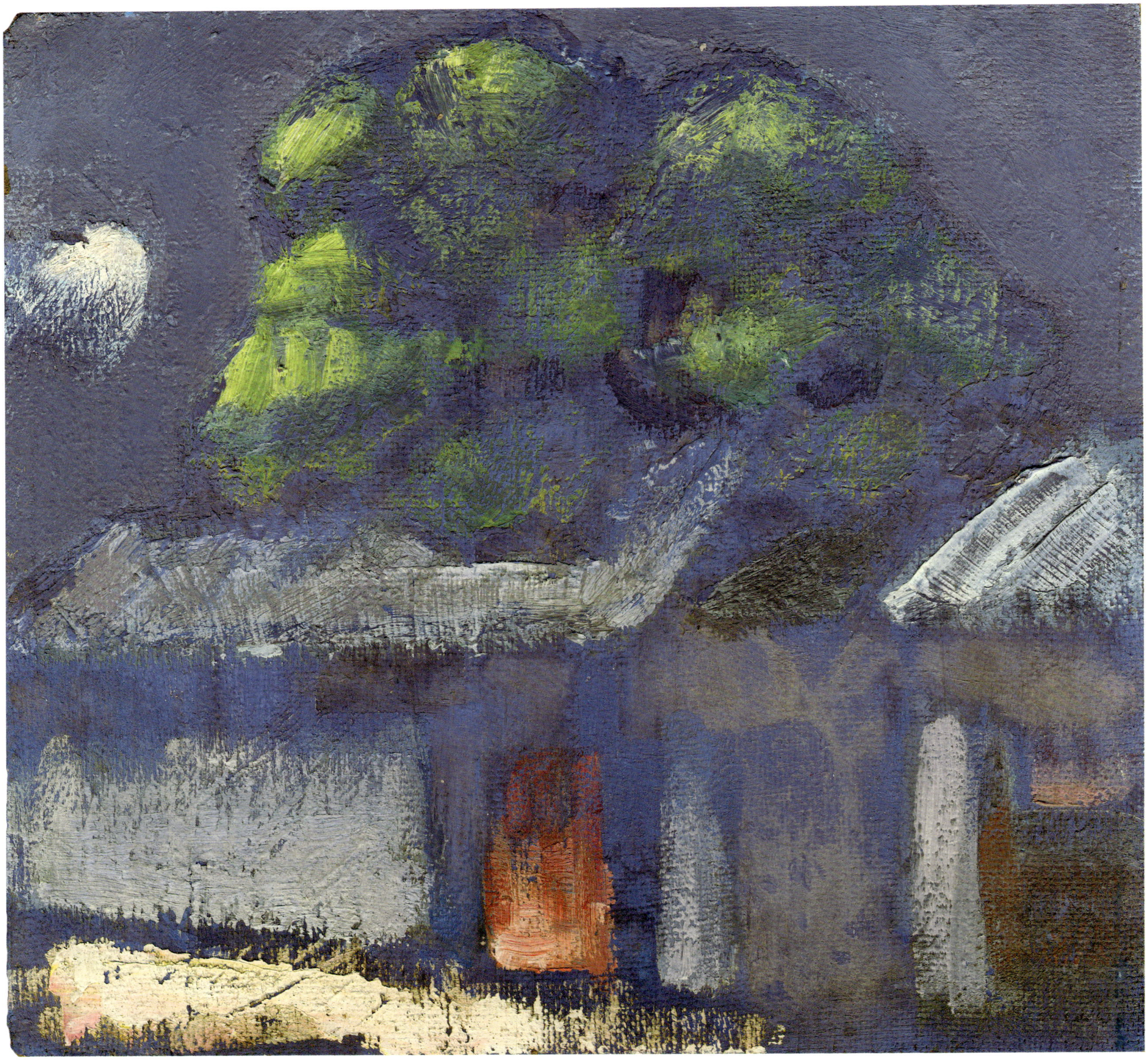

27 棉花胡同的中午 2 *1979-1980 28.4cm × 31cm* **Cotton Alley at Noontime No. 2**

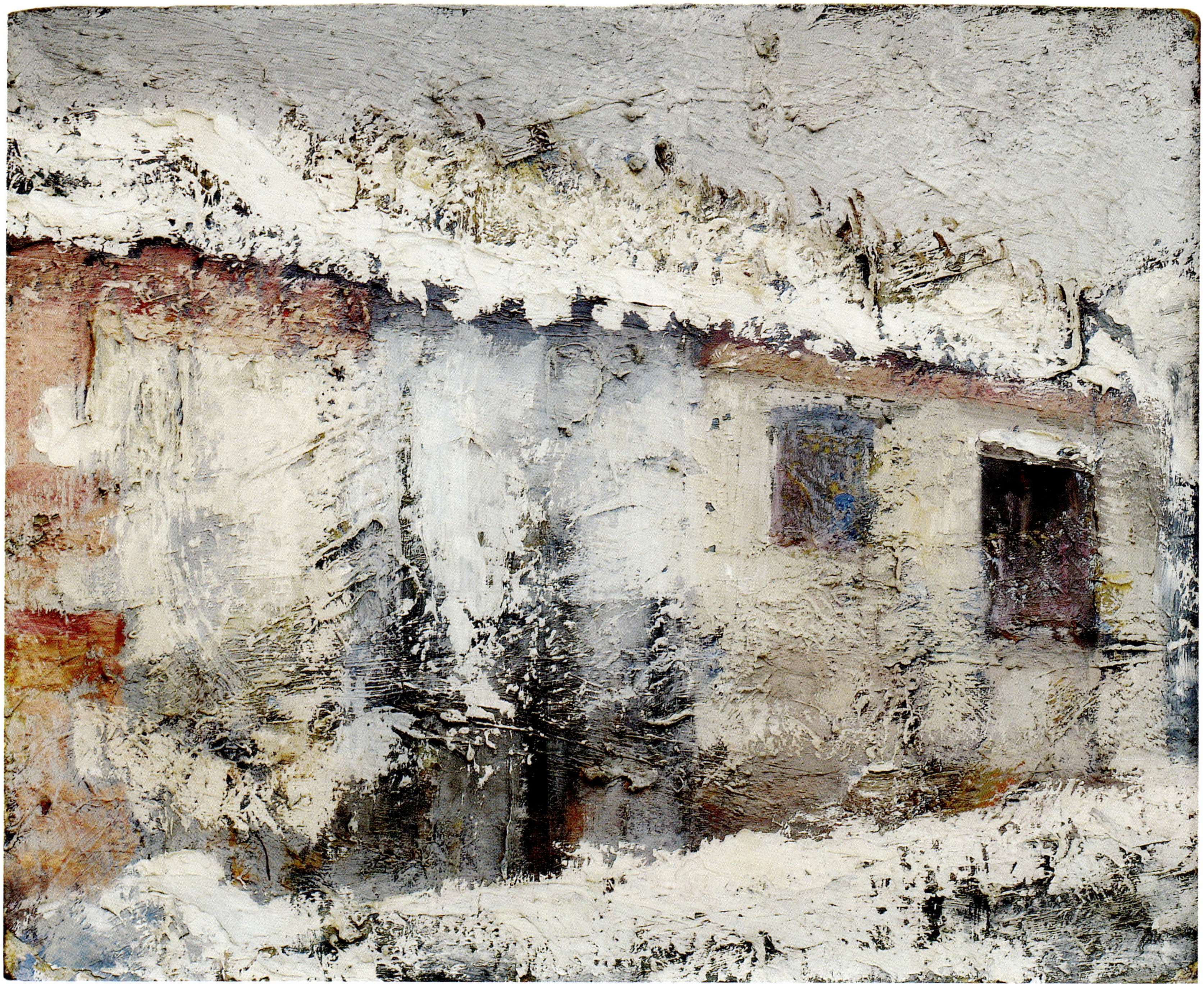

28　四川营胡同的雪 *1979-1986 43cm × 55cm* **Sichuan Camp Alley in the Snow**

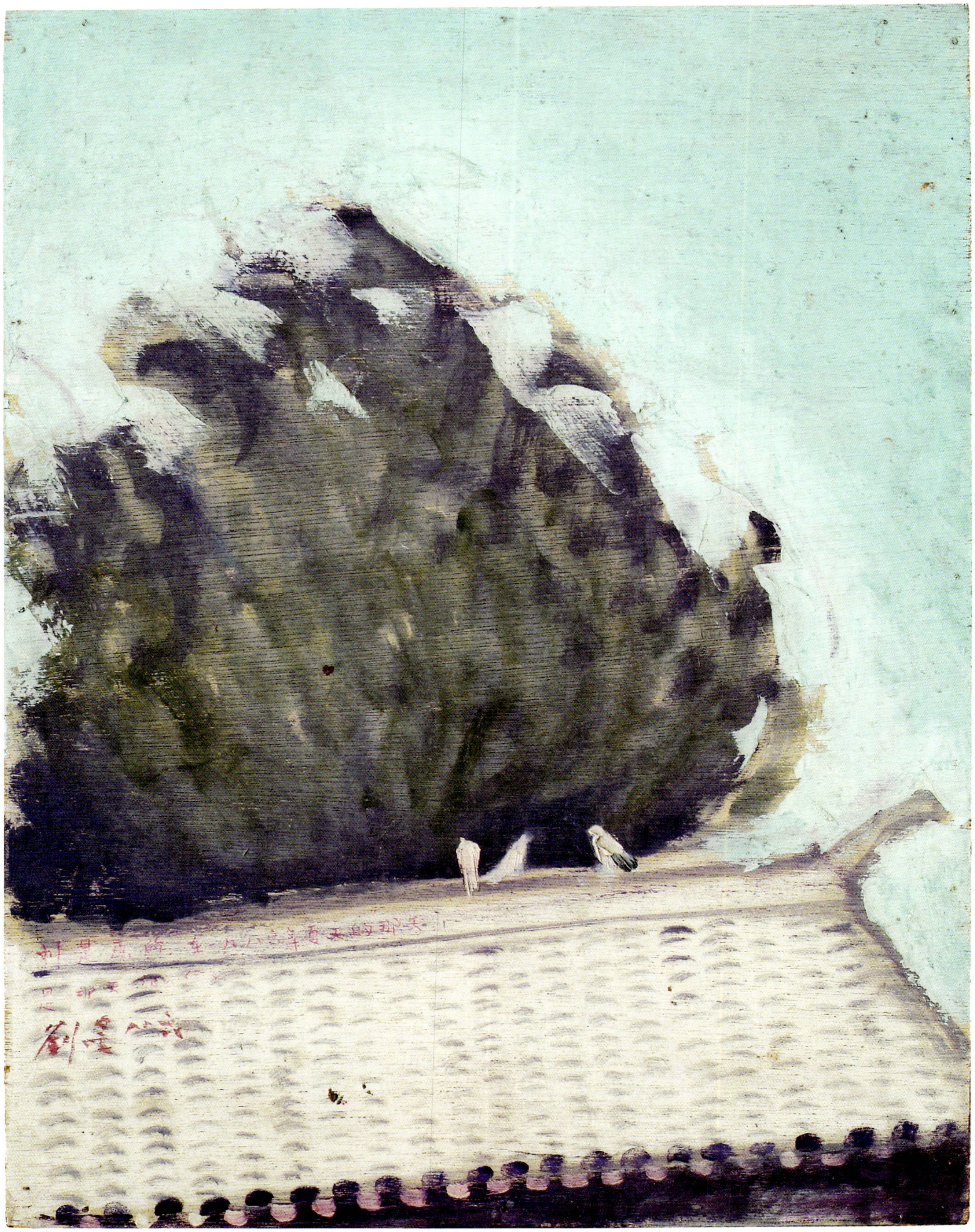

29 四川营胡同的夏 *1979-1986 60.5cm × 48cm* **Sichuan Camp Alley in Summer**

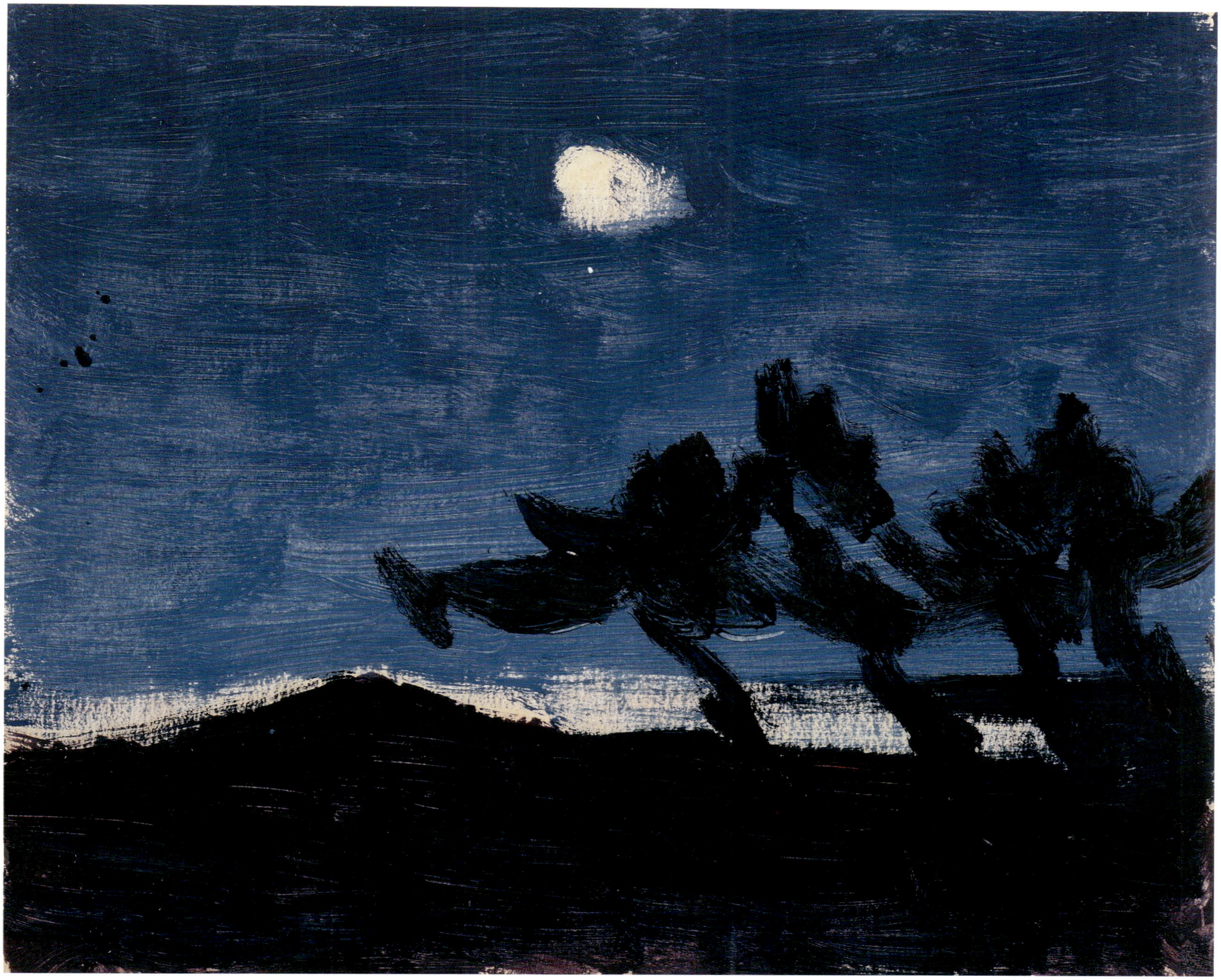

30　短松岗 *1981-1984 19.5cm × 24cm* **Short Pine Hills**

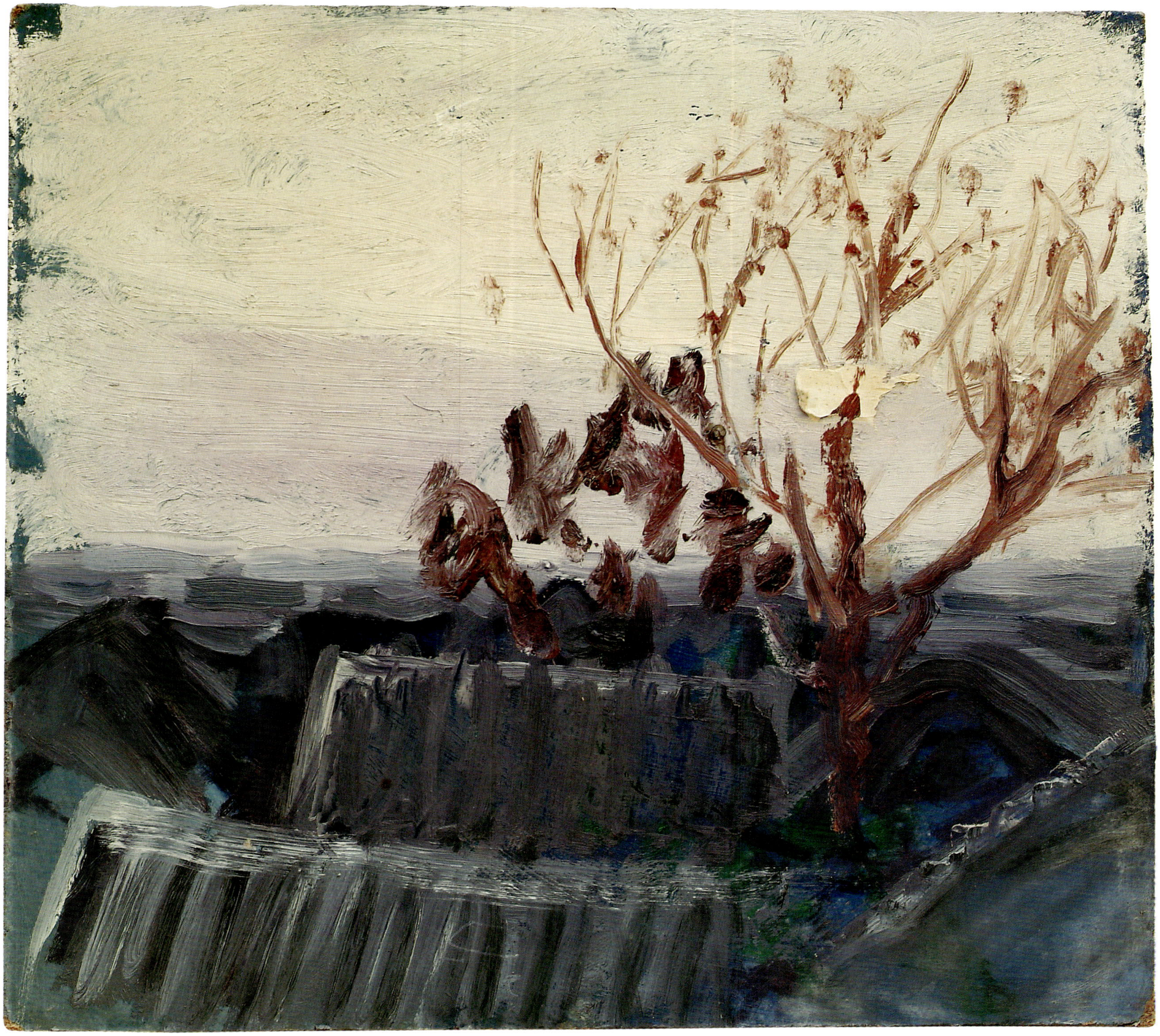

31　四川营胡同的秋 *1981-1984* *33cm × 37.5cm* **Sichuan Camp Alley in Autumn**

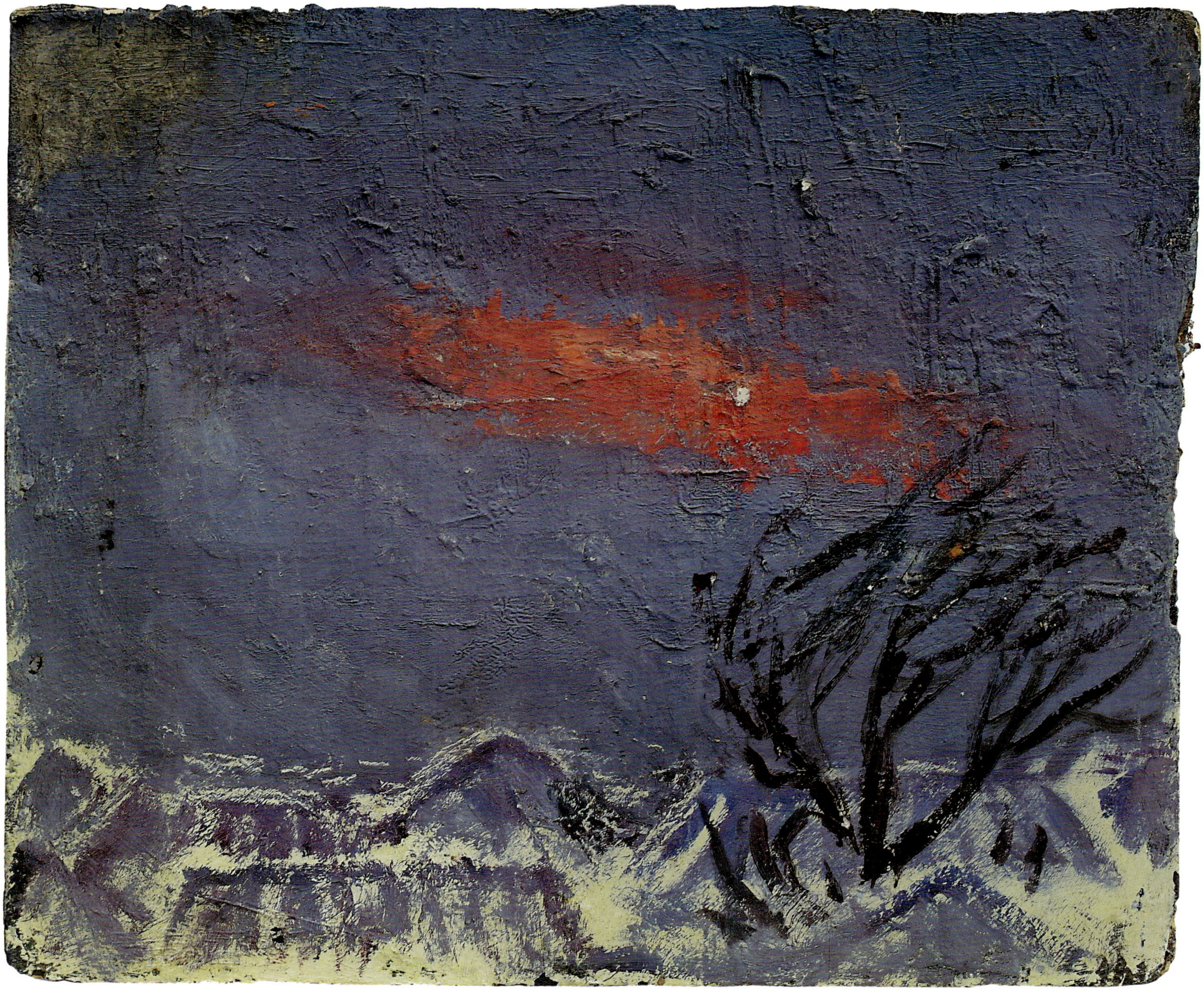

32　棉花胡同的落日 *1979-1982* *38cm × 46cm* **Sunset in Cotton Alley**

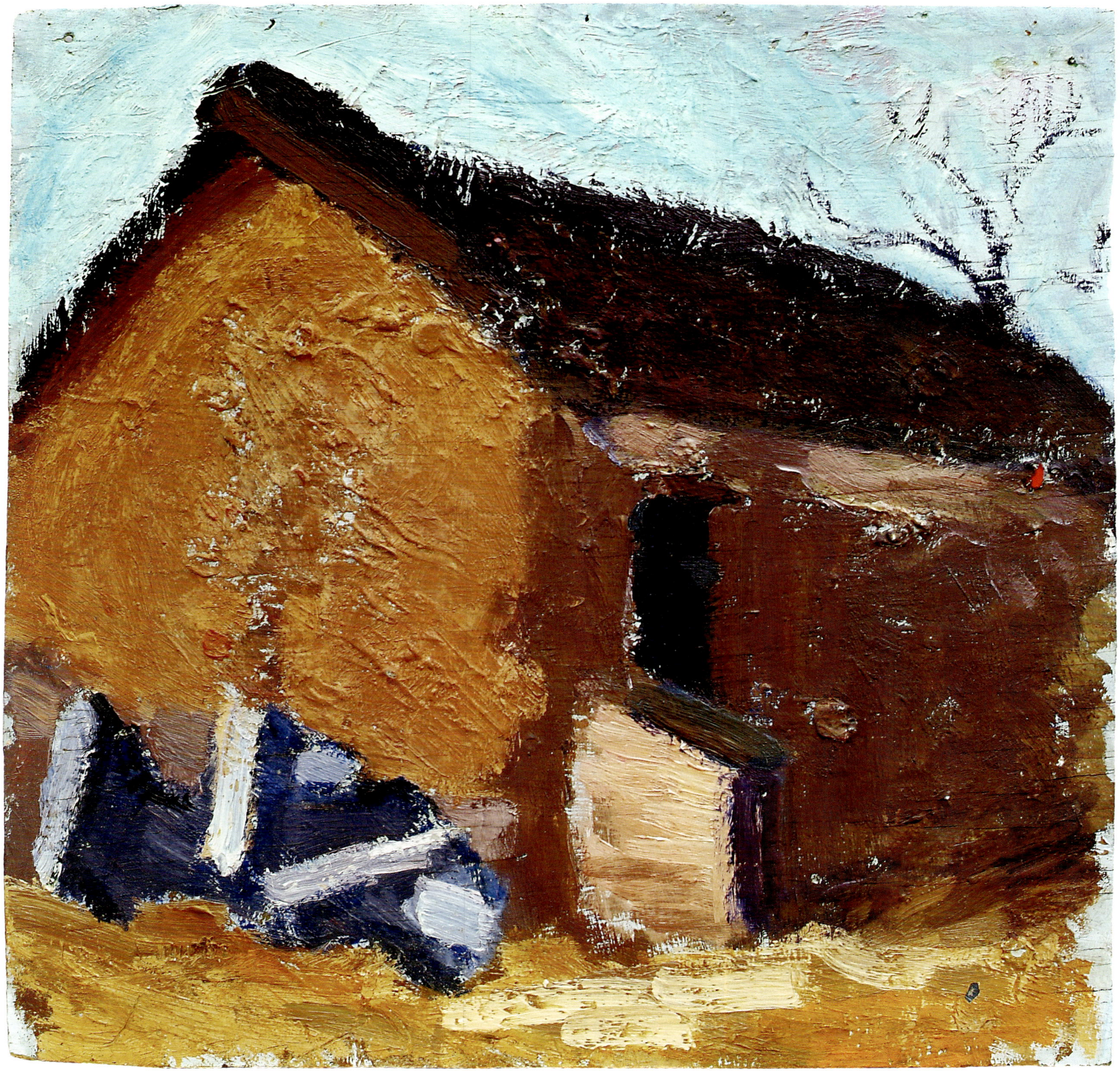

33 石板 *1980-1981 41.5cm × 43cm* **Flagstone**

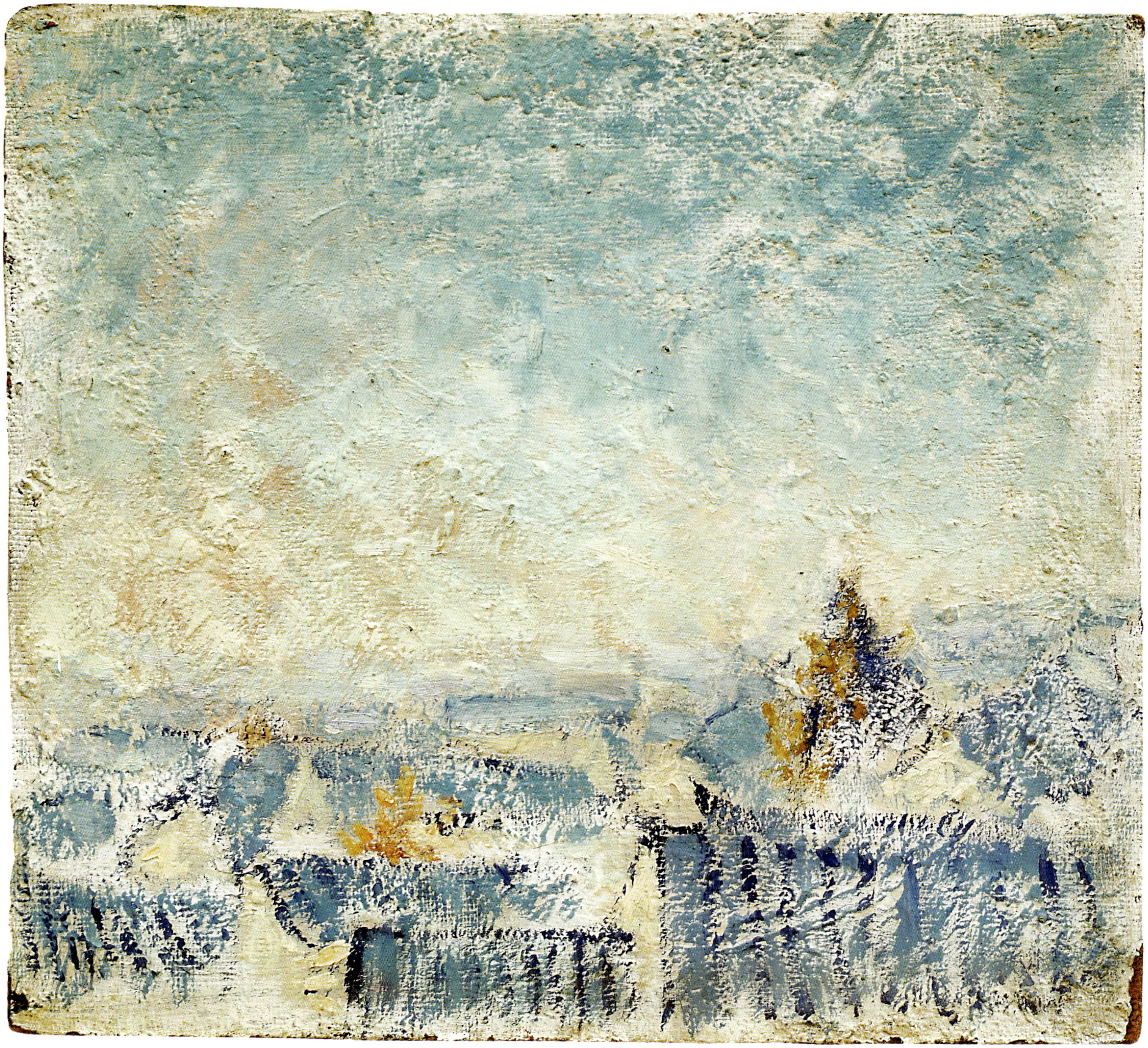

34 夏日 *1981-1982 41cm × 46cm* **Summertime**

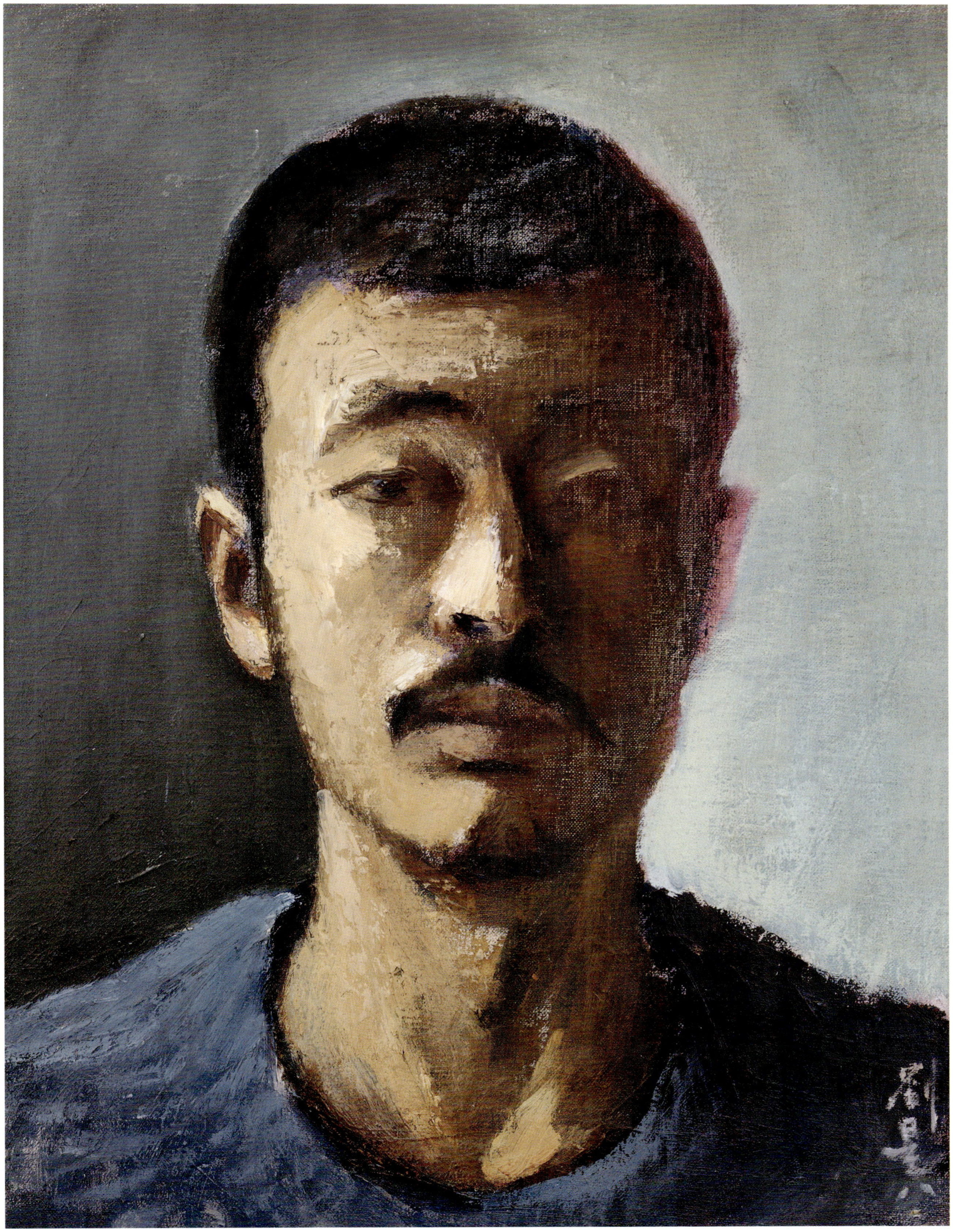

35　自画像 *1982 43cm × 34cm* **Self-Portrait**

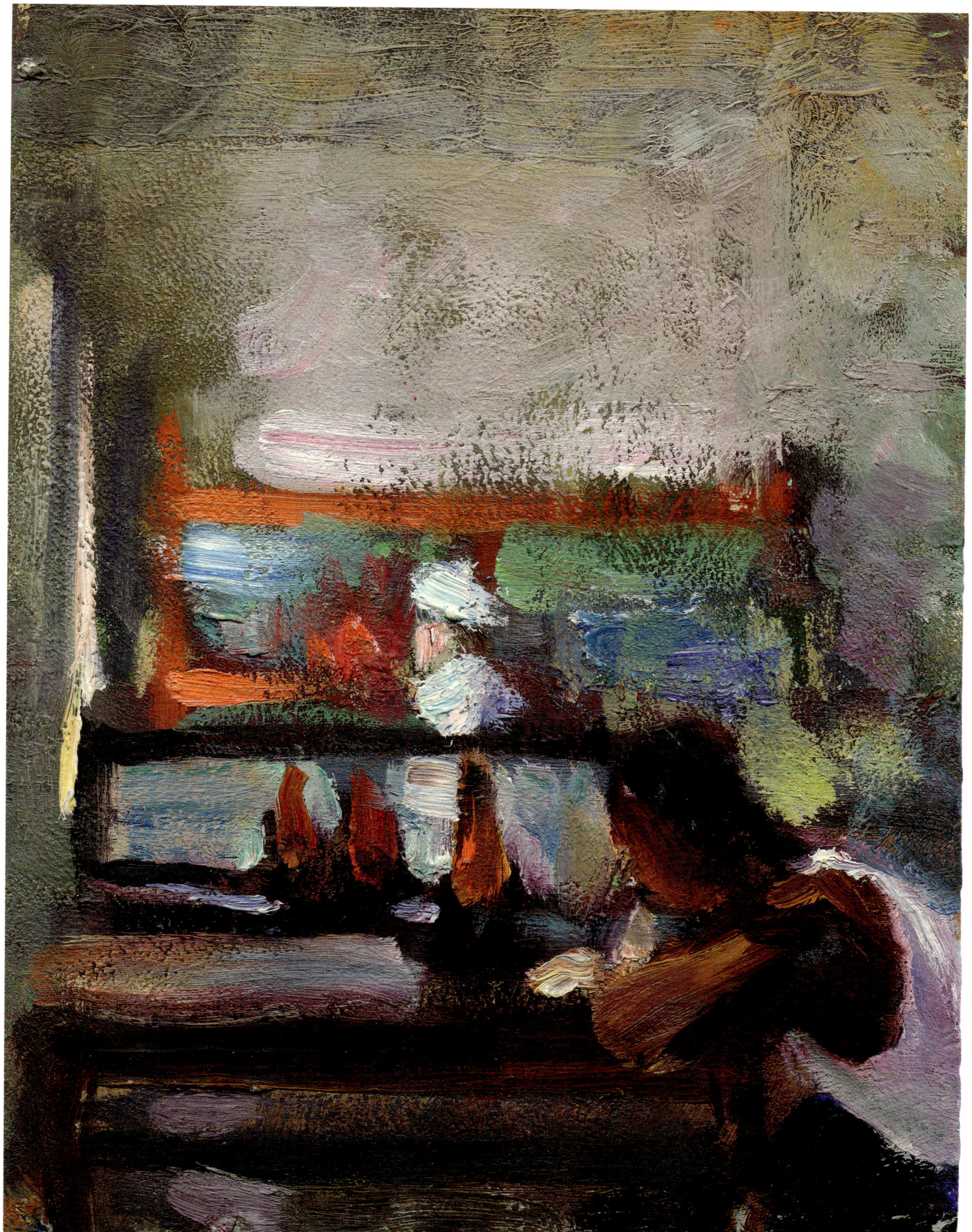

36 小酒馆 *1984 21.6cm × 16.7cm* **Little Bar**

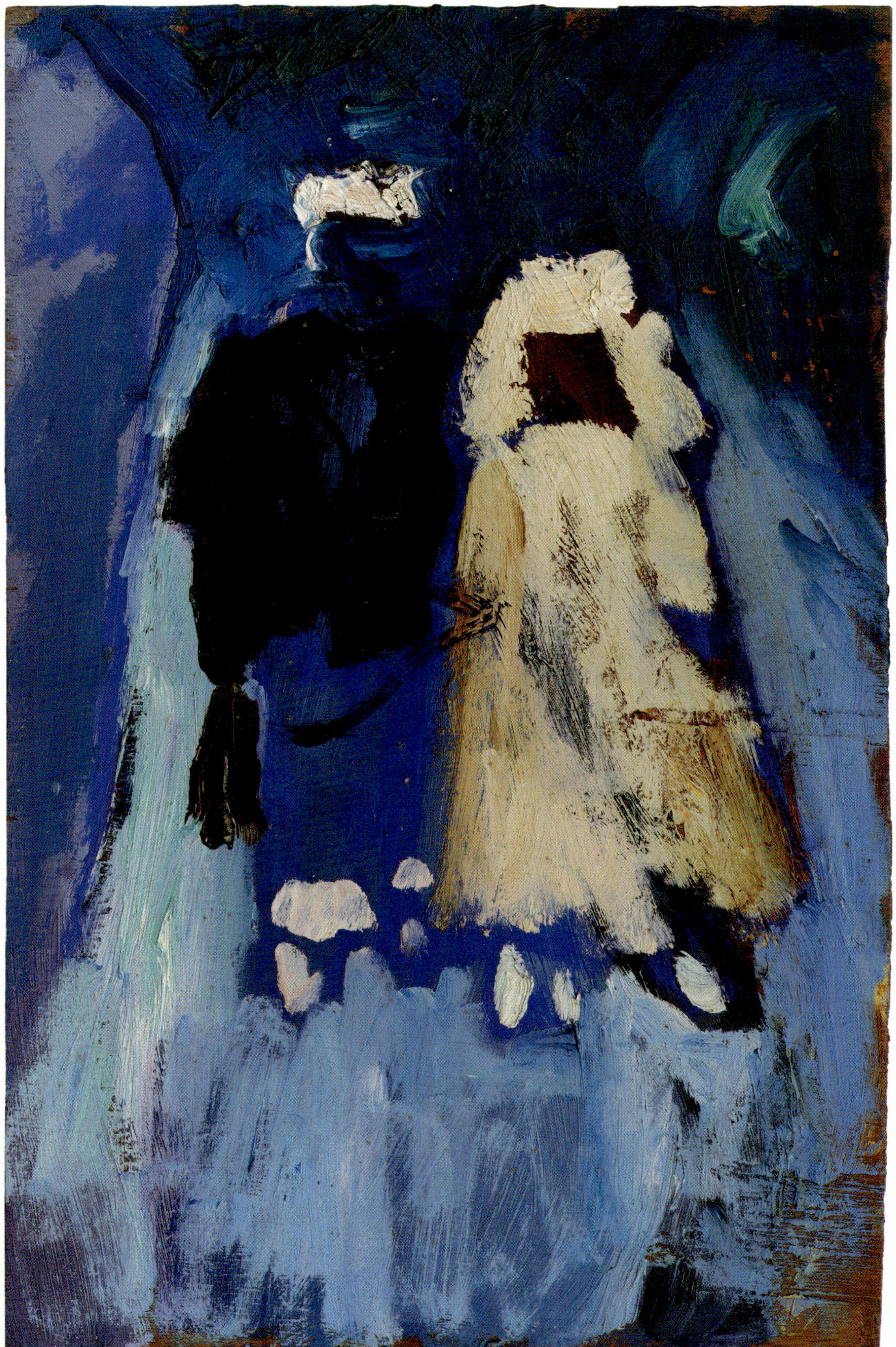

37 油条和葬礼 *1986 40.6cm × 26.7cm* **Deep-Fried Dough and Funeral**

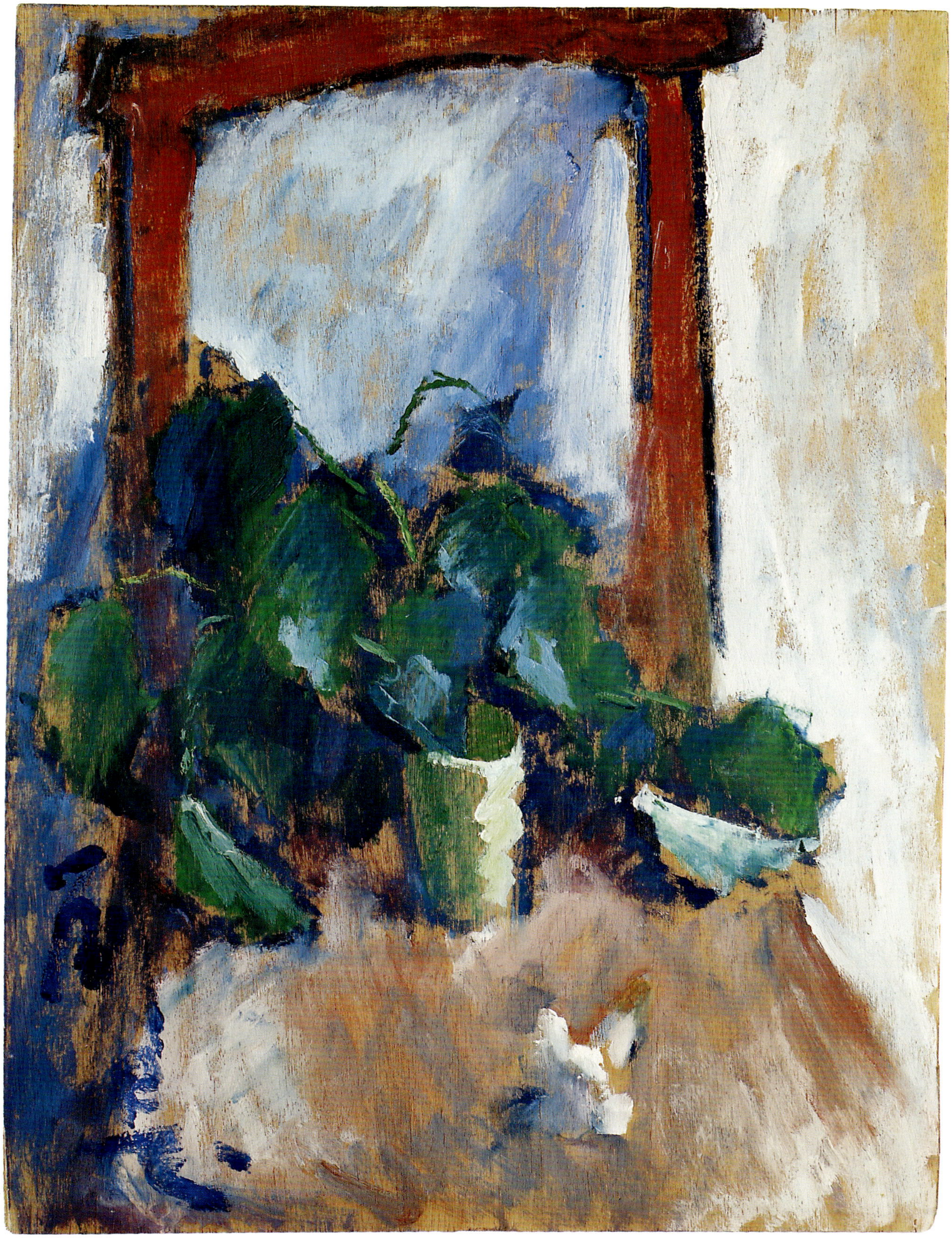

38 梧桐花与杨树叶 *1986 59.5cm × 45.5cm* **Parasol Flowers and Poplar Leaves**

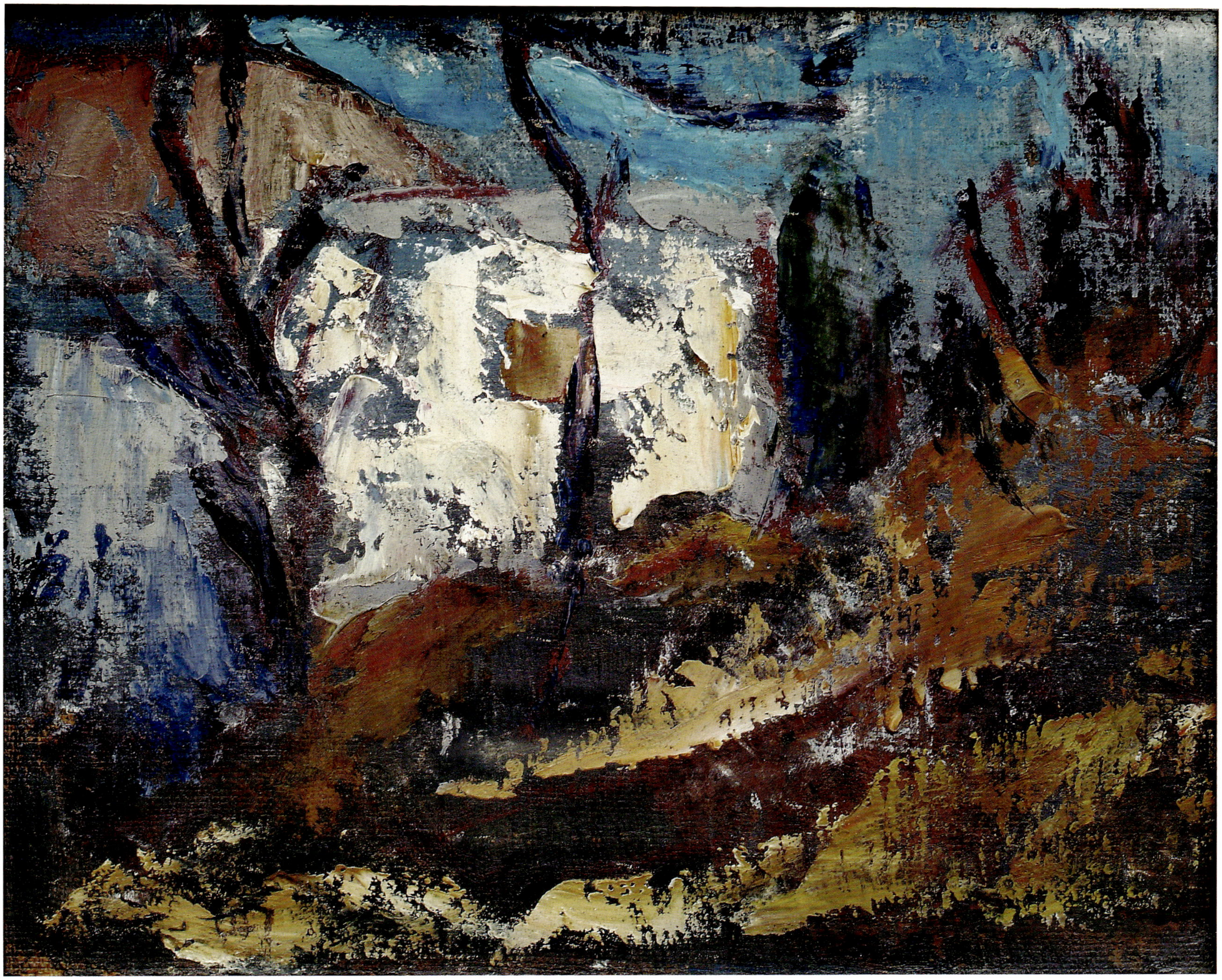

39　山坳的白房 *1986 36cm × 45cm* **White House on the Ridge**

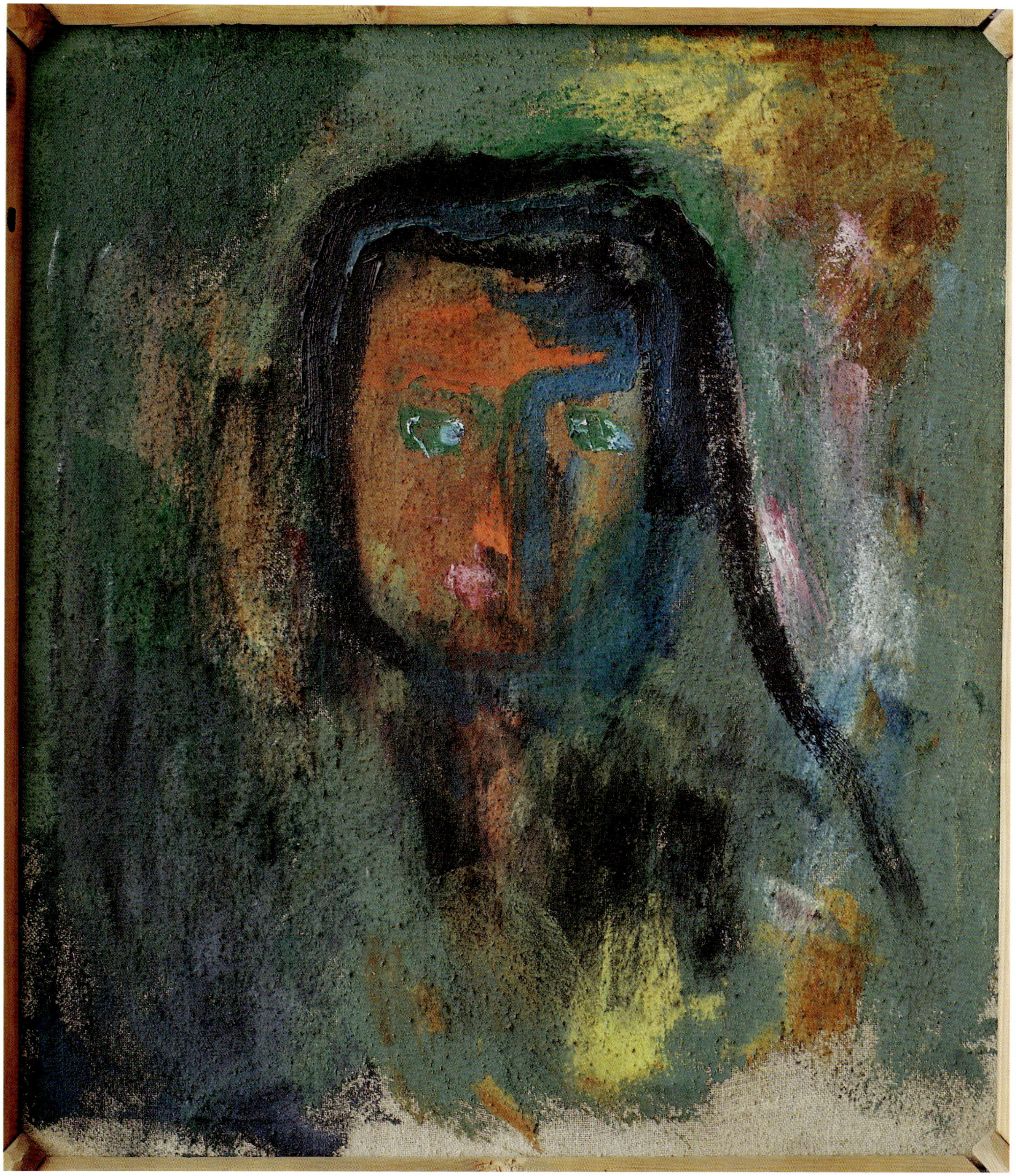

40 鬼 2 *1986 63cm × 52cm* **Ghost No. 2**

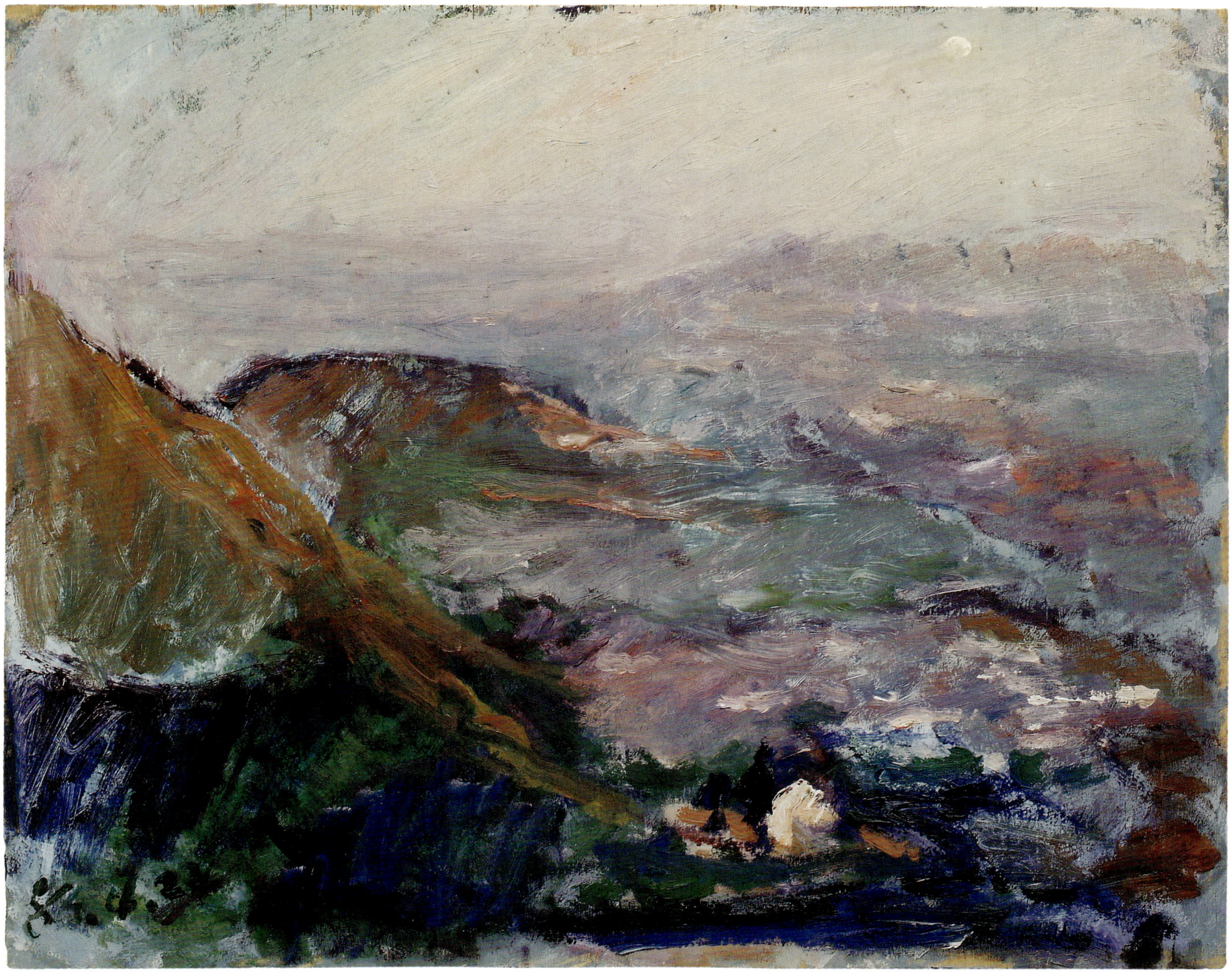

41　四月 2 *1986 61cm × 77cm* **April No. 2**

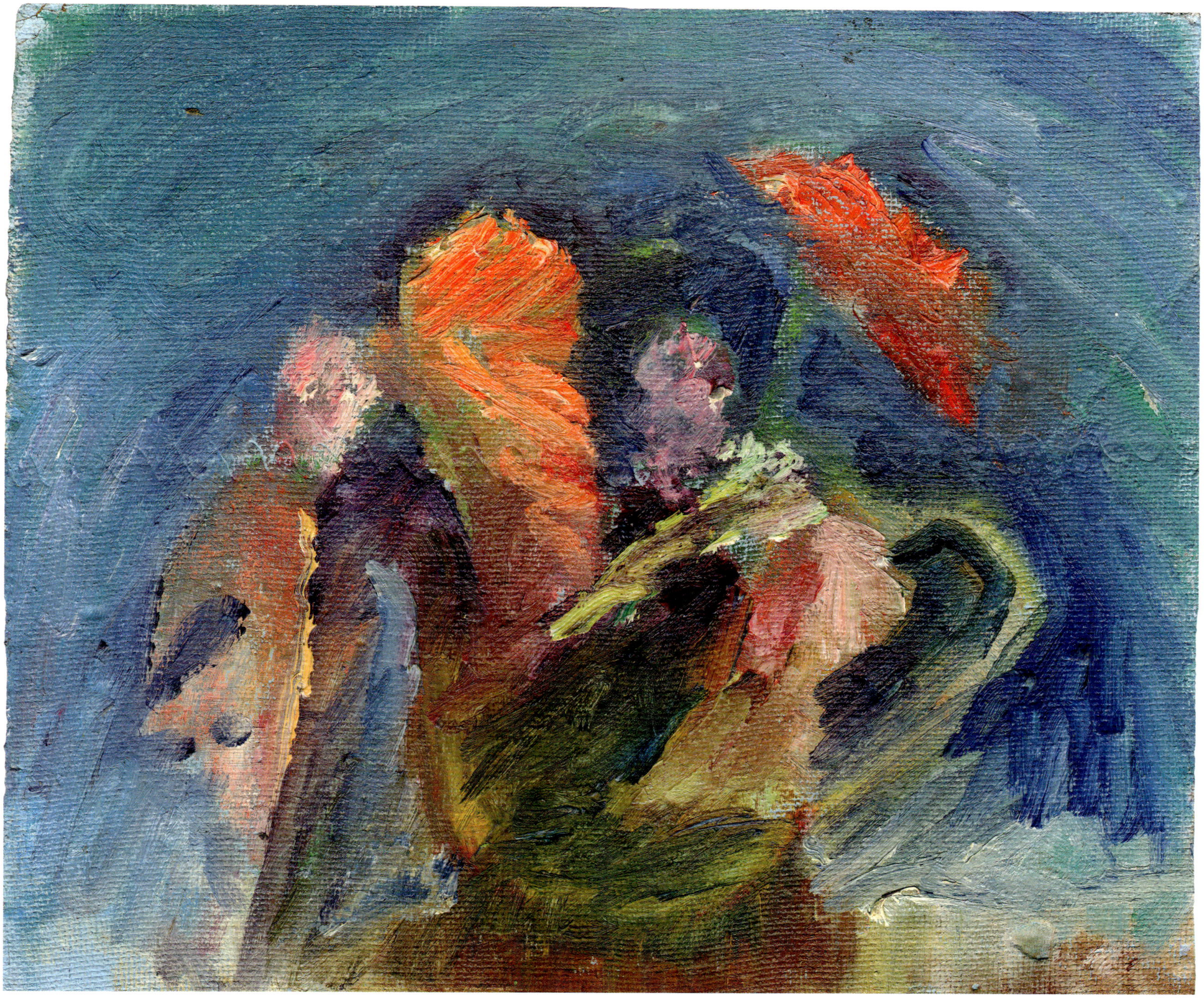

42　秋海棠 *1986-1987 29.6cm × 36cm* **Begonia**

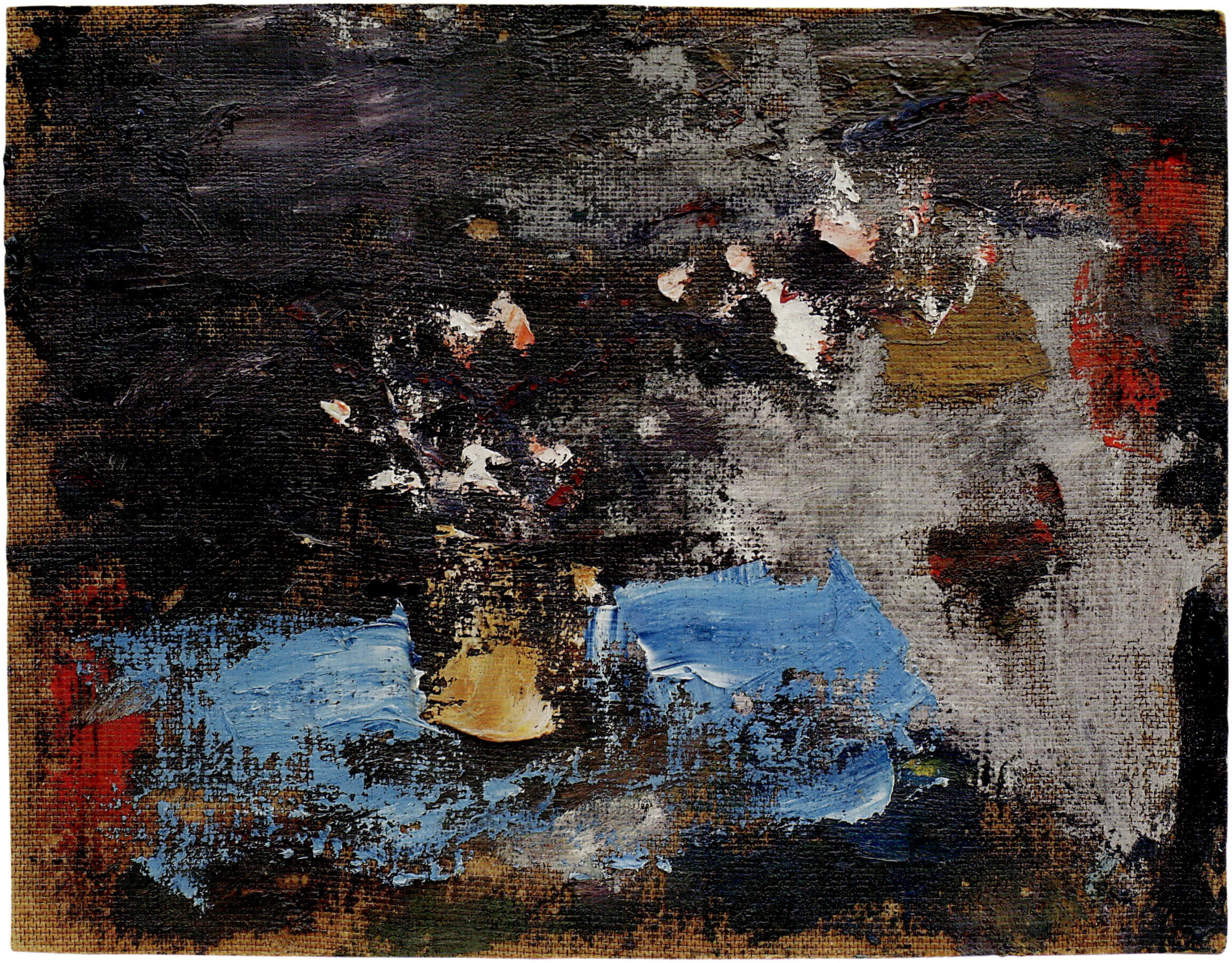

43　鲜花 *1986-1987 35cm × 45.5cm* **Flowers**

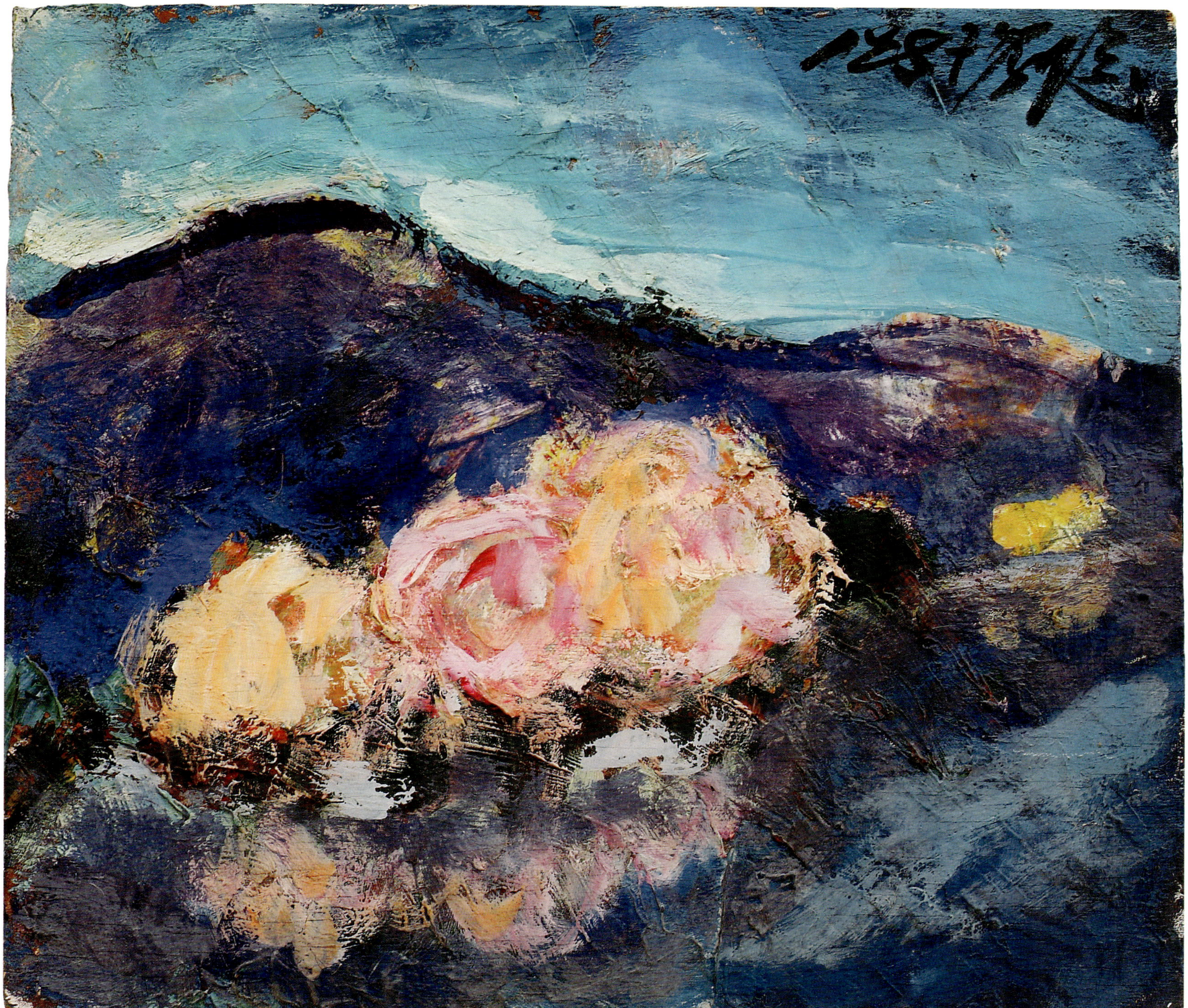

44 写生-084 *1987 31cm × 36.5cm* **Painting from Life - 084**

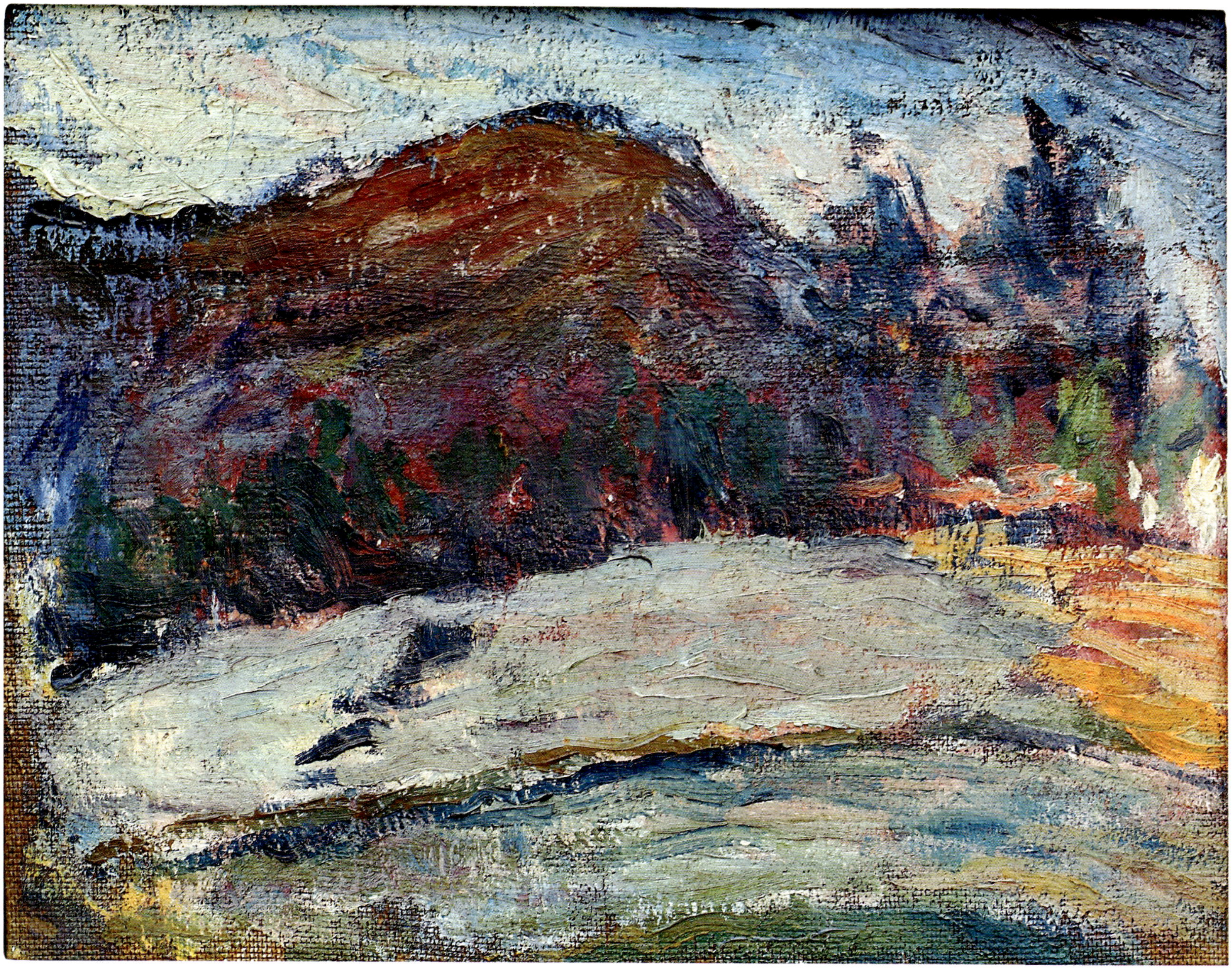

45　傍晚的池塘 *1986 35cm × 45.5cm* **Pond in the Dusk**

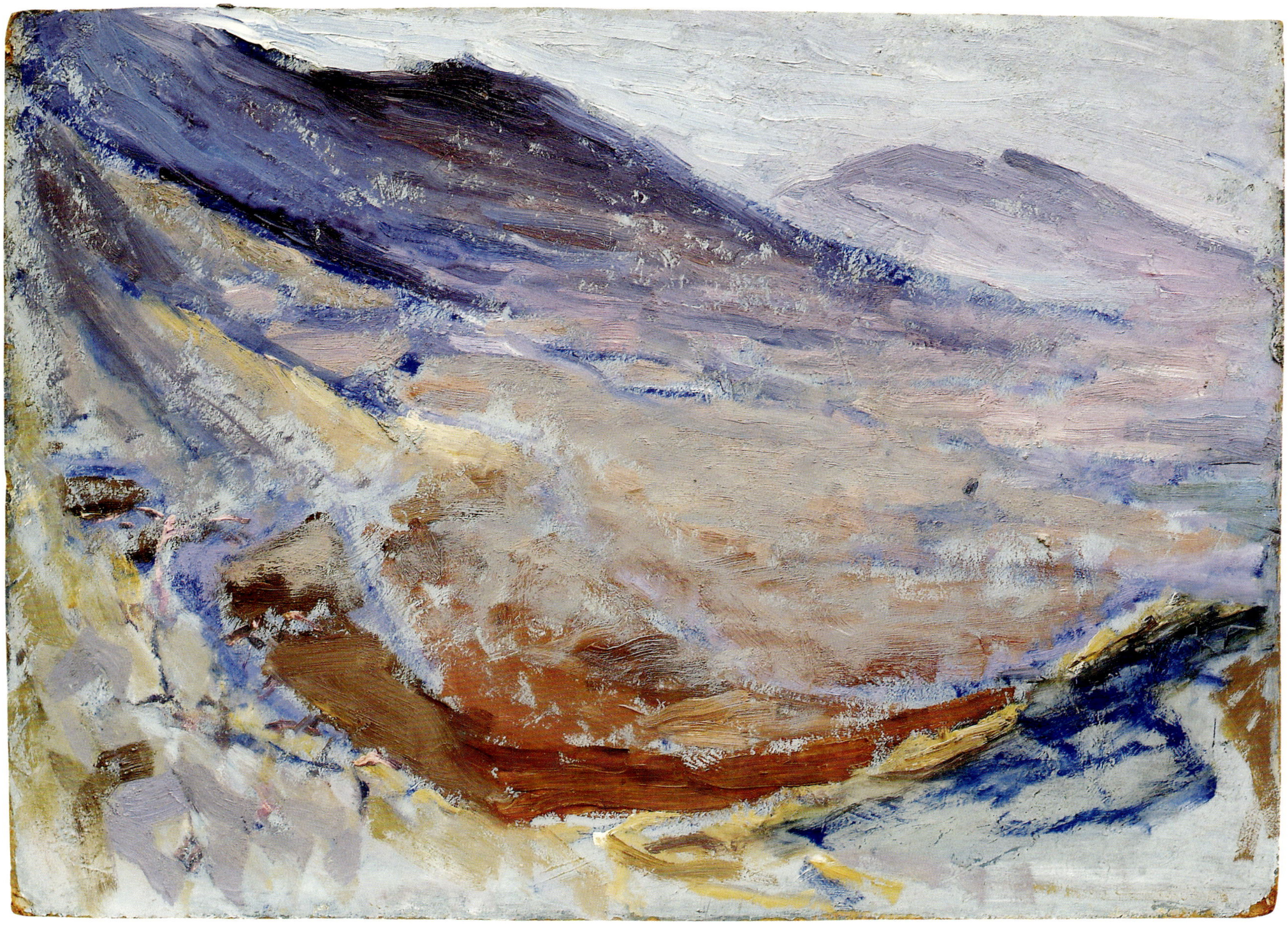

46 梯田 2 *1986 54.5cm × 63cm* **Terraced Fields No. 2**

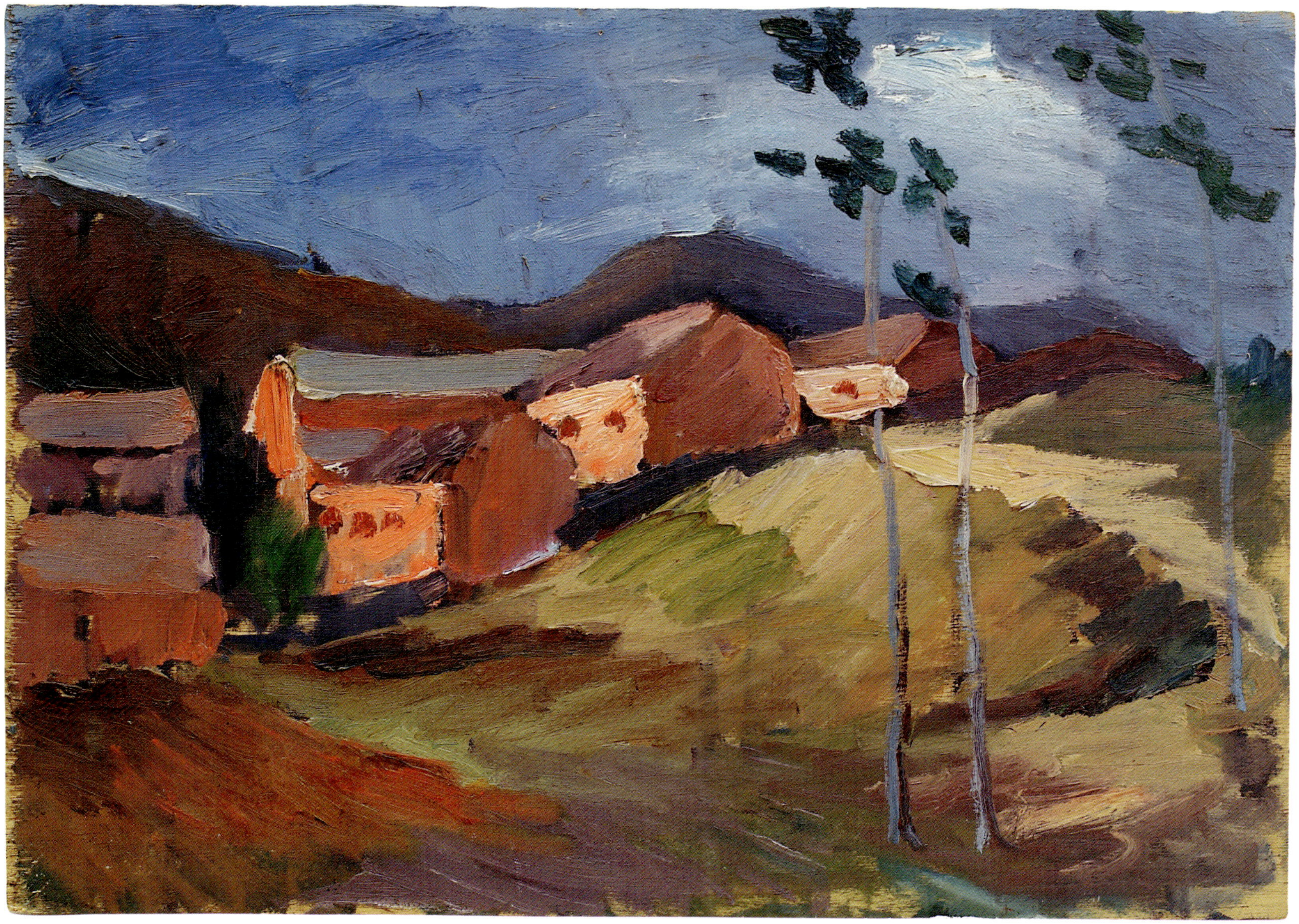

47　校办工厂 2 *1986 40cm × 55.8cm* **School-Run Factory No. 2**

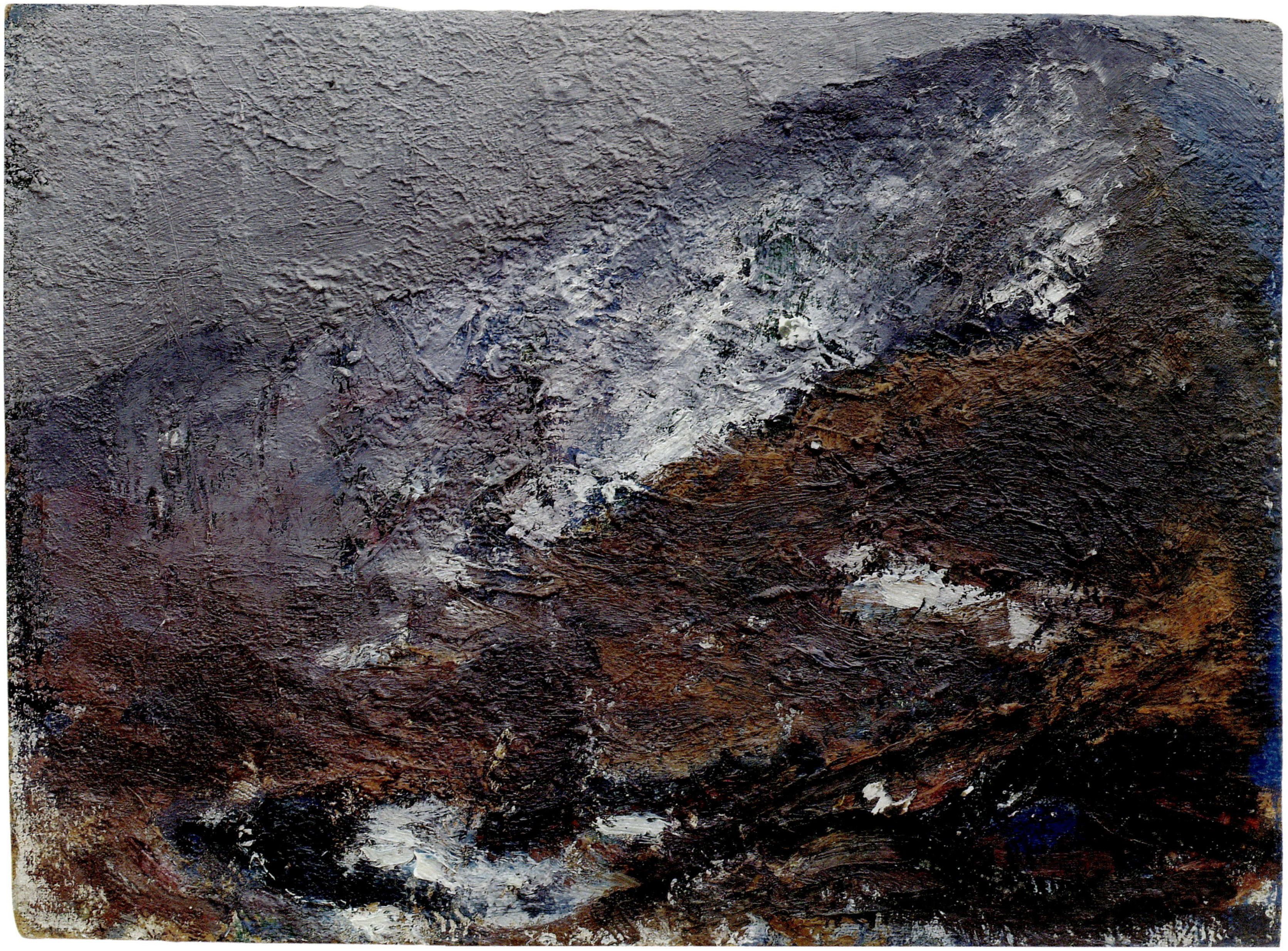

48 山坳 2 *1986 40cm × 54.5cm* **Ridge No. 2**

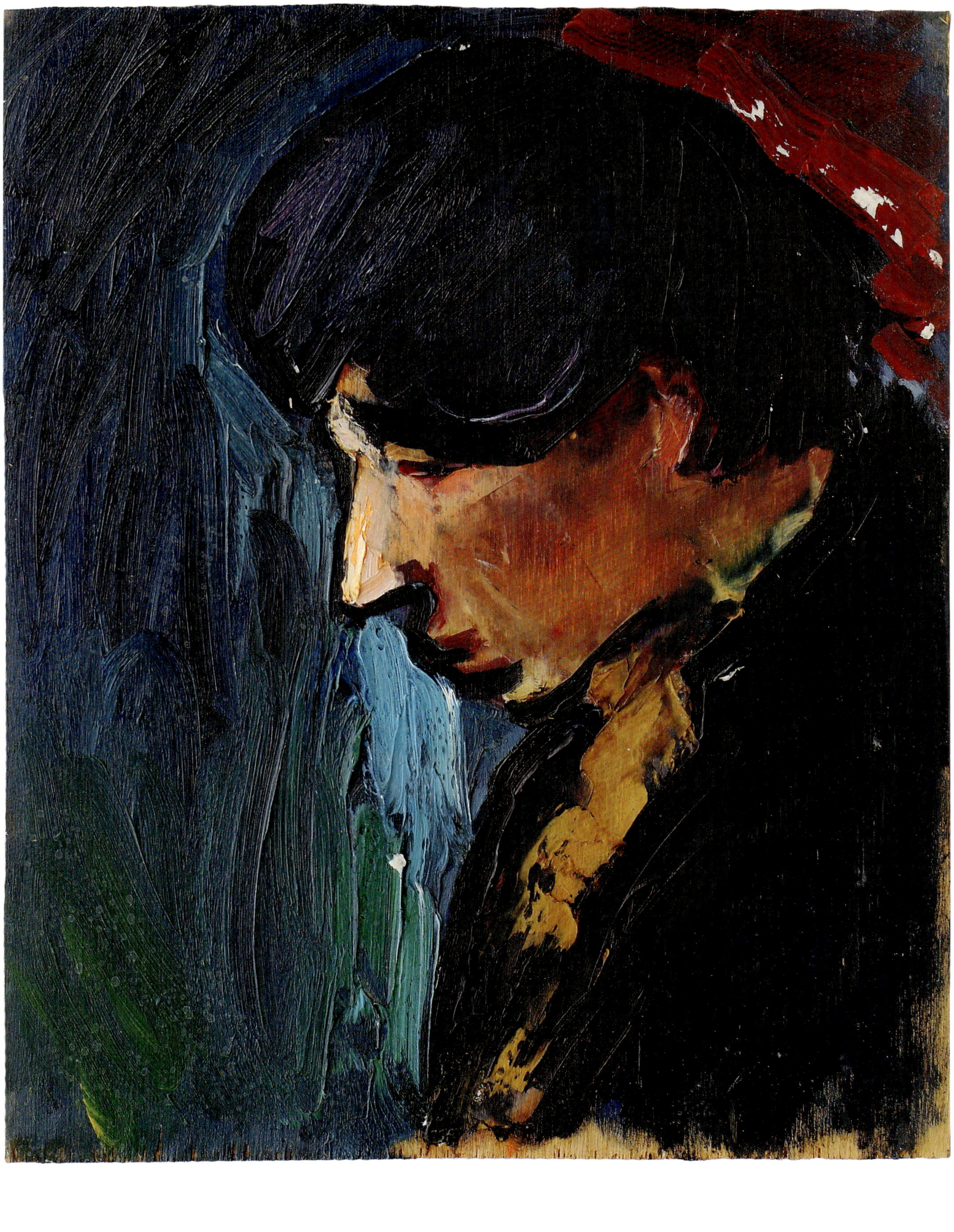

49　徐海林 *1986 49.3cm × 40.8cm* **Xu Hailin**

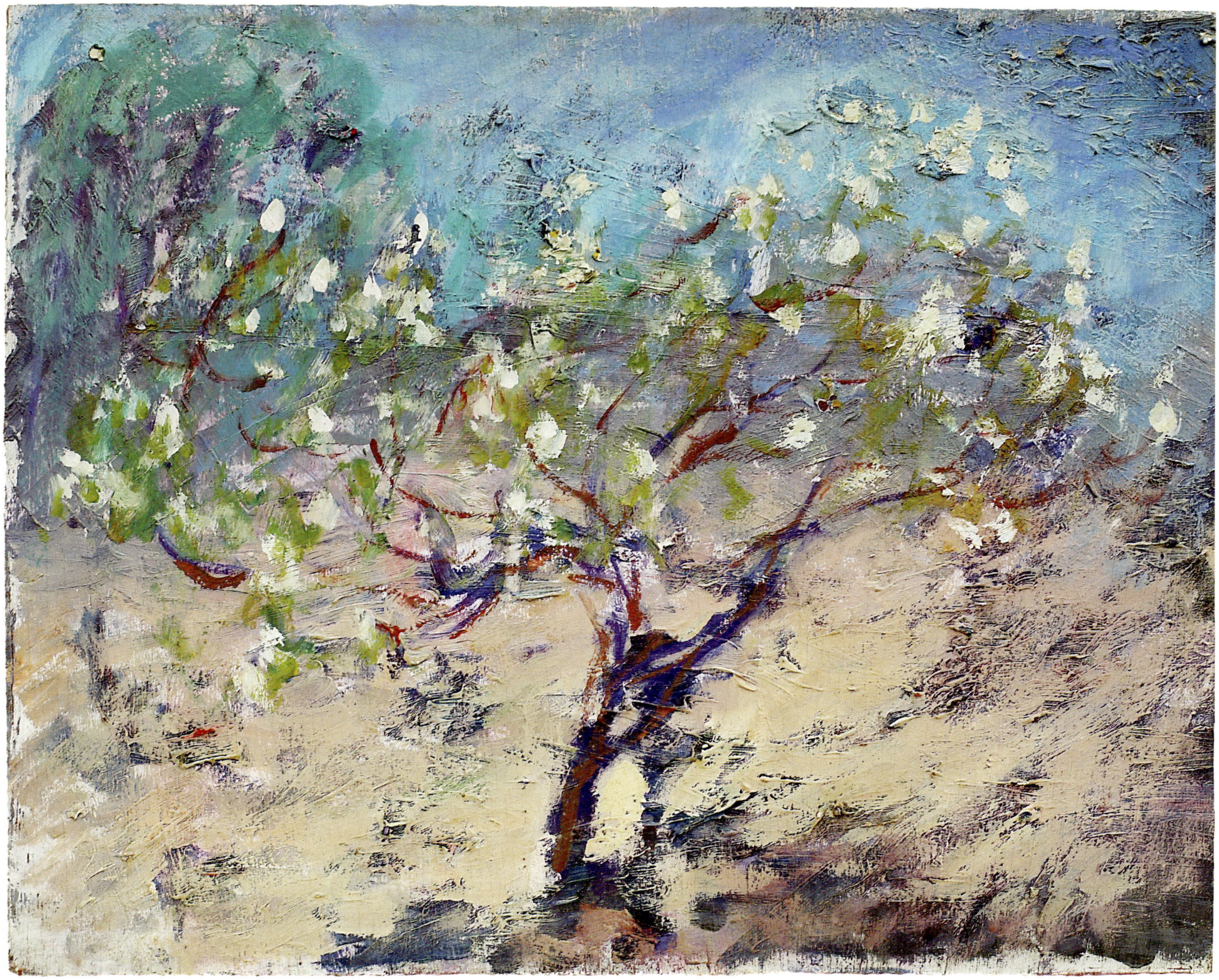

50　一树梨花 2 *1986 41cm × 50cm* **Pear Blossoms No. 2**

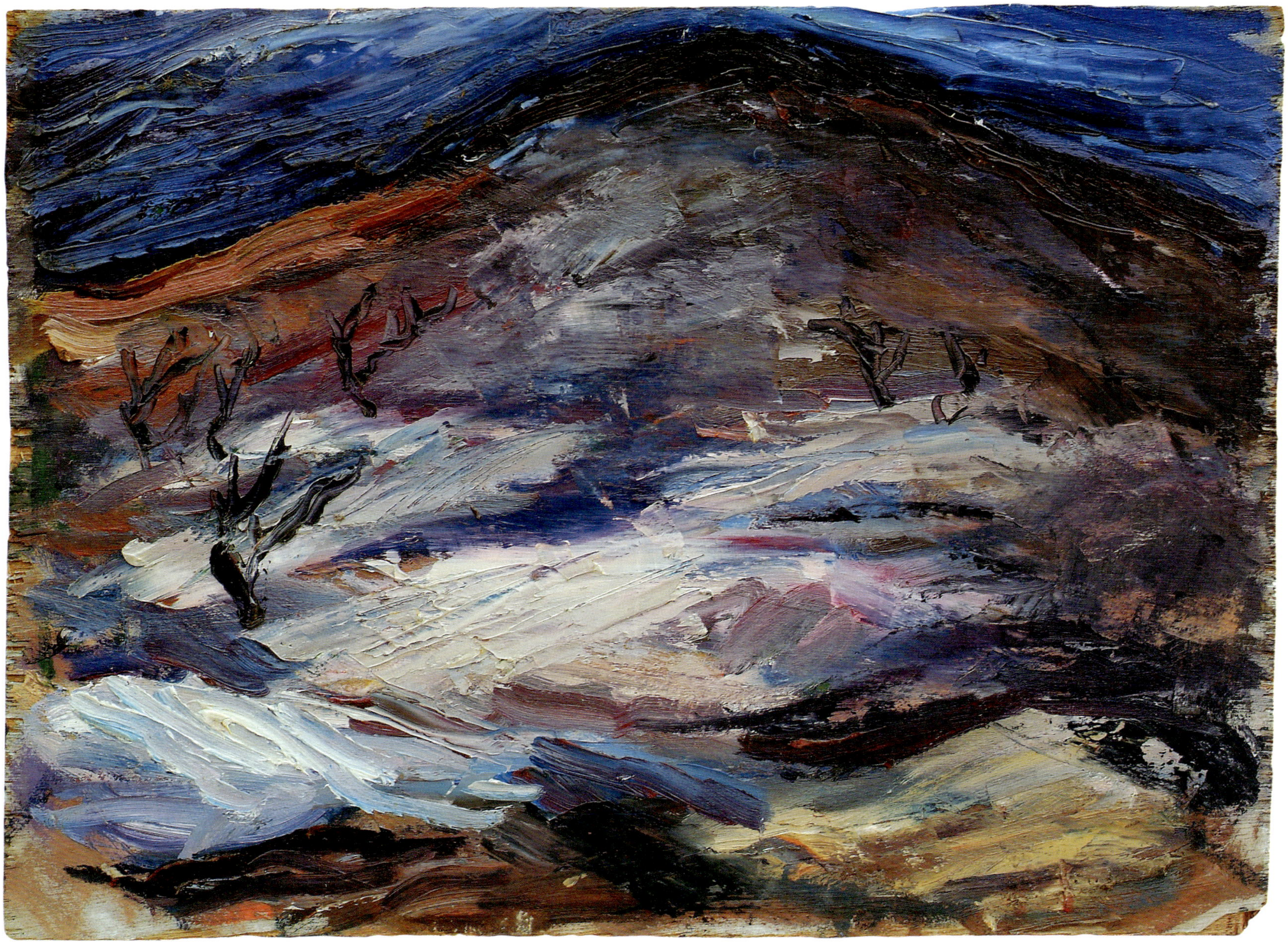

51 山坳之三 *1986 40.5cm × 55.5cm* **Ridge No. 3**

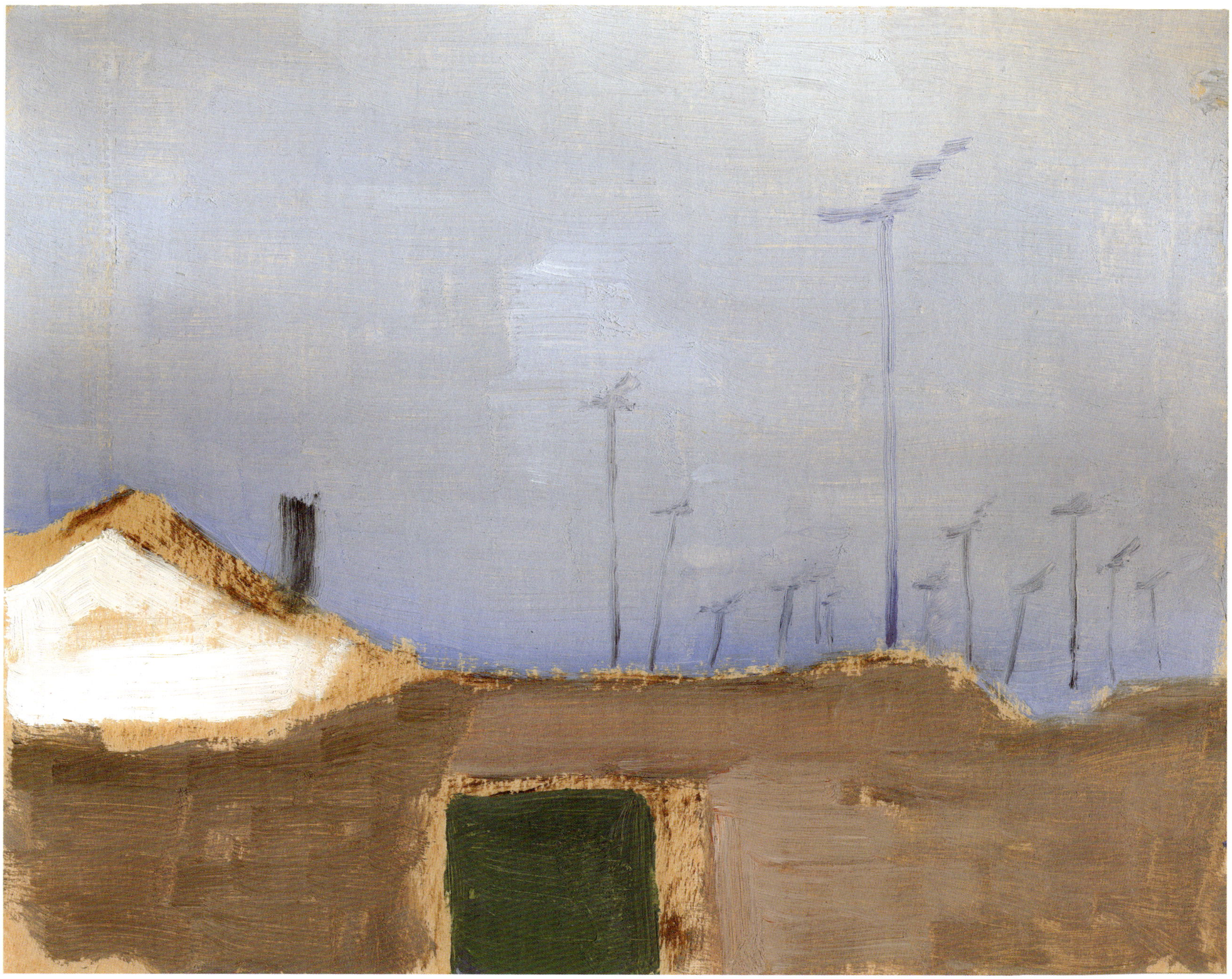

52 西北纪行 6 *1986 19.1cm × 24.3cm* **Journey to the Northwest No. 6**

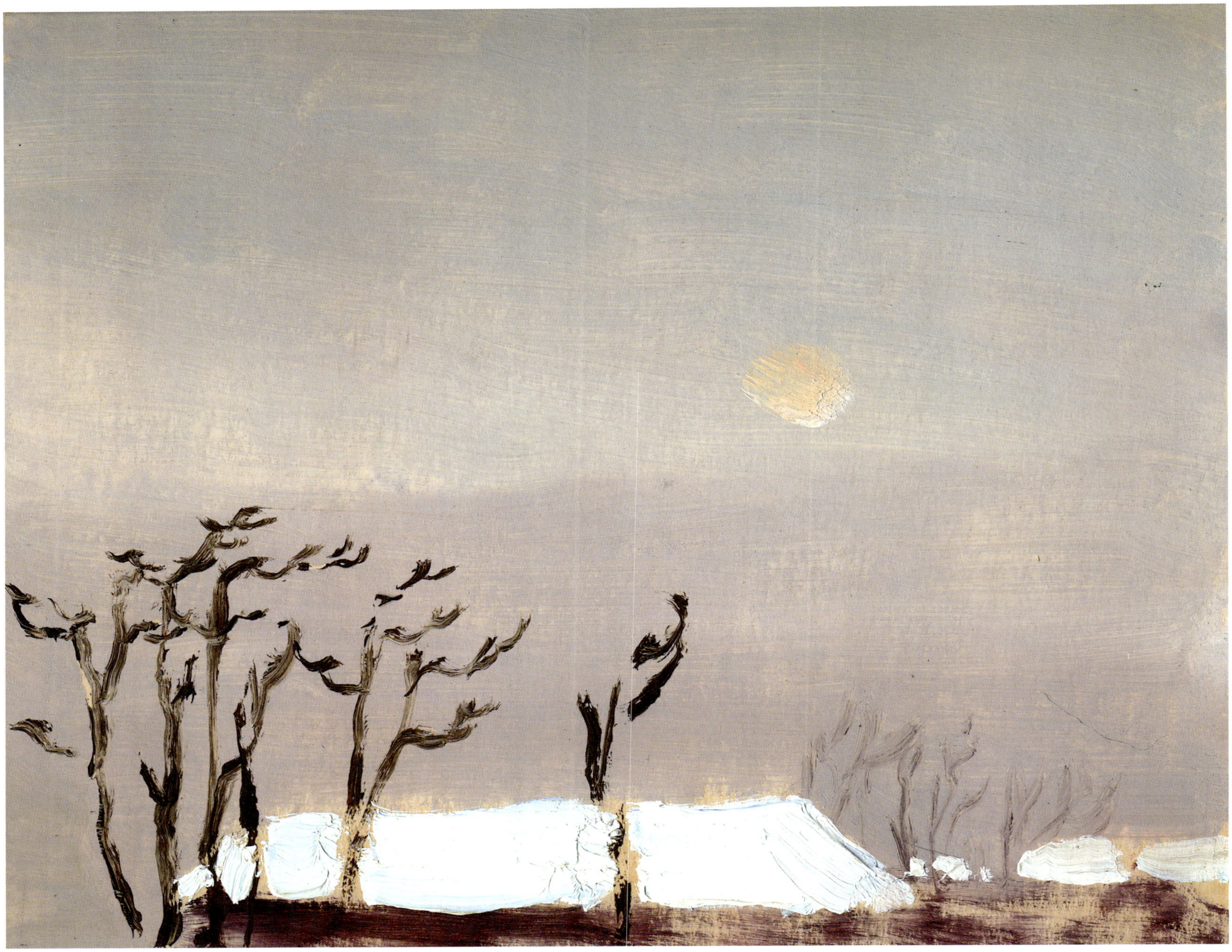

53 西北纪行 2 *1986 18.5cm × 24.3cm* **Journey to the Northwest No. 2**

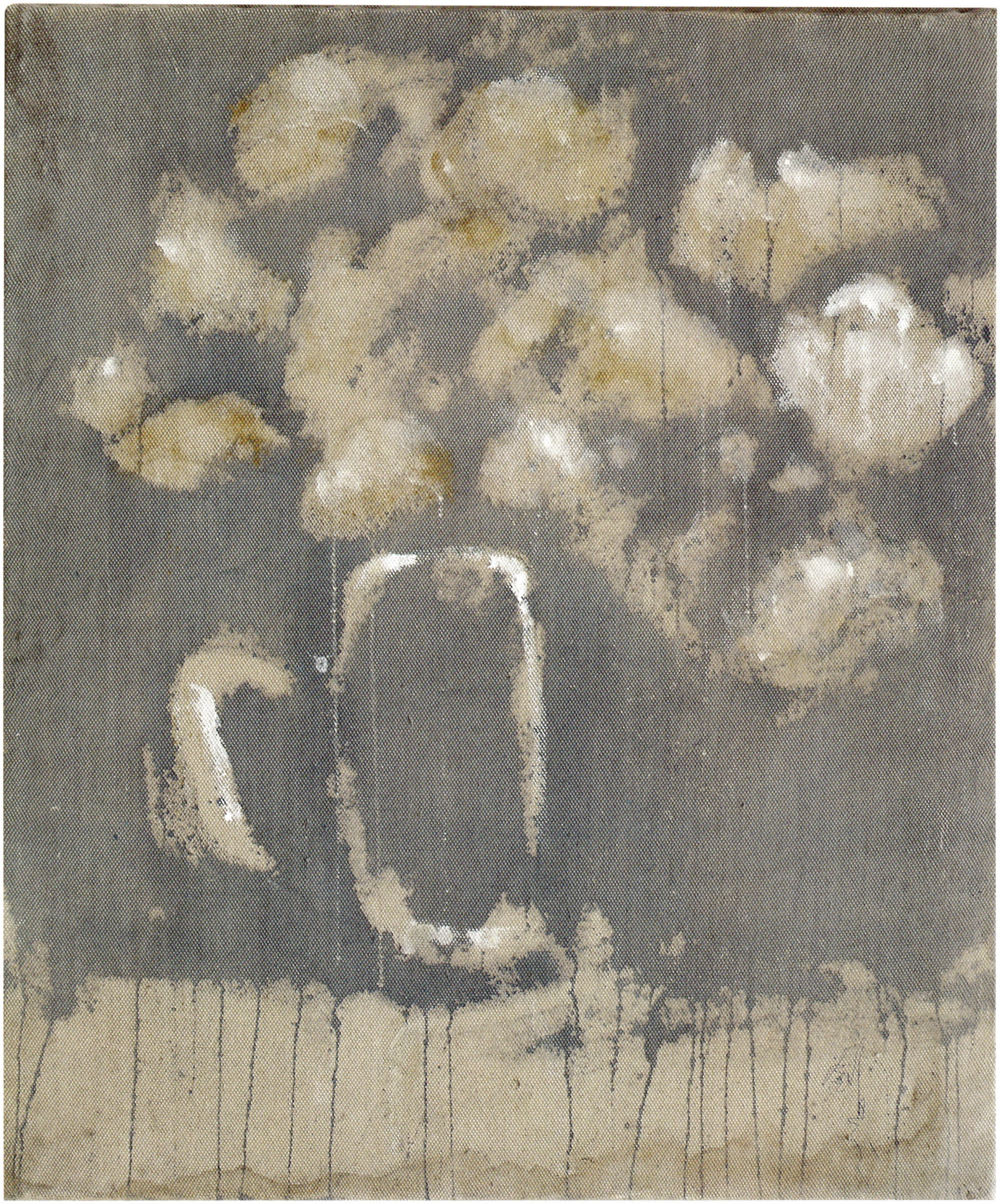

54 干花 8 *1987 69cm × 58cm* **Dried Flowers No. 8**

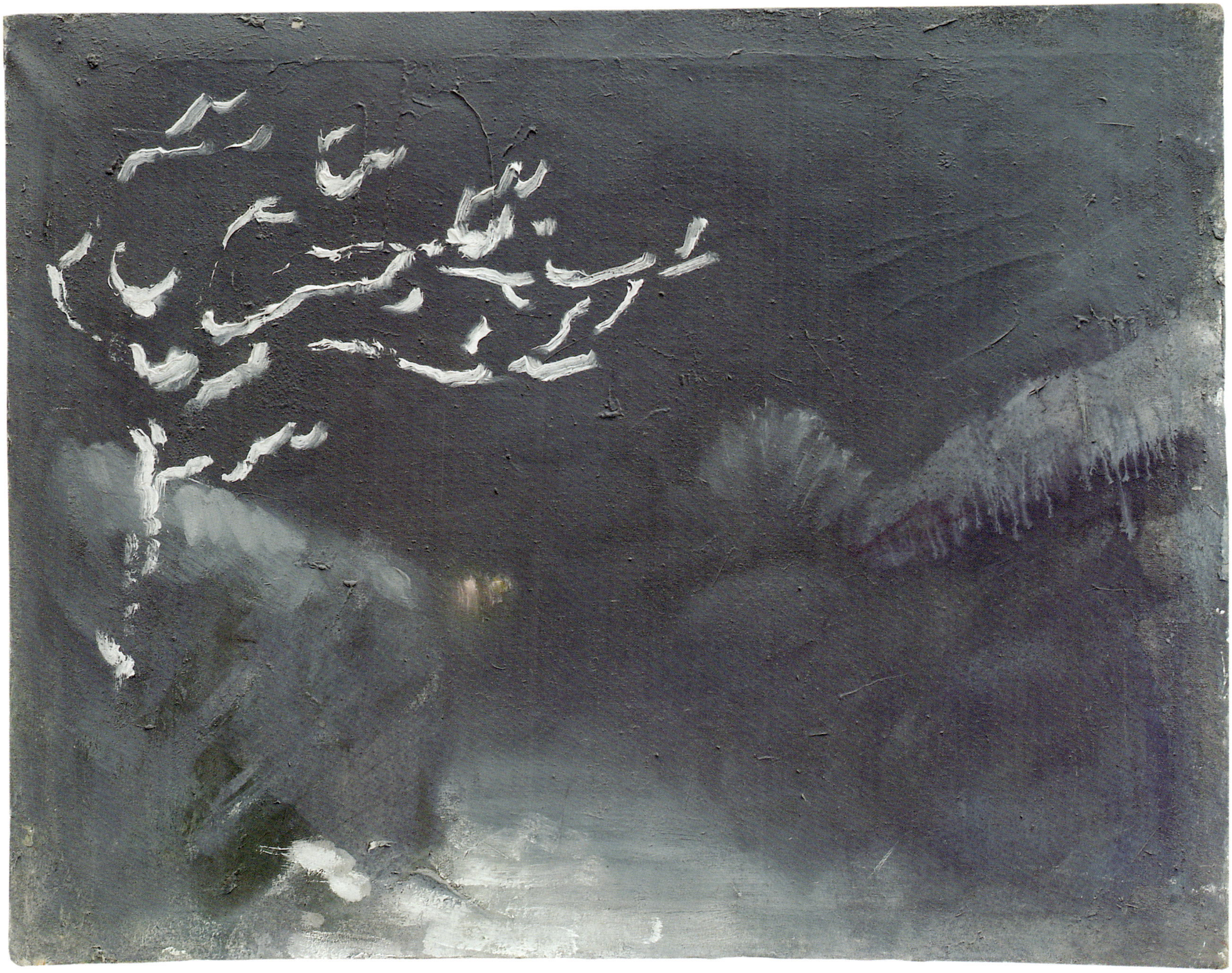

55 村口 *1987 37cm × 48cm* **Entrance to the Village**

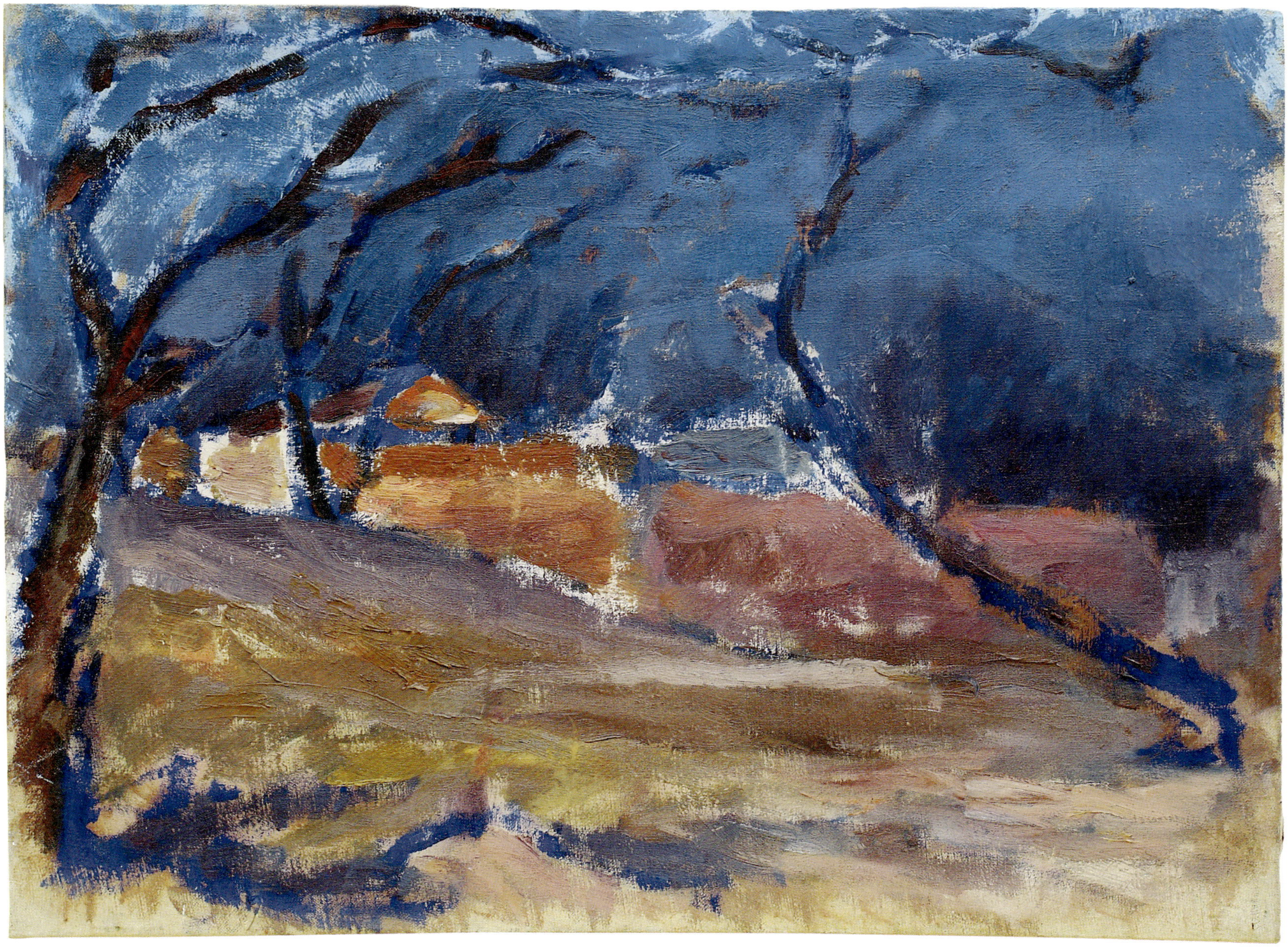

56 写生-090 *1987-1988 41cm × 56.5cm* **Painting from Life - 090**

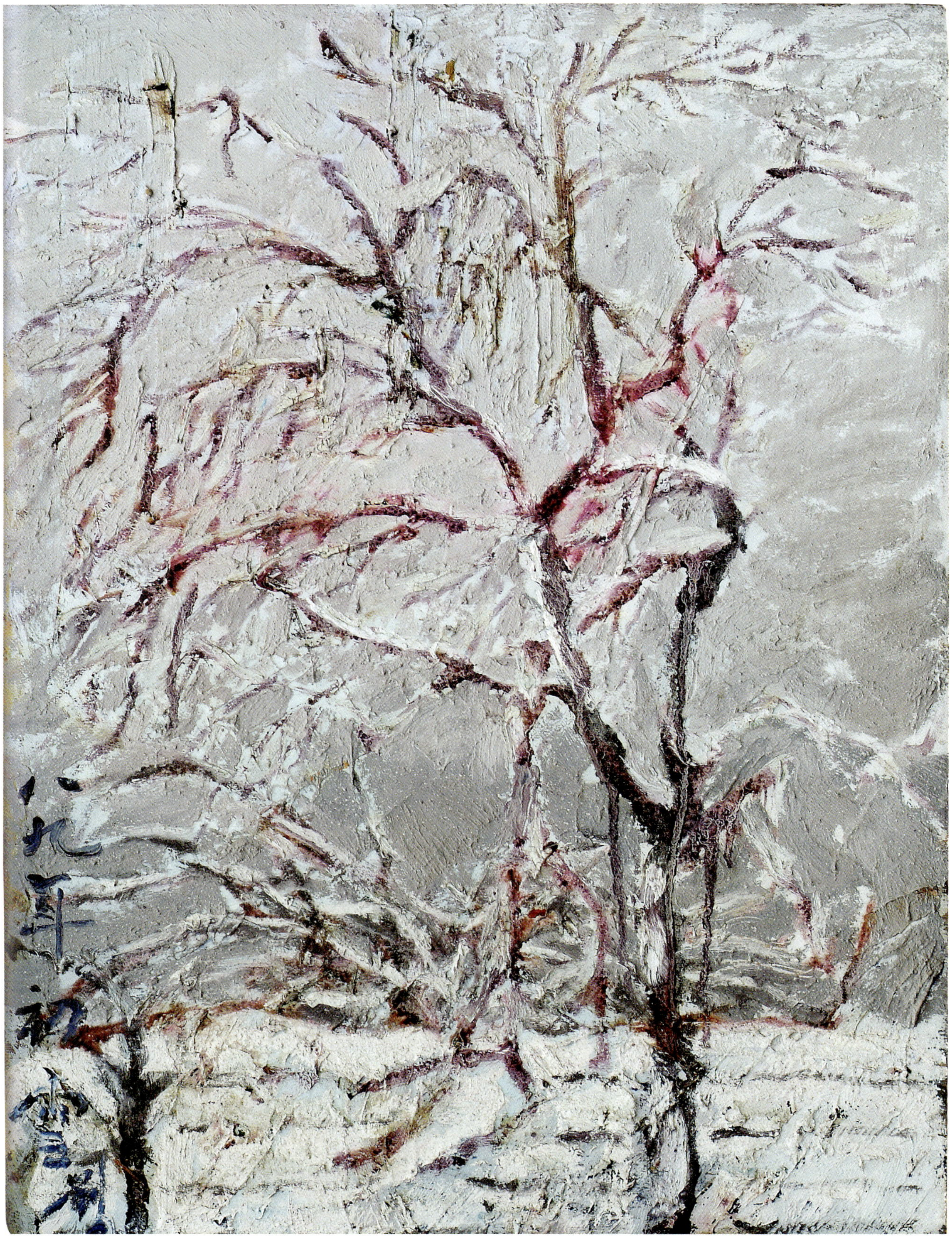

57 孙姨家的雪 *1989 73cm × 56cm* **Aunt Sun's Home in the Snow**

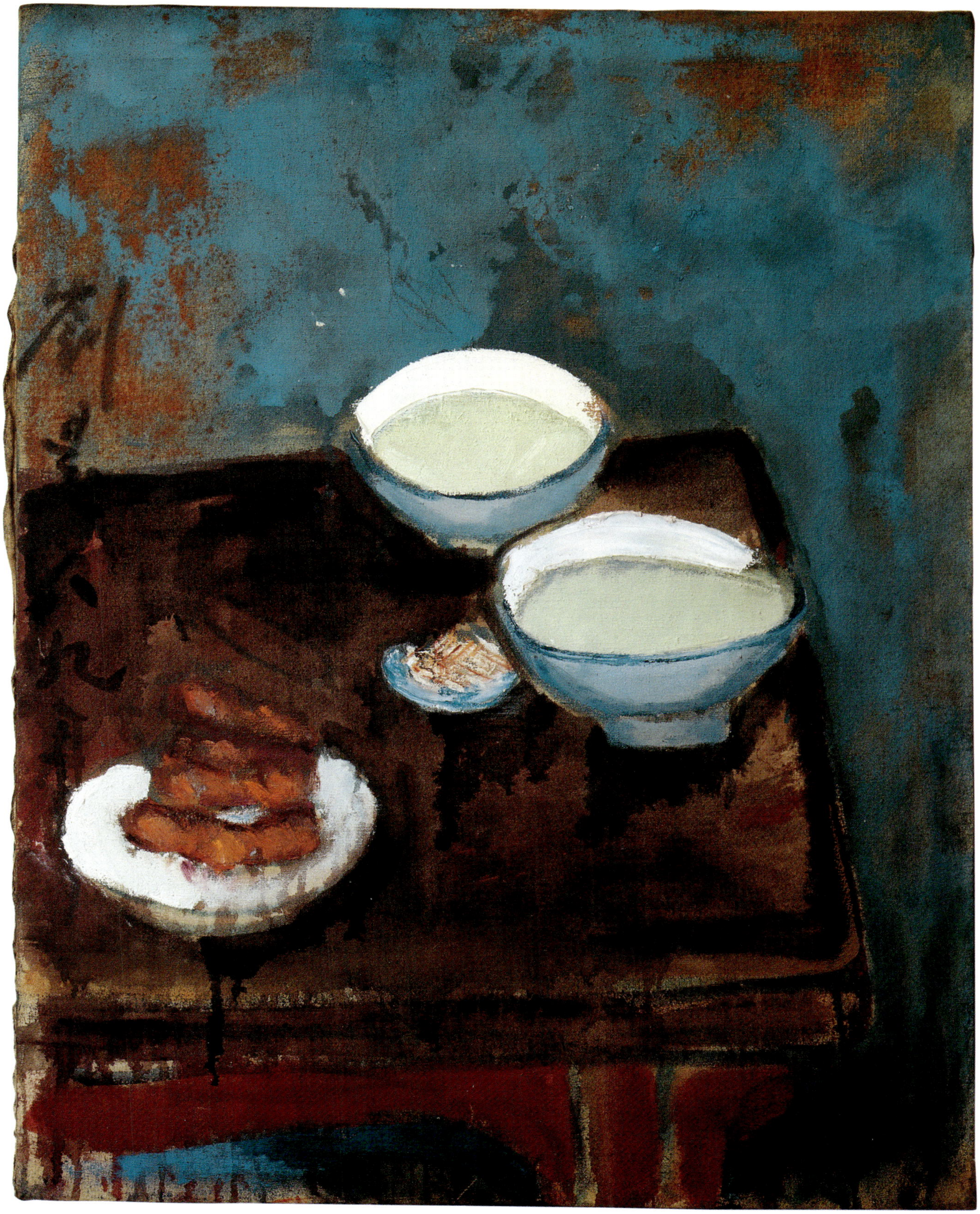

58 豆汁 *1989 76cm × 62cm* **Fermented Soya Milk**

图版目录
CATALOGUE OF THE PLATES

图版目录内容编排如下：

中文：画名、材质、创作地点*、参展纪录、收藏纪录
创作日期、规格(长.厘米×宽.厘米)
英文：画名、材质、创作地点*、参展纪录、收藏纪录
　　*创作地点除特别标明者外，均位于北京

Catalogue entry information is arranged as follows:

In Chinese: Title, medium, site of creation,* exhibition record, present location
Date of creation, dimensions (height × width, in centimeters)
In English: Title, medium, site of creation,* exhibition record, present location
　　* Sites are located in Beijing unless otherwise indicated.

图版目录中文略写注释：

1974无名展	参加1974年，"无名画会地下展览"，北京：福绥境大楼3楼5号
1979无名展	参加1979年，"无名画会展"，北京：北海公园
1981无名展	参加1981年，"无名画会展"，北京：北海公园
1989展	参加1989年，"刘是画展"，北京：当代美术馆
2006-2007无名展	参加2006-2007年，"无名画会回顾展"，北京：YQK德山文化艺术空间、TRA画廊；广州：广东美术馆；上海：上海证大现代艺术馆

Abbreviations used in the catalogue:

WM Exh. 1974	Exhibited in 1974, *The* Wuming *(No Name) Group Underground Exhibition*, Beijing: 305 Fusuijing Building
WM Exh. 1979	Exhibited in 1979, *The* Wuming *(No Name) Group Exhibition*, Beijing: Beihai Park
WM Exh. 1981	Exhibited in 1981, *The* Wuming *(No Name) Group Exhibition*, Beijing: Beihai Park
Exh. 1989	Exhibited in 1989, *Liu Shi Painting Exhibition*, Beijing: Contemporary Art Museum
WM Exh. 2006-2007	Exhibited in 2006-2007, *The "No Name" Group Retrospective Exhibition*, Beijing: TRA Gallery and YQK Deshan Art Space; Guangzhou: Guangdong Museum of Art; Shanghai: Shanghai Zhengda Museum of Modern Art
Coll.A.	Collection of the artist
P.Coll.	Private collection

1. 台阶，纸上油画，文化宫，画家本人藏
1974, 26.8cm × 20.7cm
Steps, oil on paper, Cultural Palace, Coll.A.

2. 写生-001，纸上油画，中山公园，画家本人藏
1973, 19.1cm × 14.4cm
Painting from Life No. 001, oil on paper, Zhongshan Park, Coll.A.

3. 希望，纸板上油画，刘是家，1981无名展，2006-2007无名展，画家本人藏
1975-1976, 20.5cm × 24cm
Hope, oil on cardboard, Liu Shi's home, Exh. 1981, WM Exh. 2006-2007, Coll.A.

4. 芍药，纸板上油画，紫竹院，画家本人藏
1975-1976, 12.7cm × 17.8cm
Peony, oil on cardboard, Coll.A.

5. 河边的人，纸板上油画，玉渊潭，1979无名展，2006-2007无名展，画家本人藏
1975-1976, 13cm × 18.5cm
Figure by the River, oil on cardboard, Yuyuantan, WM Exh. 1979, WM Exh. 2006-2007, Coll.A.

6. 四川营胡同之雾，纸上油画，四川营胡同，画家本人藏
1976-1978, 20.2cm × 26.7cm
Sichuan Camp Alley in the Mist, oil on paper, Sichuan Camp Alley, Coll.A.

7. 女孩，纸板油画棒，刘是家，2006-2007无名展，画家本人藏
1976, 22cm × 14cm
Girl, oil pastel on cardboard, Liu Shi's home, WM Exh. 2006-2007, Coll.A.

8. 师傅，纸上油画，青年湖，画家本人藏
1976-1977, 25.7cm × 18.6cm
Master, oil on paper, Qingnianhu, Coll.A.

9. 雪房顶，纸上油画，刘是家，画家本人藏
1976-1977, 13cm × 18.4cm
Snow-Capped Roof, oil on paper, Liu Shi's home, Coll.A.

10. 合欢树 1，纸板上油画，紫竹院，1979无名展，画家本人藏
1976-1977, 12.6cm × 17.8cm
Silk Tree No. 1, oil on cardboard, Zizhuyuan, WM Exh. 1979, Coll.A.

11. 房子的冬天，纸上油画，刘是家，2006-2007无名展，画家本人藏
1976-1977, 20cm × 27cm
House in Winter, oil on paper, Liu Shi's home, WM Exh. 2006-2007, Coll.A.

12. 回家，纸上油画，1989展，画家本人藏
1977-1978, 27.1cm × 19.4cm
Going Home, oil on paper, Exh. 1989, Coll.A.

13. 常顺儿，纸板上油画，刘是家，1989个展，画家本人藏
1978-1979, 32cm × 25cm
Chang Shunr, oil on cardboard, Liu Shi's home, Exh. 1989, Coll.A.

14. 百货大楼之夜，三合板上油画，刘是家，1989展，画家本人藏
1977-1978, 40cm × 30.5cm
Department Store at Night, oil on three-ply board, Liu Shi's home, Exh. 1989, Coll.A.

15. 嘴唇山，纤维板上油画，圆明园，1989展，画家本人藏
1978-1979, 规格不详 dimensions unknown
Zuichun Hills, oil on fiberboard, Yuanmingyuan, Exh. 1989, Coll.A.

16. 外祖父，布面油画，刘是家，1979无名展，1989展，2006-2007无名展，画家本人藏
1978, 73cm × 50cm
Grandfather, oil on cloth, Liu Shi's home, WM Exh. 1979, Exh. 1989, WM Exh. 2006-2007, Coll.A.

17. 单人床，纤维板上油画，刘是家，画家本人藏
1977-1979, 规格不详 dimensions unknown
Single Bed, oil on fiberboard, Liu Shi's homec Coll.A.

18. 火夫，纤维板上油画，刘是家，1981无名展，1989展，画家本人藏
1978-1979, 45cm × 39.5cm
Stoker, oil on fiberboard, Liu Shi's home, WM Exh. 1981, Exh. 1989, Coll.A.

19. 雪竹 1，纤维板上油画，刘是家，1981无名展，1989展，画家本人藏
1978-1979, 36.8cm × 27.3cm
Bamboo in Snow No. 1, oil on fiberboard, Liu Shi's home, WM Exh. 1981, Exh. 1989, Coll.A.

20. 画板 4，纸板上油画，刘是家，1989展，画家本人藏
1978-1979, 38.8cm × 28.4cm
Drawing Board No. 4, oil on cardboard, Liu Shi's home, Exh. 1989, Coll.A.

21. 柳的落日 2，纸上油画，紫竹院，1989展，画家本人藏
1978, 23.7cm × 38.8cm
Sunset and Willow No. 2, oil on paper, Zizhuyuan, Exh. 1989, Coll.A.

22. 同学 2，纤维板上油画，刘是家，1989展，画家本人藏
1979-1980, 44.5cm × 37cm
Schoolmate No. 2, oil on fiberboard, Liu Shi's home, Exh. 1989, Coll.A.

23. 甜水井胡同黎明，纤维板上油画，街道，1989展，画家本人藏
1979-1980, 33.2cm × 23.1cm
Tianshuijing Alley at Dawn, oil on fiberboard, street, Exh. 1989, Coll.A.

24. 夕阳，纸上油画，天坛，画家本人藏
1977-1978, 20.5cm × 25.3cm
Sunset, oil on paper, Temple of Heaven, Coll.A.

25. 满月，纸上油画，刘是家，画家本人藏
1979, 14.3cm × 20.9cm
Full Moon, oil on paper, Liu Shi's home, Coll.A.

26. 雪路，纤维板上油画，天坛，1989展，画家本人藏
1980-1981, 31.6cm × 40.7cm
Snowy Road, oil on fiberboard, Temple of Heaven, Exh. 1989, Coll.A.

27. 棉花胡同的中午 2，纤维板上油画，街道，画家本人藏
1979-1980, 28.4cm × 31cm
Cotton Alley at Noontime No. 2, oil on fiberboard, street, Coll.A.

28. 四川营胡同的雪，纤维板上油画，四川营胡同，1989展，刘征藏，北京
1979-1986, 43cm × 55cm
Sichuan Camp Alley in the Snow, oil on fiberboard, Sichuan Camp Alley, Exh. 1989, P.Liu Zheng. Beijing.

29. 四川营胡同的夏，三合板上油画，四川营胡同，画家本人藏
1979-1986, 60.5cm × 48cm
Sichuan Camp Alley in Summer, oil on three-ply board, Sichuan Camp Alley, Coll.A.

30. 短松岗，纸上油画，北戴河，1989展，2006-2007无名展，画家本人藏
1981-1984, 19.5cm × 24cm
Short Pine Hills, oil on paper, Beidaihe, Exh. 1989, WM Exh. 2006-2007, Coll.A.

31. 四川营胡同的秋，三合板上油画，四川营胡同，画家本人藏
1981-1984, 33cm × 37.5cm
Sichuan Camp Alley in Autumn, oil on three-ply board, Sichuan Camp Alley, Coll.A.

32. 棉花胡同的落日，纤维板上油画，街道，1989展，画家本人藏
1979-1982, 38cm × 46cm
Sunset in Cotton Alley, oil on fiberboard, street, Exh. 1989, Coll.A.

33. 石板，三合板上油画，郊区，画家本人藏
1980-1981, 41.5cm × 43cm

Flagstone, oil on three-ply board, suburbs, Coll.A.

34.夏日，三合板上油画，刘是家，1989展，画家本人藏

1981-1982, 41cm × 46cm

Summertime, oil on three-ply board, Liu Shi's home, Exh. 1989, Coll.A.

35.自画像，纸上油画，街道，1989展，2006-2007无名展，画家本人藏

1982, 43cm × 34cm

Self-Portrait, oil on paper, street, Exh. 1989, WM Exh. 2006-2007, Coll.A.

36.小酒馆，纸上油画，街道，画家本人藏

1984, 21.6cm × 16.7cm

Little Bar, oil on paper, street, Coll.A.

37.油条和葬礼，三合板上油画，林县，画家本人藏

1986, 40.6cm × 26.7cm

Deep-Fried Dough and Funeral, oil on three-ply board, Linxian County, Coll.A.

38.梧桐花与杨树叶，三合板上油画，林县，1989展，画家本人藏

1986, 59.5cm × 45.5cm

Parasol Flowers and Poplar Leaves, oil on three-ply board, Linxian County, Exh. 1989, Coll.A.

39.山坳的白房，纤维板上油画，林县，1989展，画家本人藏

1986, 36cm × 45cm

White House on the Ridge, oil on fiberboard, Linxian County, Exh. 1989, Coll.A.

40.鬼 2，油画布上油画，刘是家，1989展，画家本人藏

1986, 63cm × 52cm

Ghost No. 2, oil on canvas, Liu Shi's home, Exh. 1989, Coll.A.

41.四月 2，纤维板上油画，林县，1989展，画家本人藏

1986, 61cm × 77cm

April No. 2, oil on fiberboard, Linxian County, Exh. 1989, Coll.A.

42.秋海棠，纤维板上油画，刘是家，1989展，画家本人藏

1986-1987, 29.6cm × 36cm

Begonia, oil on fiberboard, Liu Shi's home, Exh. 1989, Coll.A.

43.鲜花，纤维板上油画，刘是家，画家本人藏

1986-1987, 35cm × 45.5cm

Flowers, oil on fiberboard, Liu Shi's home, Coll.A.

44.写生-084，三合板上油画，香山，1989展，画家本人藏

1987, 31cm × 36.5cm

Painting from Life - 084, oil on three-ply board, Fragrant Hills, Exh. 1989, Coll.A.

45.傍晚的池塘，纤维板上油画，林县，1989展，画家本人藏

1986, 35cm × 45.5cm

Pond in the Dusk, oil on fiberboard, Linxian County, Exh. 1989, Coll.A.

46.梯田 2，纤维板上油画，林县，1989展，画家本人藏

1986, 54.5cm × 63cm

Terraced Fields No. 2, oil on fiberboard, Linxian County, Exh. 1989, Coll.A.

47.校办工厂 2，三合板上油画，林县，画家本人藏

1986, 40cm × 55.8cm

School-Run Factory No. 2, oil on three-ply board, Linxian County, Coll.A.

48.山坳 2，三合板上油画，林县，1989展，画家本人藏

1986, 40cm × 54.5cm

Ridge No. 2, oil on three-ply board, Linxian County, Exh. 1989, Coll.A.

49.徐海林，三合板上油画，林县中学，画家本人藏

1986, 49.3cm × 40.8cm

Xu Hailin, oil on three-ply board, Linxian Middle School, Coll.A.

50.一树梨花 2，三合板上油画，林县，画家本人藏

1986, 41cm × 50cm

Pear Blossoms No. 2, oil on three-ply board, Linxian County, Coll.A.

51.山坳之三，三合板上油画，林县，1989展，画家本人藏

1986, 40.5cm × 55.5cm

Ridge No. 3, oil on three-ply board, Linxian County, Exh. 1989, Coll.A.

52.西北纪行 6，纸上油画，甘肃，1989展，画家本人藏

1986, 19.1cm × 24.3cm

Journey to the Northwest No. 6, oil on paper, Gansu, Exh. 1989, Coll.A.

53.西北纪行 2，纸上油画，甘肃，1989展，画家本人藏

1986, 18.5cm × 24.3cm

Journey to the Northwest No. 2, oil on paper, Gansu, Exh. 1989, Coll.A.

54.干花 8，油画布上油画，刘是家，1989展，画家本人藏

1987, 69cm × 58cm

Dried Flowers No. 8, oil on canvas, Liu Shi's home, Exh. 1989, Coll.A.

55.村口，油画布上油画，孙姨家，1989展，画家本人藏

1987, 37cm × 48cm

Entrance to the Village, oil on canvas, Aunt Sun's home, Exh. 1989, Coll.A.

56.写生-090，油画布上油画，女人街，画家本人藏

1987-1988, 41cm × 56.5cm

Painting from Life - 090, oil on canvas, Ladies' Street, Coll.A.

57.孙姨家的雪，三合板上油画，孙姨家，1989展，画家本人藏

1989, 73cm × 56cm

Aunt Sun's Home in the Snow, oil on three-ply board, Aunt Sun's home, Exh. 1989, Coll.A.

58.豆汁，布面油画，冯国东的店，2006-2007无名展，画家本人藏

1989, 76cm × 62cm

Fermented Soya Milk, oil on cloth, Feng Guodong's shop, WM Exh. 2006-2007, Coll.A.

English translation of catalogue entries by Wo Hoi Kwan
Edited by Greg M. Thomas